Ink Dances in Limbo

Hong Kong University Press thanks Xu Bing for writing the Press's name in his Square Word Calligraphy for the covers of its books. For further information, see p. iv.

Ink Dances in Limbo
Gao Xingjian's Writing as Cultural Translation

Jessica Yeung

香港大學出版社

HONG KONG UNIVERSITY PRESS

Hong Kong University Press
14/F Hing Wai Centre
7 Tin Wan Praya Road
Aberdeen
Hong Kong

© Jessica Yeung 2008

ISBN 978-962-209-921-0

All rights reserved. No portion of this publication may be reproduced or
transmitted in any form or by any means, electronic or mechanical,
including photocopy, recording, or any information storage or
retrieval system, without permission in writing from the publisher.

Secure On-line Ordering
http://www.hkupress.org

British Library Cataloguing-in-Publication Data
A catalogue record for this book is available from the British Library.

Printed and bound by United League Graphic & Printing Co. Ltd., in Hong Kong, China

Hong Kong University Press is honoured that Xu Bing, whose art explores the
complex themes of language across cultures, has written the Press's name in his
Square Word Calligraphy. This signals our commitment to cross-cultural thinking
and the distinctive nature of our English-language books published in China.

"At first glance, Square Word Calligraphy appears to be nothing more unusual
than Chinese characters, but in fact it is a new way of rendering English words in
the format of a square so they resemble Chinese characters. Chinese viewers expect
to be able to read Square word Calligraphy but cannot. Western viewers, however
are surprised to find they can read it. Delight erupts when meaning is unexpectedly
revealed."

— Britta Erickson, *The Art of Xu Bing*

PL
2869
.O128
Z95
2002

Contents

Acknowledgements

I am indebted to many friends and colleagues who have offered me help and support in this project. Professor Gregory B. Lee has been of critical importance in the successful completion of this project. His insights on culture and literature have illuminated my approach to reading Gao Xingjian's writing and many other cultural phenomena around me. My publisher Dr Colin Day has been extremely helpful and supportive, for which I am deeply grateful. I also wish to thank Professor Martha Cheung for her encouragement and advice; Professor Eugene Eoyang for his valuable critical feedback; Professor Jane Lai and Professor Chung Ling for their faith in my work; Ms Phoebe Chuk, Mr Patrick Li, Ms Heidi Chun and Ms Sharon Chan for their help with gathering information which is vital to the research; Mrs Ada Lee, Mr Joseph Tang, Dr Eliza Lau, Dr Sarojini and Dr Nihal Jayawikrama, Ms Monina Wong, Dr Amy Lee and Professor Mao Sihui for their friendship and unfailing support; Professor Ackbar Abbas, Professor Anthony Tatlow, Professor Rodney Davey, Professor Maureen Sabine and Professor Jeremy Tambling for their good and kind counsel; Dr Tan Zaixi, Dr Ester Leung, Ms Carina Luk, Ms Esther Kwok, Professor Zhang Xu, Dr Wang Hui, and Mr Alvin Leung for their generous encouragement; Mr Tang Shu-wing and Ms Lindzay Chan for their permission to use the photograph from their production of *Between Life and Death* on the front cover of this book. Most important, I'd like to thank Dr Mike Ingham, my comrade and companion, without whom this book and so many things in my life would never have been possible. Finally my deep appreciation goes to my family for their love and support; and to Mao Me Tung, Mao-zai-ah, Didi and Gogo for the regular distractions they provided in my toil.

This project is supported by a Faculty Research Grant from the Hong Kong Baptist University.

Part 1

Introduction

1

Introduction:
Writing across Culture

Gao Xingjian's literary works have always functioned in the interstices between China and the "West". For me they somehow evoke an image of the final scene in Bergman's film *The Seventh Seal* in which the character Death leads his train of dancing souls into limbo. Death travels between the realms of the living and the dead, generating some kind of creative power in the liminal space. Sadly in the end the spectacle of the contortions of this bizarre cortege, making such a song and dance in their journey, leads only to the nowhere of limbo. This image of dancing towards limbo cannot help but remind me of Gao's writing career up to the present. Perhaps the use of the word "dances" in my title might sound too positive. However, from the viewer's perspective such dances may appear to be more like contortions or writhing, (Reeling and Writhing) in the Lewis Carroll sense of the word.

Gao Xingjian's Writing Career and the Award of the Nobel Prize in Literature

The award of the 2001 Nobel Prize in Literature to Gao Xingjian has stirred ambivalent responses within Chinese literary circles. Some rejoiced at this news while others considered Gao an inappropriate choice. Two arguments frequently adduced to substantiate the latter response are that Gao's works do not represent the highest achievement of contemporary Chinese literature, and that Gao at the time was relatively unknown to the Chinese reading public (Tam 2001: 1). The first reservation is to do with the literary value of Gao's works, which ought indeed to be a legitimate concern for a literary award. Before a conclusion can be made in this respect, a detailed analysis of his entire output is needed. This book intends to do exactly that. The second reservation is to do with the popularity of the writer. Whether fame and reputation, sometimes determined by factors beyond literary concerns, should be criteria for the worth of literary works is debatable. After all, the classic case of Kafka shows that visionary and innovative writers might not be even understood, let alone fully appreciated, by their contemporaries. Notwithstanding, a brief survey of the development of Gao's writing career serves as a good starting point to understand his works, since the reader will find out in subsequent chapters that *contextualisation* is a key principle in my analysis of Gao's works.

Before the Nobel Prize was awarded to Gao, there had only been a modest number of critical works analysing his writings, and it is true that their popularity among the general Chinese reading public was limited. The ban on his works in China since 1995 is one reason for this neglect. But his choice of genre is another major factor. Between 1979[1] (the year he published his first piece of writing the novella *Hanye de xingchen* [Stars on a cold night]) and 1990 when his first novel *Lingshan* (translated into English as *Soul Mountain* by Mabel Lee, 2000) was published, his repertoire consisted of both fictions and plays, but it was mainly the plays that attracted critical attention. There is no doubt that *Juedui xinhao* (1982, translated into English as *Alarm Signal* by Shiao-Ling S. Yu, 1996), *Chezhan* (1983, translated into English as *The Bus-stop* by Geremie Barmé, 1984; *Bus Stop* by Carla Kirkwood, 1995, *The Bus Stop* by Shiao-Ling Yu, 1996; *Bus Stop: A Lyrical Comedy on Life in One Act* by Kimberly Besio, 1998) and *Yeren* (1985, translated into English as *Wild Man* by Bruno Roubicek, 1990) created considerable sensation in the Chinese theatre scene. Yet no matter how significant these pieces are, the theatre is restricted by time and space. Only those in the audience at the time were able to experience these works. Others could only hear about them or read commentaries on them. Moreover, theatre performance is a product of teamwork. Gao's contribution to these productions was inseparable from Lin Zhaohua's directing and the production values invested in them by the Beijing People's Art Theatre. As a result, a considerable proportion of the attention these plays attracted has been from theatre critics, who rarely evaluate the play texts on their own, but nearly always in relation to the concepts of staging (directing) and other aesthetic aspects (technical arts and acting); and also from journalists, who write about them as social phenomena in the newspapers. These plays have been published in literary journals and anthologies. But since the reading of plays in published form has not developed into a popular genre among contemporary Chinese readership comparable to fiction and poetry, one has to be prudent in estimating the extent of their influence.

In the 1980s, Gao wrote about two dozen short stories. They were published in literary journals. This was a very exciting period for Chinese fiction writing. The proliferation of highly original works and the experimental creativity of Ah Cheng, Mo Yan, Han Shaogong, Wang Anyi, Liu Sola and many others overwhelmed the critics. Gao Xingjian's short stories by contrast have never captured the same level of attention, and critical works focused on them are still lacking. His first novel *Soul Mountain* and his first and only anthology of short stories *Gei wo laoye mai yugan* (some stories in this anthology are translated into English by Mabel Lee and anthologised in one volume also entitled *Buying a Fishing Rod for My Grandfather*, 2004) were published in as late as 1990. Only then were his methods and style of creative writing revealed in a more comprehensive manner to critics and readers alike.

However Gao's literary career took off before his creative talent was widely recognised. In fact, his name was already known in the late 1970s in literary circles, and in the early 1980s he attained a higher profile. These developments were mainly associated with his series of essays published in literary journals in that period, and his theoretical work *Xiandai xiaoshuo jiqiao chutan* [A preliminary exploration of the techniques of modern fiction] (1981). By introducing European Modernism in these essays, he systematically advocated an anti-Realist stance in contemporary Chinese fiction writing. He consistently championed the writings of French Modernists, especially Sartre, and the Chinese Modernist writings of Wang Meng. In this way, he established a coherent literary position. This stance came directly into conflict with that sanctioned by the State. At the time literature was expected to adhere to a hard-line Socialist Realism in conformity with Mao's 1942 "Talks at the Yan'an Conference on Literature and Art". Gao's subversive position thus established him as an icon of literary dissidence. His first literary achievements were indeed those of a critic, before he put into practice his own literary credo in the capacity of playwright, and later novelist. It would thus be fair to say that before he received the Nobel Prize in 2000, his early theoretical writings on Modernism had been the most notable works in his *oeuvre*.

Gao Xingjian is the first Chinese writer to be awarded a Nobel Prize in Literature, but he was not the first to be nominated for the prize. Literary giants of modern Chinese literature such as Ba Jin, Lao She and Shen Congwen also received nominations. Prestigious international prizes such as the Nobel carry much significance because they attract international attention. One of the by-products of colonialism and globalisation has been the internationalisation of academia and the publishing industry. This has been followed by an extension of the literary canon to include literatures outside the European and American "great traditions", to refer to F. R. Leavis' famous title. Comparativists who aspire to build up a world canon might see themselves as in the process of realising Goethe's ideal of a *Weltliteratur* ["World Literature"], but the presence of some or the absence of other literary traditions in the international arena has become directly related to the politics of power and representation in international literary studies. Along with other post-colonial critics, Edward Said makes the scathing criticism on Comparative Literature as a discipline that it was a field "epistemologically organized as a sort of hierarchy, with Europe and its Latin Christian literature at its centre and top" (Said 1993: 52). Such critical comments have inspired scrutiny of the power relations involved in the global reception of non-European-North-American literary traditions. Under such circumstances, the first Nobel Award for a Chinese writer has assumed great significance in making visible the entrance of Chinese literature into the international canon, or the canon of "World Literature". This event also subjects itself to the scrutiny of Post-Colonialist discourses.

Zhang Xudong and Tam Kwok-kan in their respective articles summarise this reality faced by Chinese literature with Charles Taylor's concept of "the Politics of Recognition". They have both observed a keen anticipation among Chinese literary circles of a Chinese Nobel Laureate (Zhang 2000: 18–23; Tam 2001: 4). One can easily understand such an anticipation, and the frustration caused by previous failed nominations. Had the glory of the first Nobel Prize in Literature award to a Chinese writer befallen some grand literary figure extolled by mainstream discourses of Chinese literary history and accepted as representative of the Chinese tradition, it would have served as a metonym of legitimisation of modern Chinese literature within the international canon. However as it turned out, the glittering prize was awarded to Chinese literature, but not on Chinese terms. Something is being legitimised here, but that something is associated with a body of works that are explicitly allied with the Modernist tradition of western Europe. What is being celebrated by the Award is therefore not the autonomy and achievement of the Chinese tradition, but the influence of the European tradition on "other" literatures. Instead of the grand climax of Chinese literature receiving recognition in the world, the Prize proved to be rather an anti-climax. One might of course question whether the assumption of a "Chinese tradition" is valid, since the existence of heterogeneity within the Chinese canon cannot be ignored. Yet the issue here is not the reality or otherwise of a closed tradition, but the *desire* for recognition for something *Chinese*, as opposed to *Western*. This desire must be understood in the context of China's self-interpellation at the dawn of the new Millennium as it begins to assert itself in the world after more than a century of subordination.

This is not to say that the Swedish Academy intended such a scenario. In fact there is never any way of knowing anybody's intention about anything for certain, all that we can assess are outcomes and implications. The mission of the Nobel Prize committee is to acknowledge outstanding achievements in literary arts. This general principle is honourable, but the process by which this principle is put into practice is more complex. The incongruity between the popularity of Gao's works with the Swedish Academy and their lack of popularity among Chinese readers raises doubts as to the validity of the Prize with respect to the Chinese tradition(s). The knee-jerk responses frequently observed in internet discussions at the time of the Award include the following: Are Gao Xingjian's writings really that good? Are they really the most worthy writings in contemporary Chinese literature? Are they representative of the achievements of contemporary Chinese literature? In other words: Does it represent sound judgment on the part of the Swedish Academy to have given him the award? Upon reflection it has to be concluded that all these are irrelevant questions. After all, the Nobel Prize is a European institution. Its criteria and judgments have to be understood within its own conventions, not within the Chinese tradition(s). For a non-Chinese institution, possessing expertise and knowledge of Chinese literature is one thing, whether it adopts the Chinese values and acts on behalf of the Chinese tradition(s) is another thing altogether. The Academy speaks for itself, not for the Chinese tradition(s). It represents its own perspective on Chinese literature, and not a perspective from within the Chinese tradition(s). Furthermore, to assume that the Academy can in any way represent a value system that transcends its own perspective and thereby achieves universality is completely unrealistic. Philosophy in the twentieth century has denounced the teleology of God, so it is surprising that some of us are still bothered by the idea of the teleology of the Swedish Academy. The incongruity between the Academy's opinion of Gao's works and the reception of these works by Chinese readers only serves to accentuate difference rather than to prove universality.

Xihua: "Westernisation"

Perhaps a more relevant question to ask is: What is there in Gao's works that appeals to the Swedish Academy? The obvious answer is that Gao writes in a way that can be understood in the literary convention the Academy is accustomed to. Gao's entire *oeuvre* has evinced considerable western influence. In fact, as mentioned above, his first noted literary project was to advocate European Modernism in Chinese literature. Having graduated in French in 1962, Gao's vision of literature was understandably informed by European, especially French, traditions. Yet Western influence in China, and indeed in many other places subjected to colonial and imperialist domination, is never merely an idiosyncratic or a personal choice, but often takes on more profound significance. Like his May Fourth predecessors who instigated literary and social reform through *xihua*, Westernisation, European Modernism served for Gao as a springboard for literary reform in the 1980s. To understand what *xihua* signifies in China, and consequently in Gao's works, one needs some understanding of this phenomenon in modern China.

Major nation-building campaigns in China in the late nineteenth and almost the whole of the twentieth centuries were very much the result of China's interaction with Europe and America. Both Li Hongzhang's and Kang Youwei's reform plans in the late Qing Dynasty, and Deng Xiaoping's Economic Reforms in the 1980s, were provoked by the disjuncture between China's political, economic and military power and that of foreign capitalist and imperialist superpowers. The link between Westernisation and modernisation is not a matter of coincidence, but a function of China's being forcibly "opened up" to and exploited by militarily superior foreign powers. In fact, the same dominant world forces led China to upgrade her economic and military power twice in the modern period, first at the turn of the twentieth century, and then after the Cold War. At the end of the Qing Dynasty, Li Hongzhang, serving the Qing Court, aimed to build up strong armed forces with foreign technology in order to strike a military balance with the foreign powers, whilst his contemporary, the republican-leaning Kang Youwei attempted a thorough reform of the social system. Kang advocated the introduction of Western technology to Chinese industries and engineering with the aim of improving China's economic power and ultimately strengthening its political power in the world. Sun Yatsen's model of party politics and the republic reflects his early education and experience in Hawaii. In the early years of the Republic the writings of students and scholars overseas together with translations of foreign books created a strong interest in Europe and the USA, which was most intensely expressed by the May Fourth generation of concerned patriots who clamoured for "total Westernisation" [*quanpan xihua*] of Chinese society. Students on overseas scholarships who held different political and ideological convictions formed new political forces by direct political involvement (Zhou Enlai and Song Jiaoren for example occupied important positions in their own political parties), or by performing the crucial backseat functions of writing and teaching (Lu Xun and Cai Yuanpei for example committed themselves respectively in the fields of writing and education). It is worth noting that it was through the constant reminders of China's political and economic inferiority in a world socio-economic scenario dominated by Europe and the USA, and the various attempts at national modernisation modelled on the latter, that the image of the implacably supreme and infinitely superior West was constructed. In addition, the writings of the first group of Chinese Modernist writers of the 1930s such as Shi Zhecun, Liu Na'ou and Mu Shiying also constituted the construction of the image of the advanced West through its constant association with the modernised city.

This connection between the modern and the West was at its most conspicuous in the Chinese theatre. European Naturalistic theatre was introduced as the progressive form as opposed to the traditional Chinese theatre *xiqu*, which was deemed backward, conservative, and emblematic of feudal values. Although the history of imperialist oppression by these countries often generated certain xenophobic emotions, Westernisation has served as the model for national reform frequently enough to be associated with national rejuvenation. This Chinese-Western dichotomy extends into the binarisms of tradition versus progression, conservatism versus modernisation, even dictatorship versus democracy and thus oppression versus liberation. The construction of such associations has received willing collaboration on the part of the West through numerous apparatuses such as the media, international political organisations, trade and charity institutions, which have contributed to the perpetuation of the dividing image of the Orient and the Occident to the present day. Even nowadays, the Chinese are locked in a dichotomous mode of thinking over the issue of Westernisation: either they support it, or they reject it.

Westernisation took on similar associations right after the Cultural Revolution. In the Communist Party Congress held in August 1977, Deng Xiaoping, once a student in France himself, stressed the development of technology and science in the Ten Years Plan of national growth. In the new constitution promulgated by the Fifth National People's Congress held in March 1978, science and technology occupied an important role in the agenda. On both occasions, the scientific and technological achievements of the European and American world were held up as a model to be emulated. This model of reform aimed at the development of industrialisation and capital accumulation in the Western mode, but reflection on the established political ideology or structure was left aside. The purpose of reform was to strengthen the existing model of government by means of stronger economic and military power. *Xihua*, Westernisation, became a symbol signifying a progressive attitude in Chinese life throughout the entire twentieth century. The identification of Westernisation with modernisation, thus of the West with the modern, is perpetuated in the post-colonial era after the Second World War, and in the new millennium by the increasingly fierce consumerism that operates globally.

The conspicuous association of Gao's writings with the West prompts a reading of them through the prism of the politics discussed above. This is true not only of his early works directly advocating European Modernism, but also of his later works which can be read as displaying features of both Modernist and Post-Modernist writings. The adoption of Western literary models has been evident throughout Gao's entire repertoire and formed the backbone of his creative methods. His early writings show striking resemblance to some European Modernist classics, while his later works attempt to articulate Post-Modernist views on literature and on the world. The intimate intertextuality between Gao's works and those European works demonstrates itself in terms of both concepts and structures. These writing paradigms were translated into Gao's works. It is no wonder, therefore, that the Swedish Academy recognises its own image in them.

Translation

I understand the close intertextual relationship between Gao's works and European writings as a translational one, and Gao's writings as translation of the European Modernist and Post-Modernist writing paradigms. Translation is not mere cloning. It involves much adaptation and transformation. In Gao's translation of the European writing paradigms into Chinese literature, seemingly similar textual features generate different meanings across cultures. His translations of the Modernist writing paradigm are so successful that through them Modernism made its way into the mainstream Chinese literary system in the 1980s. This phenomenon is examined in Chapters Two, Three and Four. On the contrary, his translation of the Post-Modernist writing paradigm is less successful. This phenomenon is examined in Chapter Five.

Readers will have noticed that my use of the term "translation" goes beyond its most common scope of reference which refers to a one-to-one linguistic transfer of texts. In fact it has been a recent development in translation studies to move away from the product-oriented approach and emphasise the intertextuality between and among texts. Indeed in some cases the texts in question are often not recognised in the traditional view as translations in a strict sense of the word. Translation is now sometimes taken as a critical concept rather than a category of textual equivalence or a linguistic exercise. Some disciplines outside literary studies have already taken advantage of this new approach to the concept of translation and used it to refer to the adaptation of a system from one structure into another structure. These studies often emphasise the changes the system in question goes through in the process of transfer, so that it fulfils the needs and requirements of the target users, and becomes successfully acculturated into the target structure.[2] Instead of celebrating equivalence, this new approach shows a hermeneutic orientation and focuses on discrepancy (rather than similarity) between the source and the target text. I find a good many concepts and theories in translation studies of this type helpful in my understanding of the relationship between Gao's works, especially the early pieces, and their sources of influence. Among these theories is Itamar Even-Zohar's Polysystem Theory. He situates translated literature within the literary polysystem of the target culture. In this theoretical model, the position of a work of translation within the target system rather than the source system is emphasised. Translated literature is therefore understood as literary-cultural reality in the target society. Gideon Toury, Even-

Zohar's colleague of the Tel Aviv School, elaborates the linguistic aspect of the systemic correlation between the target text and the target context, suggesting that linguistic norms in the target language and the target culture are determining factors in making translation decisions. Toury's theory meticulously weaves contextual and cultural details into the linguistic constructions of translated texts. He also suggests that other modes of intercultural writings such as "pseudo-translation", a category of original writing disguised as translation, can be analysed with the same model. The objects of investigation in Even-Zohar's and Toury's theoretical models are the "whys" and the "hows" of transformation when writings or modes of writing travel from one culture to another.

A good description of this kind of transfer is offered by Ovidio Carbonell. He makes a distinction between "cultural translation" and "textual translation", emphasising the cultural-contextual dimension rather than the textual-linguistic dimension of a translation (Carbonell 1996: 79). In his theory, translation is understood as "a paradigm of culture contact" (Carbonell 1996: 79). This resonates with the Polysystem and the Systemic Theories of the Tel Aviv School. Carbonell's notion of "cultural translation" signifies more than the translated text itself. It refers to the text and its relation with the whole network of issues surrounding it — be they textual, cultural, hermeneutic or political — which are involved in cross-cultural reproduction and production of meaning. Carbonell in particular pays attention to the activities of cultural transfer against the background of power-play of colonisation and decolonisation. The translational relationship between the source and the target texts is not one of equivalence, or one that seeks equivalence, but an intertexutual one that is embedded in existing structures of power, ideology and other cultural and intercultural realities. It is in this sense I refer to the intertexutuality of Gao's repertoire and its European source of influence as a *translational* one. Moreover, in order to gauge the degree of translatability of Modernism into Chinese literature in the 1980s, and also to identify Gao's translation strategies, I resort to Even-Zohar's Polysystem Theory. It helps me understand the interplay between Gao's texts and their contexts as a systemic one. Readers will notice that from Chapter Two to Chapter Five, these two theoretical concepts, "cultural translation" and the Polysystem, have significantly informed my approach to Gao's early writings.

It should be noted that there is no existing English translation of Gao's early introductory essays on European Modernism. Therefore a detailed description and study of these texts is provided in Chapter Two. In my analysis of these essays, emphasis is put on what aspects of European Modernism are stressed and what others are played down, so that common ground between this "new"[3] and the existing literary paradigms are foregrounded, with the result that this new writing paradigm could make its (re-)entrance into the Chinese polysystem. Chapters Three and Four examine the short stories and plays Gao wrote before

1988 when he took up residence in France. The theory of Gao's works as translation of the European Modernist writing paradigm is followed through in these two chapters.

I need also to stress that my description of Gao's writings as cultural translation carries no derogatory insinuation or intent. Anybody with any experience of translation will agree that translation is as creative as any "creative" writing, and indeed hermeneutically even more complicated, since it has to deal with more levels and realms of reality, namely the primary realities of both source and target culture as well as the secondary reality represented in the source text. And it is exactly this complexity in Gao's works that requires them to be looked at as translations rather than "adaptations" or "re-creations". These last two concepts are unsatisfactory because they tend to be product-oriented. Related ideas such as "importation", "loan" and "influence" carry an innuendo of uni-directionality. By invoking translation as a critical concept, I hope to highlight the following questions: How does the transferred paradigm differ from the source one? Why is this so? What transformations have taken place in order for it to assimilate into the target culture? What functions does this new paradigm perform in the target system? These are exactly the questions I will ask about Gao's early writings. In the three chapters to follow, I will try to answer the following questions: How are Modernism and Post-Modernism negotiated within the texture of Gao's writings in Chinese? Under what conditions are these negotiations made? As a point of cultural contact, what functions have these cultural translations fulfilled in the target culture? I have grouped these three chapters together under the heading of "Translation as Transfer".

Exile

In 1987 Gao left China and has stayed away in the subsequent twenty years, being *persona non grata*. His departure from China has drastically changed the functions of his writing. Following China's proscription of his works in 1989, they have become marginalised in the Chinese polysystem. The conditions for both production and reading of his works have been very much altered. What has remained consistent is the cross-cultural factor. Instead of translating a Western paradigm into China, a Chinese subjectivity is being written under the conditions of writing in the West. In view of the general ban on his works in China, the intended readership has to be those Chinese living in Taiwan, the former European colonies of Hong Kong and Macau, and the Chinese diasporic communities in South East Asia and other continents. These readers, though ethnically Chinese, do not necessarily possess many qualities of an assumed "Chineseness" in terms of their understanding and values. This is simply because more often than not, the differences in the actual material and cultural lives they live out in their respective countries have outweighed any legacy of Chinese culture they have inherited from their immigrant forefathers. Since leaving China, Gao's writings were predominantly written for such a readership. "China" means something completely different for them from what it does to those who live out the everyday reality of the contemporary nation of China.

Any subjects in the diasporic situation could easily find themselves confronted and confounded by an exilic alienation. To remain relevant to the reality of their host countries they would have to review their relationship with their own past and seek new connections with their present communities. The latter half of this process is described by the critic Mary Besemeres as "cultural self-translation" in the context of her discussion on Edward Said's and André Acimen's descriptions of their experience as immigrants (Besemeres 2003: 32). The need to articulate meanings generated from one's native culture and native language in another cultural and linguistic framework involves much re-fashioning of the material, so that the "narrated self" can be understood in the target culture. Gao's works written outside China reveal two impulses: first to articulate China's mythical past and the reminiscence of his life in the past in China; secondly to withdraw into an individualistic isolation. Gao's plays written in the 1990s, instead of simultaneously achieving a double-membership of both cultures, attest to the phenomenon of "non-membership". In the analysis of these works from Chapters Five to Seven, I will ask the following questions: In what ways can these two impulses be understood as the result of exile? In what ways are these texts relevant to China? In what ways are they relevant to their immediate environment? What kind of cultural and political identity has been constructed in them? What light does this phenomenon shed on diaporic writing? I have grouped these three chapters under the headings "The Translated Man" and "Translating the Self" respectively.

There is one more aspect in Gao's works that is related to translation: some of his works are received through translations. Even in the early stage of Gao's writing career, a small but significant proportion of his readers do not belong to the (diasporic) Chinese communities but are sinologists, academics and translators of Chinese literature, cultural critics or simply the more interested members of an international reading and theatre-going public. The latter categories of reader have gained access to his works through translation. The Nobel Prize award has made reception of his works through translation ever more important. There are problematics and politics involved in translation that are relevant to the entrance of Gao's works into the global literary arena. These issues will be examined in the concluding chapter entitled "Reading across Culture".

Methodology

To sum up, in this book, the relationship of Gao Xingjian's writings to the "West" (in terms of both their production and reception) is taken to be the corollary of contextual understanding of the repertoire. His works of different periods have functioned as one kind of mediation or another between the Chinese and the Western literary polysystems. Therefore, the different aspects of the concept of cultural translation are evoked to illustrate those various functions of mediation I note in Gao's works.

There are two points in my methodology that need to be clearly stated. First, I emphasise Gao's works as a repertoire. This perspective has enabled me to conduct internal comparisons and draw internal references within his repertoire. My intention is thus to highlight the importance of interactions between the writings and their conditions of production, which I find particularly pertinent in the case of Gao Xingjian's writing. Second, I have made the decision not to include the plethora of exegeses of his own work by Gao as the object of my study. Although they provide important hints as to the directions one could take in their interpretation, they are inevitably susceptible to subjective bias on the part of the writer. In many instances I find Gao's treatises to be more the expression of the writer's own artistic aspirations than an objective description of the texts. In some other instances, I find his practice simply at odds with his treatises. After all, a text articulates not only the conscious but also the sub-conscious and the unconscious. I see it as the critic's job to go beyond what the writer is conscious of in order to open up other possibilities of interpretation. Having said that, I have consulted that particular body of material and they have served as a reference point in this study.

Except for the first reference to them in each chapter, all titles of Gao's works are referred to in this book in English rather than in the transliteration of their original Chinese titles, simply for the sake of convenient reading. As regards those texts that are published in English translation, I conform to their translated titles as much as possible, also for convenience of reference for non-Chinese readers. A few of his plays have multiple translations, and for these I have chosen the ones I find best translated. In the cases where I find my interpretation of the titles different from existing translations, I provide my own. All quotations of Chinese sources are translated into English by myself, except where otherwise stated.

Part 2

Translation as Transfer

2
Essays on Modernism 1980–1983:
Negotiating Modernism

The Post-Cultural Revolution Context

Gao Xingjian belongs to the generation of writers who started their literary careers after the Cultural Revolution (1966–1976). He graduated from university in 1962 but did not get published until 1980, not because he was a late developer, but because normal prospects for young people in the 1960s were blighted by the Cultural Revolution. On many occasions Gao refers to having burnt manuscripts of his own writing to avoid getting into trouble. It was only in the relatively relaxed atmosphere in the years after the Cultural Revolution that he was able to get published. It is therefore important to contextualise his early writings within the framework of post-Cultural Revolution literature.

The year 1976 represents a watershed in modern Chinese life. The deaths of Zhou Enlai in January and Mao Zedong in September that year engendered enormous changes in the political climate and power structure of the country. Among the many aspects of modern Chinese life that were intensely affected by these changes, literature was both radically influenced by and expressive of them. The gathering at Tiananmen Square in traditional April mourning for Zhou Enlai turned into an opportunity for many people to express their doubts openly about the leadership and the direction of the Cultural Revolution. Poems by anonymous authors were posted in the square expressing discontent. The importance of these poems was underlined by their tone of defiance towards the prevailing official ideology. This informal manner of publication signified an outpouring of sentiments subverting the official line laid down by the stultifying restrictions of Party sanctioned literature since the establishment of the People's Republic. This boom in heterodox expression came as a breath of fresh air to the monotonous Maoist "Socialist Realist"[1] works lauded by the repressive authority that had for ten years been particularly heavy-handed in curbing free artistic expression. It was no surprise that such freedom was swiftly suppressed and condemned by the Central Cultural Revolution Committee. This clamp-down was followed by the arrest and political persecution of many of the poems' authors and supporters. Nevertheless the poems came to represent the struggle for freedom of speech and autonomous literary production; both of these goals would continue to be pursued in the post-Cultural Revolution decade.

The post-Cultural Revolution Economic Reforms launched by Deng Xiaoping's new leadership allowed many areas of socio-economic development to take on more progressive characteristics. In terms of literature, the first discussion of literary activity on a large-scale after the Cultural Revolution was held in November in 1976, when the editorial board of *Renmin wenxue* magazine [People's literature] organised a forum on short stories. This generated a discussion on writers' creative autonomy regarding matters of theme and style. But this call for diversity did not achieve much success in practice. Instead, it encouraged the production of scar literature [*shanghen wenxue*], represented by Liu Xinwu's short story *Banzhuren* (translated into English as "Class Counsellor" by Geremie Barmé and Bennett Lee, 1979) published in the November issue of *Renmin wenxue* in 1977 and Lu Xinhua's *Shanghen* (translated into English as "The Wounded" by Geremie Barmé and Bennett Lee, 1979) in the newspaper *Wenhui bao* on 11 August 1978. These works of scar literature are commonly characterised by their expression of discontent with the Cultural Revolution. They tell stories of unjust and cruel purges of innocent people. The sentiments in many of these works are true and honest, but they also uniformly conclude with their hope and trust in the new leadership. This was literature produced under the regulated freedom of expression. They closely followed the government's policy of the period of "bringing order out of chaos" [*boluan fanzheng*]. This was adopted as the overarching new policy to restore social order under the new leadership which replaced the Gang of Four and their followers. In terms of literary techniques, the majority of scar literature works adopt a loosened style of Socialist Realism with a sentimental tone. This is not to say that there were no experimental writings among scar literature. Ru Zhijuan's *Jianji cuole de gushi* (translated into English as "A Story out of Sequence" by Fan Tian and John Minford in 1981) published in the February issue of *Renmin wenxue* in 1979 received major attention for its non-chronological narration of events. But these kinds of experimental writings were in the minority, sometimes risking criticism for their alleged literary elitism.

It is within this context that Gao Xingjian advocated the adoption, or re-adoption, of European Modernism into Chinese literature. In a discussion of the nature of European Modernism, Malcolm Bradbury and James McFarlane suggest that the innovative and experimental approach to the arts during the Modernist Movement was initiated

> ... not only for formal reasons. The crisis is a crisis of culture; it often involves an unhappy view of history — so that the Modernist writer is not simply the artist set free, but the artist under specific, apparently historical strain. (Bradbury and McFarlane 1976: 26)

Bradbury and McFarlane refer specifically to the explosive growth of production technology, and hence capital, in Europe in the nineteenth century, which brought about drastic changes in civilian life and led to the destructive capabilities of modern weapons in the First World War. The discontent felt in Gao's contemporary literary circles, on the other hand, was more of a national scale. China's relative economic backwardness had not been reversed since the establishment in 1949 of the People's Republic. Neither a unidirectional reliance on the leadership of the Party nor a sense of complacency regarding China's five thousand years of cultural heritage helped to secure a comfortable cultural identity for the intellectuals. In particular their disillusion with Party ideology sowed the seeds for alternative perceptions of the world. In Gao's writings published after his first visit to Europe can be perceived an eager yearning to continue the Westernisation of modern Chinese literature, a path that was taken by the May Fourth writers but spurned after the establishment of the PRC for its incompatibility with the new Republic's ideological foundation. Between 1980 and 1981, Gao published over a dozen essays introducing European Modernism. Most of them were later collected in his theoretical work *Xiandai xiaoshuo jiqiao chutan* [A preliminary exploration of the techniques of modern fiction] (1981).

A Preliminary Exploration did not include all of Gao's essays on Modernism, but only those on the general features of this writing paradigm. Case studies were featured in three other essays on French Modernist writings. French literature has in general significantly informed Gao's literary orientation. His entire career up to this point was connected with the education in French literature he had received before the Cultural Revolution. Upon graduation in 1962, he was first assigned the job of translator at the Foreign Languages Press. Although there was an interlude of five years from 1970 to 1975 when he was sent to the countryside for labour work during the Cultural Revolution, he was "rehabilitated" [*fuyuan*][2] and returned to Beijing to assume work with the press in 1975. In 1977 he was transferred to the Foreign Affairs Unit of the Writers' Association of China. Until then his work had mainly been translating between French and Chinese. At the Writer's Association, although also working as translator, his responsibilities were different. One of his duties was to accompany a delegation to France and Italy led by the veteran May Fourth generation writer Ba Jin, who was himself a very proficient French speaker, having been at one time a student in Paris and a translator of Russian and other European writings into Chinese. This position at the Writers' Association allowed Gao much greater exposure and more opportunities.

Although he already had a novella published in *Huacheng*, a reputable literary journal published in Guangzhou as early as 1979, his literary career did not take off until after this visit to Europe. *Hanye de xingchen* [Stars on a cold night] follows the realist formula of scar literature both in form and in content. It is a competent piece of writing but does not stand out among other works of the same type, nor has it attracted much attention from critics and readers. But immediately after the visit to Europe, the number of his publications increased dramatically. He had six journalistic pieces related to this trip published between the end of 1979 and the beginning of 1983.[3] They record his observations on the theatre, literature and culture of the places he visited. In that period going abroad was no simple and casual matter. Apart from the financial expenses that were prohibitive for anyone on a Chinese salary, a visa was hard to obtain, even for official purposes. Moreover, the government exercised tight control over the circulation of information, especially anything pertaining to the West. As a result, the Chinese reading public had strictly limited contact with the contemporary West. Gao's six articles were well written. They served as both pleasant easy reading, and also an induction to European culture for the Chinese reading public. In this context, Gao performed the function of self-appointed cultural mediator.

As mentioned earlier, in addition to these six pieces of easy reading, he also had three articles on French literature published in early 1980. These three pieces were written as hard-core literary criticism. Although published in three different literary journals, they form a series of introduction to major French Modernist writers, including Sartre, Camus, Robbe-Grillet, Prévert and others. Compared to his controversial and well-known book *A Preliminary Exploration of the Techniques of Modern Fiction*, these three articles might appear more conservative as they often conclude with dogmatic Marxist evaluation of the revolutionary relevance of the writings in question. They may not be of great interest if critics are looking for the explosive moments of post-Cultural Revolution Chinese Modernism. But their significance should not be under-estimated, especially if one is concerned with the *process* of Modernism's transfer into China in this period, as well as the cultural negotiation involved in that process, and the role played by Gao's works.

"*Falanxi xiandai wenxue de tongku*" [The agony of modern French literature]

"*Fanlanxi xiandai wenxue de tongku*" [The agony of modern French literature] was published in *Waiguo wenxue yanjiu* [*Foreign Literature Studies*], No.1, 1980.

It was, and still is, one of the literary journals on foreign literature held in the highest esteem by literary critics nationwide. This article offers a comprehensive survey of some of the most important literary figures of French Modernism and their writings. It opens with two questions: "What is literature? What can literature do? The article suggests that French literature has been "agonising" [*tongku*] about these two problems since the Second World War (Gao 1980b: 51). Then it starts its discussion on the writers in question. The first one is Jean-Paul Sartre. He is commended as "the pioneer of existentialist literature, and the most influential writer after the War" (Gao 1980b: 51). The main example cited is his 1938 novel *La Nausée*. A brief summary of the plot is provided, and the theme of the novel is understood to be the protagonist's feeling of nausea at the "sheer lack of meaning of existence" (Gao 1980b: 51). Yet no further elaboration on Sartre's philosophy of existence is offered. There appears to be a deliberate suppression of Existentialism as philosophy in the article. The discussion is restricted to literary issues. The article suggests that the novel form is the best vehicle for the representation of Sartre's Existentialist vision of life, because Existentialism is "not a meticulous system of philosophy, it is better understood not through scholarly inquiry, but through his literary creation" (Gao 1980b: 52). It is interesting to compare this with Iris Murdoch's analysis of Sartre's literary works. She also holds that Sartre's novel is a more effective means to propound Existentialism than his theoretical writings, but her reasons are very different. According to her,

> It is not surprising that such a thinker should use the novel as one of his modes of expression … The novelist proper is, in his way, a sort of phenomenologist. He has always implicitly understood, what the philosopher has grasped less clearly, that human reason is not a single unitary gadget the nature of which could be discovered once for all. The novelist has had his eye fixed on what we do, and not on what we ought to do or must be presumed to do. He has as a natural gift that blessed freedom from rationalism which the academic thinker achieves, if at all, by a precarious discipline. He has always been, what the very latest philosophers claim to be, a describer rather than an explainer … The novel is a picture of, and a comment upon, the human condition, and a typical product of the era to which belong also the writings of Nietzsche, the psychology of Freud, the philosophy of Sartre. (Murdoch 1953/1969: 9–10)

Sartre's two critics arrive at the same conclusion but for different reasons. Murdoch's reason is the phenomenological potential of the novel form and she looks upon it as a merit, whereas Gao blames a disciplinary deficiency on the part of Existentialist philosophy. In his article, Existentialism as a description of life and as a philosophy is played down. Unfortunately, without a good understanding of Existentialism, it is impossible to demonstrate the value of Sartre's novel, since it is exactly the apocalyptic awareness of man's existentialist situation unfolded in these novels that has constituted their greatness. Therefore the article has not successfully illustrated the value of Sartre's works. Its generally positive attitude towards Sartre's writings is somewhat related to Sartre's well-known anti-capitalist and anti-colonial stance, and the overt political inclination in his novels. Yet even this is checked by a major criticism:

> But Sartre did not really understand modern proletariat revolution. He could neither understand the problems that the proletariat revolutionary had struggled against in its historical progress, nor the complexity of these problems. And neither was he able to propose a set of strategies and policies for revolution. All he offered amounts to no more than a call from his passionate soul for an abstract and absolute idea of social justice. No wonder he had not found the correct way to bring changes to the capitalist society. (Gao 1980b: 52)

This argument is typical of Maoist Materialism. Not proposing concrete strategies and policies for proletariat revolution is taken as a fatal flaw in any analysis. This position might make the article read as conservative by today's standard, but it must be remembered that China in 1980 still required a doctrinaire Maoist approach to literary criticism. Going against this stance could create problems in getting published. With this understanding in mind, it is noticeable that the above criticism stands out rather abruptly on its own as a kind of statement, with neither examples for illustration nor arguments leading to its conclusion. In fact it tends to arouse suspicion that such criticisms are inserted to enable the article to meet the demands of the more doctrinaire censors. But as a result, the article oscillates between a positive and a negative view of Sartre's works, and thus conveys an almost embarrassing indecision.

Along the same Maoist Materialist lines, the article also criticises Albert Camus for "understanding even less about revolution than Sartre does" (Gao 1980b: 53). Camus' two novels, *L'Etranger* and *La Peste*, are discussed. The thoroughly Existentialist view on life in these novels is interpreted as the result of a revolutionary "passion not being sustained", and therefore is concluded as constituting "a return to loneliness and spiritual agony" (Gao 1980b: 53). According to the article, this is exactly where the value of Camus' works lie: they fully reflect and represent contemporary French minds. For Gao Camus' agony represents the agony of modern French intellectuals. The article suggests that the greatest achievement of critical realism is:

> ...its function as criticism of social injustice as opposed to antidote prescribed for moral perfection; its expression of purpose to change social reality as opposed to the desire for a sense of assurance and relief secured by the presumed value of human existence." (Gao 1980b: 53)

This indeed is an apt description of existentialist literature. But this comment stands in sharp contrast with the dogmatic view presented earlier in the same article criticising Sartre's writings for their lack of concrete strategies and policies for proletariat revolution. There is an inconsistency between its view of Sartre and its view of Camus, but the article as a whole shows no attempt either to reconcile them or to put them into some kind of negotiation with each other. They are simply juxtaposed in the same article, and so an interesting tension is created.

An equally ambiguous stance is taken with reference to the writings of André Malraux. Malraux is represented as being very different from both Sartre and Camus, because his "literary creation is intertwined with his political activities" (Gao 1980b: 53). Although Sartre and Camus were equally committed and active in anti-Fascist and anti-colonial struggles, ideologically their works are more subtle because of their philosophical orientation. In Gao's article, Malraux's *La Condition Humaine* and some of his other writings are considered "the highest achievement of Western Humanism", demonstrating "no hesitation, no regret" in "seeking for the meaning of life and literature" (Gao 1980b: 53). Yet, this is not to say that Malraux was immune to the French "agony". In his last work *Anti-Mémoire*, he expressed frustration with the events of 1968 and the social reality of France. In the last years of his life, he "agonised" because, looking at contemporary France, he was no longer able to affirm the value of his life, a life that had been devoted to political participation. Yet Gao in this article suggests that it was the very commitment to political struggles that had infused his literary creations. Such scepticism therefore diminishes the value of his writings. However the article stops short of launching into a dogmatic Maoist criticism on this "agony" which can potentially be seen as revisionist.

François Mauriac is the only figure represented in the same article to be free of this French "agony", because he had found salvation in Catholicism. But he was only given a mention of less than 100 characters in this article which extends beyond 3500 characters, perhaps because his relief in salvation renders him incongruous in this article about "agonising" French literature, or because spiritual salvation through religion is dismissed in both Maoist and Existentialist discourses. This brief mention is basically informative rather than analytical, but it has already given voice to Mauriac's position, thereby adding to the conglomeration of voices in the article.

There is not much discussion in the article on the use of language and literary devices in the works of these writers. Indeed one would not take them as good examples of the full-blown Modernist style. In fact their reliance on the description of external reality and the protagonists' rational understanding of events constitute an objectivism akin to European realist novels. In his comments on Existentialist and Absurd Theatre, Martin Esslin expresses dissatisfaction with Sartre's dramatic and linguistic strategies (Esslin 1961/1987: 24). He finds Sartre's dramatic realism not as effective as some other non-realistic plays, such as those of Samuel Beckett and Eugène Ionesco, in constructing the Existentialist view of the world Sartre's own philosophy has inspired. Iris Murdoch shares a similar view on Sartre's fiction, but she attributes his stylistic choice to his desire to bring about changes through literature:

> ... Sartre is an amateur psychoanalyst and a moral teacher, as well as being a philosopher. A driving force in all his writing is his serious desire to change the life of his reader. It is perhaps this which makes his philosophical consciousness stop short of a critical awareness of language ... (Murdoch 1953/1969: 9)

Whether Murdoch is correct or not in her speculation about Sartre's desire to change his reader, she is right in her observation that Sartre's novels show an absence of a "critical awareness of language". Their not being experimental in form might explain why Gao focuses on their content rather than their language. However, a different approach is adopted in his analysis of other French Modernists. Their experimentation in narrative structure and their "critical awareness of language" are justly given due attention. A comprehensive summary is offered on the experimentation conducted by writers including Louis Aragon, André Breton and his fellow Surrealist poets who seek to give representation to the subconscious, and on the works by Marcel Proust, André Gide, Samuel Beckett, and also those by writers of the *Nouveau Roman* including Alain Robbe-Grillet and Claude Simon. In hindsight, one could almost have pointed to exactly those aspects of French Modernism Gao discussed in this article that came to exert strong influence on his own creative writings. Many of the dominant features in the writings Gao was to produce later coincide neatly with those given special attention in this article. One example is his discussion on the unconventional treatment of the personal pronouns in Aragon's novel *Les Communistes* [*The Communists*]. It foretells the use of the second and third person pronouns as narrative subjects in Gao's later novels and plays. Even more amazing is his description of Malraux's *Anti-Mémories*, which could almost serve as an articulation of his own artistic principles in the novel *Lingshan* [*Soul Mountain*] which he was to finish a decade later:

> He has merged historical facts with fiction, and created an alternative self to engage in a dialogue with the author. The book demonstrates the author's wisdom and breadth of knowledge in its extensive discussion of political figures in history, of arts and literature, and of modern culture. (Gao, 1980b: 53)

This extract matches the explanation of the structure employed in *Lingshan* that Gao himself has offered on a great many occasions. In his plays the actors are required to expedite a fluid entrance and exit of their characters by referring to the characters they play by third person pronouns. This has probably stemmed from Malraux's influence. Later on, Gao's wholesale rejection of an objectivist view on language, his translation of another European Modernist idea, can also be traced back to this article, in which a tradition of the subjectivist use of language is constructed to include the poetry of Baudelaire, Mallarmé, Apollinaire, the Surrealists, and the theories of Freudian psychoanalysis and phenomenology. At this point, he suggests that in these writers' works an objective external world has given way to privilege the expression of:

> ... the subconscious, dreams, and psychological processes visualised in images. A language is invented to match them. This language has also prompted a change in the way people think. To a certain extent, a conceptual way of thinking is replaced by an intuitive thinking through images. The boundary between external reality and internal feelings is transgressed ... They [the Modernist writers] were enchanted by this language, and this enchantment was often taken as the aim of literary creation, but they could not find the bridge of language that would lead them to the other shore. Therefore the majority of them became isolated in their own minds, not understood by others ... (Gao 1980b: 55)

One can understand the difficulty of summing up in one short paragraph the entire phenomenon and the intentions and constraints of a subjectivist use of language. Parts of this short exegesis strikes the reader as rather obscure; for example, it is not clear what is being referred to by "that other shore" the unachievable "bridge of language" is supposed to lead to. Nevertheless the commentary shows an early interest in linguistic experimentation that came later to dominate Gao's writing. The only one of his writings that does not show heavy Modernist influence is *Hanye de xingchen* [Stars on a cold night], a novella written prior to his visit to Europe, which also predates his suite of three articles on French Modernism. This first one of the three pieces reads remarkably like a preface to his entire *oeuvre*, or like the synopsis of a play.

"Faguo dangdai wenxue de yige zhuti — zhuiqiu: ping liangpian faguo duanpian xiaoshuo" [A theme in contemporary French literature — quest: on two French short stories]

Gao's subsequent two articles read less like a survey than the preceding one. There is a clear structure for the suite: the first is an overview, followed by two case studies. The two case studies echo the brief conclusion in the first one, which states that French literature is engaging in an agonising search for a meaning for its own existence, and this self-awareness is what renders French literature of special importance among Western literatures (Gao 1980b: 57). The second article of this suite was also published in 1980, but in another literary magazine *Shiyue* [*October*], also among the most prestigious literary magazines circulated nation-wide. This article analyses two short stories of the French *Nouveau Roman*, "*Lazare aux mains vides*" by Vercors from his collection of stories *Sept sentiers du désert*, and "*La plage*" by Alain Robbe-Grillet from his collection of short stories *Instantanés*. The former is an interior monologue reflecting the protagonist's psychological process, while the latter is an elaborate description of the external world without any interpretations of its psychological relevance to the protagonist or its metaphysical implications.[4] Both are unusual by comparison with conventional Realist writing. The focus of Gao's analysis is placed on the formal innovations of these two texts, and on how subjective reality, the new focus in literature after Freudian psychology, is differentiated from objective reality of the Realist tradition. Their common theme of a man insisting on his quest for an ideal is taken to be meta-literary. Lazarus' fervent religious quest in "*Lazare aux mains vides*" and the protagonist's quest for the sea-bird in "*La plage*" are both read as allegories of the *Nouveau Roman*'s quest for new narrative methods. Such a quest is taken to be of significant aesthetic and philosophical profundity:

> Eternal quest has become the very aim of their existence. The theme of both stories is questing without attaining the goal. The characters are no longer simply artistic images but elevated to become the embodiment of philosophical profundity. The meaning of life is being recognised in the process of their quest. (Gao 1980c: 250)

Literary experiments and the characters' spiritual quests are read as an analogy. In this way, literary experiments become richly endowed with the passion and religious purity embodied by the persona of Lazarus, and also with the nobility in man's devotion to an ideal as exemplified by the character in "*La plage*". This is true even, and especially, when it is unattainable, as suggested in these stories. The act of literary experimentation itself is highly romanticised. It acquires a positive and almost heroic image. Again, this anticipates the obsession in Gao's subsequent writings with literary experimentation. In Gao's theories, literary experimentation often occupies a certain moral high ground by being equated with the struggle for individual autonomy under the oppression of political hegemony. One way to understand this is to see it as a direct reaction to the heavy-handed censorship which *A Preliminary Exploration of the Techniques of Modern Fiction* and his subsequent experimentations have confronted.

"Faguo xiandaipai renmin shiren Puliewei'er he ta de Geciji" [The French Modernist poet Prévert and his *Paroles*]

By late 1980, translations and introductory writings of modern and contemporary Western literature had already aroused suspicion on the part of the conservative ideologues. They found the stance, or the lack of one, on class awareness in these works highly dubious. Politically loaded discussions were starting to make an appearance in major literary journals (Tan 1996: 321). The famous debate on Realism versus Modernism which was to put huge political pressure on Gao was getting underway. Gao's position on Modernism in this next article is much more overt than in his previous ones.

The article is dedicated to a discussion of Jacques Prévert's writings. Gao's own translation of some lines from *Paroles* were provided there to illustrate Prévert's stylistic features. It discusses in considerable detail how Prévert's works promote proletariat and anti-imperialist ideologies; how poetic imagery rather than political slogans move his reader; how humour and satire, rhythm and rhyme, and the abundance of colloquialisms contribute to a rich texture in these works; and also how they are influenced by the cinema, Cubist painting and Surrealism. Gao takes pains to justify Prévert's well-known criticism on Realism. He suggests that Prévert's chief objection is directed at Naturalism, "an inferior imitation of Realism" (Gao 1980d: 223). He also differentiates Prévert's achievements from some experimental poetry that could come across as obscure, and emphasises that Prévert's Modernist poems are not only understood by, but are also popular with, the *"renmin dazhong"* [the people and the masses]. Two points are made in relation to this: first, the poet had taken care to make sure these poems could be set to music and sung by the people; second, the poet himself is loved by the people and often referred to as the *renmin shiren* [the poet of the people]. The article's main idea is clear and direct: Modernist writing does not have to be elitist. Prévert's poems are good demonstrations of how Modernist poetry can "reach the people and the masses" and propagate the "correct" kind of ideology, which is the ultimate revolutionary purpose that proletariat literature seeks to fulfil (Gao 1980d: 221). This article represents Gao's first attempt to resolve the perceived contradiction between literary innovation and ideological "correctness". It is also his answer to literary critics who attacked his advocacy of Modernism.

Xiandai xiaoshuo jiqiao chutan [A preliminary exploration of the techniques of modern fiction]

Xiandai xiaoshuo [Modern fiction] in the title of this book refers to *Modernist* fiction. The book represents Gao's most vigorous theoretical endeavour to advocate

Modernism. Seven of the seventeen chapters of the book were already published in the form of individual articles in literary journals.[5] The book consists of approximately 50,000 Chinese characters, rather short for a Chinese book. It reads more like an extended essay. In a short book like this, it is impossible to include all the methods and features of Modernism, let alone to elucidate the philosophies behind them. But the book did serve a purpose, not only as introductory reading and quick reference, but also as an argument for allowing the transfer of Modernism into the centre of the Chinese literary polysystem.

The book comprises seventeen short chapters. Each chapter describes one literary characteristic the author identifies with Modernist writings. They are organised in the following order:

1.[6] Transformations of fiction
2.   Narrative language in fiction
3.   Shifting of personal pronouns
4.   The third person "he"
5.   Stream of consciousness
6.   The Absurd and the illogical
7.   The symbolic
8.   Artistic abstraction
9.   Modern literary language
10. Manipulating language
11. From plot to structure
12. Time and space
13. The sense of reality
14. The sense of distance
15. Modern[ist] techniques and Modernist schools
16. Modern[ist] techniques and the national spirit
17. The future of fiction

The general stance of the book on Modernism is established in Chapters 1 and 2. Changes in literary methods are presented as a natural evolution of the genre. The author argues that the narrative structure of a piece of work should match the vision of the world constructed in it. Therefore, formal experimentation is not only legitimate, but necessary, in a good piece of writing. A differentiation is drawn between sincere experimentation and meaningless formalism. The latter is described as something that "bears no correlation to the content; perhaps it is the only trick to play since these works are so destitute of anything to say" (Gao 1981a: 2). In the various chapters, a plethora of formal explorations by a range of writers, both foreign and Chinese, of different periods in the twentieth century are discussed to show that formal experimentation is a universal phenomenon. Works discussed include those by foreign writers such as Chekhov, Gorky,

Turgenev and the French school of the *Nouveau Roman*, and by Chinese writers such as Lu Xun, Liu Xinwu and Wang Meng. The Chinese examples have been carefully selected to avoid controversy. Lu Xun is the literary figure most consistently lauded by the Chinese Communist Party. Liu Xinwu and Wang Meng were figures of political correctness at that time for their highly successful works of scar literature that went in perfect harmony with the post-Cultural Revolution official policy of political rehabilitation.

Chapters 3 to 9 make up the most important part of the book. The main features of Modernist writing are introduced in these chapters. These features later on are to provide the basis of the recurrent style in Gao's *oeuvre*, both fictional and dramatic. Chapters 3 and 4 discuss different narrative perspectives and the possible effects of adopting the first, second and third person narrative positions. Special attention is given to the use of "you" when the reader is given direct address:

> Sometimes, when an author tells a story, he wants to arouse intense emotional response from the reader. Instead of "he was so emotional that he burst into tears", he will write: "could you but shed tears for him?" Even if the reader does not really shed tears for the protagonist, he will at least pause and think, put himself in the protagonist's shoes, imagine himself in the same situation and ask whether he would cry. (Gao 1981a: 13)

In this exegesis, second person address is taken purely as a device to arouse the reader's emotional response. It is then suggested that Aragon has "adopted a very lively narrative language" in *Les Communistes*, in which the first, second and third person perspectives "are used interchangeably". Later in another paragraph, a bolder proposal is put forward:

> Is it possible to change the dominance of "he" and the supplementary use of "you", and put them side by side in the same narrative? Is it possible to use "I" and "you" interchangeably in the same novel? I think it entirely possible. This would greatly enrich the narrative language, help to break away from the rigid structure and established methods of the novel, and enhance the power of language as an art of expression. (Gao 1981a: 15).

At this stage, this proposition was merely an idea. No suggestions were put forward as to what kind of narrative schemes might be possible. Later on, this idea is put into practice in the narrative structure of his first novel *Lingshan* [*Soul Mountain*]. In hindsight one can see the idea already germinating at this early stage. It is a very good example to show the two steps of the process in which Modernist writing methods are translated into Gao's own Chinese writing, namely inspiration and application.

Chapters 5, 6 and 7 are introductions to stream of consciousness, the Absurd and Symbolism. Gao explains that stream of consciousness is characterised by an emphasis on sensations, a non-linear time sequence of narration and a fluent shifting of first, second and third person perspectives. The Absurd is understood to be an endeavour to express what is beyond the comprehension of logical thinking, and Symbolism the use of concrete figures to express ideas. Sometimes, symbols can be ambiguous, but ambiguity is accepted as a necessary aesthetic quality of Symbolism rather than a drawback. These three chapters consistently argue that these writing methods are not simply rhetorical devices, but are expressions of the Modernists' vision of reality. Stream of consciousness is their attempt to foreground the subjective consciousness in constituting the individual's perception of "reality"; the Absurdists present their detached view of the world; the Symbolists express their ideas of the world in condensed artistic images. The chapters repeatedly argue that these writing methods are effective expressions of universal human faculties, namely the subjective and the subconscious, the illogical and irrational, the conceptual and the poetic, that are present in everybody, whatever their political inclinations. In the discussion of stream of consciousness Gao stresses that this writing method merely imitates the psychological makings of human consciousness; the content of this consciousness can be anything. It can be the consciousness of a petty-bourgeois, or it can be that of a member of the proletariat. The mode of writing is not politically loaded. It is itself neutral:

> The language used to describe corrupt capitalists and reactionary politicians is not necessarily a corrupt and reactionary language. Likewise, classical Chinese is innocent despite being used to record the deeds of kings and emperors. (Gao 1981a: 27)

In order to hammer this point home, he argues that the Absurd possesses a tremendous revolutionary potential because many phenomena generally accepted in society would reveal themselves to be utterly unreasonable if they were looked at from the unusual perspective provided by the Absurd. The perspective of the Absurd is critical in nature; it can lead to progress and revolution (Gao 1981a: 41). It follows that there is no reason to associate Modernism with the decadent and with Capitalist Western culture. To allow them to monopolise these modes of writing would be "too generous" of the proletariat (Gao 1981a: 39). The unspoken conclusion is: *Let Chinese writings adopt these modes of expression.*

Subsequent chapters of *A Preliminary Exploration* elaborate on the literary effects Modernist writing devices can bring, among which is psychological time privileged over objective time, and narrative structure over plot. Two principles stated in the opening chapters are regularly reiterated; these are: formal experimentations are natural and necessary in literary development, and the choice of literary methods have no bearing on the author's political ideology. These two points make up the central thesis of the book. The book as a whole displays a strongly consistent argument and there is a rigorous argumentative force running though each short chapter. Each chapter follows a roughly uniformed structure: first, an explanation of either one Modernist device or one effect of these devices; second, examples of Western and/or Chinese writings employing that device; finally, a conclusion on the ways in which this writing method is ideologically progressive and in tune with revolutionary ideals, hence suitable for China.

First Step of Transfer: Introduction and Translation of Texts

In the veteran comparativist Itamar Even-Zohar's theory about translation as a process of transfer, translation is understood as a dynamic process characterised by a flow of entities from one system to another across borders. He stresses that translations are both informing and informed by other elements within the target culture. His theory of the Polysystem looks at literature as one (poly)system among the many other systems that conglomerate and interact with each other to form a nation's cultural life. The literary polysystem is further divided into sub-systems, such as children's literature, feminist literature and translated literature. Translated literature should not therefore, be studied as a secondary, derivative and parasitical category. It does not necessarily occupy a peripheral position in the literary polysystem. Sometimes translated literature can be so influential that it becomes the dominant component of the literary polysystem in the target culture. In Even-Zohar's own words, translated literature playing "a central position in the literary polysystem means that it participates actively in shaping the centre of the polysystem" (Even-Zohar 1978: 193). But this does not happen haphazardly. It is often "identified with major events in literary history" and "it is the leading writers (or members of the avant-garde who are about to become leading writers) who produce the most conspicuous or appreciated translations" (Even-Zohar 1978: 193). He has made a list of the situations under which this is likely to happen:

> (a) when a polysystem has not yet been crystallised, that is to say, when a literature is "young," in the process of being established; (b) when a literature is either "peripheral" (within a large group of correlated literatures) or "weak," or both; and (c) when there are turning points, crises, or literary vacuums in a literature. (Even-Zohar 1978: 194)

Even-Zohar's description is a perfect match with the situation of May Fourth literature. It was a time when Chinese literature was starting to be written in *baihua* [the modern vernacular] rather than classical Chinese. This new literature was still in its infancy struggling against the powerful tradition of the classics, in its language, its generic forms and the values it embodied. It came into being as its writers felt a crisis in Chinese literature: the classical form and language did not possess the capacity for expressing the modern. This new literary movement was one and the same process of China's modern nation building which reached a climax in the 1911 Revolution resulting in the establishment of the Chinese Republic. Many foreign literary works were translated into Chinese in the early years of the Republic. Hu Shih and Luo Jialun's 1918 translation of Ibsen's *A Doll's House* in the literary journal *La Jeunesse* became a major inspiration. Many other translations of mainly European and some Japanese literature were produced by prominent writers who wrote in *baihua*. Their popular slogan of *quanpan xihua* [total Westernisation] shows how influential translation and introduction of foreign literatures were in the formation of the new Chinese literature.

Comparable conditions emerged after the Cultural Revolution whereby translated literature could assume a central position in the Chinese literary polysystem. A crisis in literature was generally felt. The country had been battered by the political turmoil. In this situation Maoist Socialist Realism, tailor-made to nurture unquestioning loyalty for the Chinese Communist Revolution, did not allow room for any expression of doubt and discontent directed towards the Communist authorities. Yet these were the exact sentiments that needed articulation after 1976. Once again writers looked for alternative models. The Government's re-evaluation of its international relationship signified by Kissinger's and Nixon's visits in 1971 and 1972 respectively allowed opportunities to express interest in foreign cultures. In this situation translators, the legitimate agents of cultural exchange, occupied an interesting position. Gao's involvement as translator with both the Foreign Languages Press and the Writers' Association gained him access to foreign writings that were not for public circulation (Quah 2004: 7–8). Other translators with the Foreign Languages Press who have also become part of the literary *avant-garde* include Bei Dao and Han Shaogong. Bei Dao is one of the leading poets of *Menglongshi* [misty poetry]. Han's fictions offered powerful criticisms on Chinese culture and stirred up many controversies in the 1980s. In Bonnie McDougall's reminiscence of her days with the Foreign Languages Press in the 1980s, she has given a very interesting description of the situation: Literary translators had no choice as to what material to translate and no communication with the editors who were at liberty to change their translations. In most cases translators had no control over their own work, and the published texts often bore no translator's signature, except for those done by very famous translators such as Xianyi and Gladys Yang. But this kind of translation activity within the official framework was not all that was happening. Some translators might translate other literary writings of their own choice during their own leisure time, since the workload at the Foreign Languages Press was seldom heavy. Some translators, such as Bei Dao, Han Shaogang and Gao Xingjian, even turned to creative writing.[7] The work situation there also provided good opportunities for contact between the Chinese and the foreign experts, although sometimes such contact could be warned off by the authorities (McDougall, 2005). Compared to the general reading public who were completely dependent on translation and anthologies of approved and edited texts, the position of the Chinese translators/writers at the press did entail several advantages, one of which was the exposure to foreign literary works. The personal contact and other activities among this circle developed into vigorous cultural exchange. The actual translating that took place and other relevant activities were indeed more intensive and open than represented by the published products. In the case of Gao Xingjian, the only translations that bear his signature are the two poems from *Paroles* published together with his introductory essay on Prévert for the purpose of illustrating the poet's style. They should be contextualised and understood as one of the many activities that happened during this boom in interest in and contact with Western literature of the post-Cultural Revolution period. These activities first took place within the translators' circle before published translations and introductory writings helped to spread the phenomenon. The first step of the transfer of Modernism into China in the post-Cultural Revolution era was not textual translation of literary texts, but intensive cultural translation in the form of exposure and inter-personal exchange.

A Preliminary Exploration has attracted much attention from Gao's critics as the definitive moment of his introduction of Modernism into the post-Cultural Revolution Chinese mainland. However important as it was, it did not constitute an explosive *Eureka* moment impinging on the consciousness of the talented individual. To achieve an accurate evaluation on the importance of this work, two points should be noted. First, the book needs to be evaluated as part of the small body of Gao's early theoretical writings on Modernism in this period. Second, this body of texts needs to be read within the wider context of translation and literary activities in Beijing at the time. The range of activities that helped transfer Modernism into the Chinese polysystem include translation, selection and anthologising, editing and publishing, trips of cultural exchange, involvement of foreigners as bearers of cultural content in the foreign language speaking circles, the popularisation of the image of Western modernity promoted through the mass media which was more relaxed and open compared to the previous period and so on. But the success of transfer depends heavily on the compatibility of the new paradigm with the target system. There is always much mediation required. Negotiation and adaptation are necessary. Gao's theoretical writings in this period show that negotiation between the home literary paradigm and the imported one was growing in intensity. The first three articles merely introduce Modernism as a literary phenomenon that occurred in France as it did elsewhere. There is no apparent advocacy for its adoption or adaptation at home. Especially in "The

Agony of Modern French Literature", Modernism is presented as nothing more than a certain expressive writing method to narrate the problematic reality of the modern French society. Like the other two articles, it emphasises the anti-Facist and anti-Capitalist stance of the French writers, therefore dissociating Modernism with Western Capitalism to make its reception favourable at that time in China when Capitalism was still viewed negatively. But care is also taken to include dogmatic Maoist criticism, such as criticising Sartre for being idealistic, in order for the article to maintain a critical distance from its topic. This can account for the ambiguous and inconsistent attitude running through the article. There is a practical reason for such calculated reservation. The tight political control on literary creativity since the 1950s had made literary and political stances inseparable.[8]

Presenting Modernism in this way avoided setting it up in direct opposition with the party-sanctioned Maoist Socialist Realism. Any confrontation of that kind would have induced the premature death of Modernism in China. The mild and cautious introduction in Gao's first article was a test of the water. This exploratory foot very soon found solid ground thanks to the increasing attention and interest in Modernism among writers and readers. His two subsequent articles assume a more overt position. By the time the article on Prévert was published, translation, publication and discussion of Modernism was already in full swing. June 1981 saw the publication of Liu Fangtong's *Xiandai xifang zhexue* [Modern Western philosophy], and in September *Ershi shiji waiguo wenxue congshu* [The twentieth century foreign literature series] by the Foreign Literature Press. Gao's article on Prévert responded directly to the discussion of the time. By stating that proletariat literature does not necessarily exclude Modernist literary experimentation, it is arguing against the Maoist doctrine of "*kandedong*", literally meaning "comprehensible" and referring to a transparent and simple style which can be easily understood by the general reading public. This article is without doubt the boldest of the three. This firm stance is only taken after a theoretical foundation has been firmly laid in the preceding articles within the author's own repertoire aligning Modernism with what is accepted in the target culture. In *A Preliminary Exploration*, Chinese writings by prominent literary figures such as Lu Xun are cited as examples for the Modernist features they too have displayed, which further legitimise the principles of Modernist writing as both universal and ideologically appropriate for China. Moreover, this systematic presentation in book form consolidates what is being understood as Modernism in China. It facilitates definition, identification and categorisation of other writings of this strand. The concept of Modernism in post-Cultural Revolution Chinese literature has obviously taken root.

This repertoire consisting of three articles and a small book is not merely introductory, nor is it a straight-forward case of advocacy. Rather, it reveals a continuous process with its own internal rhythm and advancing at its own pace, and in which Modernism undergoes cultural and political negotiation and finds its way into the Chinese polysystem. It is a modest-sized but highly significant body of work in the context of post-Cultural Revolution Chinese literary history, not because it is the only one that advocates Modernism in Chinese writing, since it is not; nor is it the first critical call, since chronology of response to the *zeitgeist* is seldom the main criterion for greatness. It is important because it shows cultural translation as a process with its own internal development. It reveals a systematic and continuous process of exploration and negotiation between the home and the imported paradigms. It shows that cultural mediation, and literary development in this case, is not an event, but a *process* that takes place between two systems. It is important to see the movement within the process as well as to see the dynamics within the Chinese literary polysystem at that time. Any critical writing that fails to engage on this level of complexity would risk confusion of "general procedures" with "particular" ones, and also "exaggerated perspectives", in Even-Zohar's words (Even-Zohar 1990: 74). It is precisely to avoid such a risk that this particular group of Gao's works has been read in the context of translation and cultural transfer.

3

Fictions 1979–1987:
Adopting Modernism

From Fact to Fiction

Before Gao left China in 1987, eighteen of his short stories were published. Like his essays on Modernism, these stories show a similar transition from a relatively conservative to a more experimental position. This change is most obviously marked by a shift from the dominance of naturalist realism to psychological realism. It is particularly interesting to compare these stories with European high Modernist writing in early twentieth-century Europe, because such a change in the definition of reality and realism is the very core of Modernist philosophy and Modernist writing. By aligning with this basic principle, Gao in these short stories has slotted himself neatly into the Modernist mode.

At the turn of the twentieth century, the techniques employed to imitate objective reality in literature, generally known as Realism (as first coined in an article in *Mercure Francais* in 1826), gradually lost their attraction among many writers, since Modernist writers no longer understood reality as merely constituted by the "objective facts" of the world. One of the major factors that brought about such a change was Sigmund Freud's influential study of human psychology. At the same time, many philosophers also questioned the so-called objectivity of reality. Instead, they postulated a formative relation between perception and "reality". Cassirer's description of cognition and interpretation has shed light on the understanding of psychological and mental activities:

> ...none of them [cognition and interpretation] is a mere mirror, simply reflecting images of inward or outward data; they are not indifferent media,

> but rather the true sources of light, the prerequisite of vision, and the wellsprings of all formation. (Cassirer 1923 / Manheim 1961: I: 111)

According to him, reality is not out there in the world with an objective essence. Instead, its formation depends on the beholders' perception. Cognition is not a passive process of recognition, but an active process of construction. Therefore:

> Through them [perceptions] alone we see what we call "reality", and in them alone we possess it: for the highest objective truth that is accessible in the spirit is ultimately the form of its own activity. (Cassirer 1923 / Manheim 1961: I: 111)

Under the influence of innovative psychological and philosophical treaties, many writers turned inward from "external reality" to "mental", or "psychological reality", and depicted how the minds of their characters work instead of the events that happen to them. The operation of human psychology was now taken to be more important in literature. Indeed, it became the object of depiction in many significant works in the early twentieth century. For example, James Joyce's *A Portrait of the Artist as a Young Man* emphasises the development of Stephen's psychological responses to events more than any of those events that happen in the novel, not to mention the domination of the overall structure of *Finnegan's Wake* by the imitation of the way human minds work. This is also the principle that governs the narrative structure of other influential Modernist writers such as Marcel Proust, Virginia Woolf, Henry Miller and William Faulkner.[1]

Gao's early short stories show a radical swing from a position of factual authority to one of relative and subjective reality. The first of these stories to get published is the novella "*Hanye de xingchen*" [Stars on a cold night] in 1979 in the third issue of the Guangzhou literary journal *Huacheng*. It was published five years after he had gone back to Beijing from his labouring work in rural areas, and the year after he accompanied Ba Jin on the trip to Europe. However, according to the date he appends to the piece, it was written between April and December of 1978, which means less than two years after the downfall of the Gang of Four and the official end of the Cultural Revolution in 1976. In other words, it was at the time of the Beijing Spring, also known as the Democracy Wall, period, which also saw figures such as Bei Dao and Gu Cheng emerge. That means it was written around the time of his European trip. The plot of the novella focuses on the sufferings endured by an old cadre and his family during the Cultural Revolution. The slightly over-the-top depiction of the protagonist as tough and faithful also reveals traces of revolutionary heroes of Socialist Realism. On the whole the story reveals definitive features of scar literature, which consist of overwhelming sympathy for the hero victimised in the Cultural Revolution, and explicit condemnation of the destruction it had wreaked on people. The last quarter of the novella mostly contains statements of views on national politics at the time, packaged in the form of dialogue between the narrator-character and the old cadre, who is the main protagonist.

The overall structure of the novella is moulded on the style of Reportage [*baogao wenxue*]. This kind of writing was very much in favour among readers and publishers in the late 1970s as the popularity of journalist Liu Binyan's accounts of real life stories confirms. This new enthusiasm for factuality built up a rapport with readers who had shared the experience of being force-fed on a diet of empty political slogans and larger-than-life stereotypical heroic stories invented by the state authority. Many writers were keen to adopt the device of referring to events and personas from real life in their stories. This proved an important factor in promoting an atmosphere which encouraged and celebrated the rehabilitation of people persecuted in the Cultural Revolution. Gao Xingjian's "Stars on a Cold Night" reflects the aspirations of the period, but he does not only follow this prevailing spirit of factuality, he takes it further. The popular journalistic style turns into an obsession with presenting the story of the main character as a "true" case. The overall structure of the story is unusual, with the main body of the novella divided into eighty-nine small sections. Each section tells a fragment of the story from the perspective of one of the characters or the narrator. This fragmented structure helps to facilitate the ambitious attempt of telling in epic form the life of the old cadre in the ten-year period of the Cultural Revolution. The narrative proceeds smoothly, jumping from one event to another with differing temporalities intervening between the sections. Continuity is preserved since in the main it follows a chronological order. In the beginning the narrative adheres closely to the "diary" format. Subsequently the narrator's own recollection of events gradually take over and the diary functions rather as an expression of the protagonist's emotions, since the diary "records" how he "felt" about the events. This has facilitated a much greater flexibility in the narrative as events can be related together or explained in a way which would be unnatural if attributed to a personal diary. The narrator's voice is used to complement the cadre's in order to represent a wider picture in the story. Although at this point the diary ceases to function as the factual source, the details of the events related in the narrator's voice still aspire to factuality, since they are supposed to constitute "correct information" he had acquired in confidential talks with the old cadre before the latter died.

But the most interesting feature of the story's structure is the *daixu*, meaning someone writing a preface to the story for the author. It states that the main body of the story is the diary of an old cadre, therefore authorship of the story should be attributed to him while the author should only be credited as the editor. The writer ascribes the existence and retention of this diary to exceptional luck:

> It is a miracle that he had managed to keep this diary. In those years even for someone who was lucky enough to enjoy some personal freedom, it was impossible to keep a tiny piece of paper with him ... This [the retention of the diary] was one small piece of fortune in great misfortune, an exception among general cases. This is how this diary has survived. (Gao 1979: 146)

Again, in the epilogue he tries to counter the possible incredulity of the reader:

> Our sons and descendants may be shocked when they read this. Wouldn't they suspect this to be purely fictitious? (Gao 1979: 218)

As with the enthusiasm for expressing anti-Cultural Revolution sentiment, the desire to "tell the truth" [*shuo zhen hua*] was an eruption of repressed emotion after the tight control over freedom of speech in the preceding decade. This desire was so often raised in various fora and published discussions on literature that it became almost like another slogan. But such a trend is necessarily ephemeral because its principle limits the potential of literary production to an easy confinement within the bounds of, yet again, Socialist Realism. Moreover, the claim of factuality in a story like "Stars" invalidates the story itself since first, it provides no guarantee of the factuality it claims, and secondly, any credibility it may have is diminished by the process of writing, if we accept that representation is more an expression of subjective interpretation than a faithful copy of the objective fact. This ironically is a position that Gao repeatedly argues for later on in his theoretical writings. Therefore, it soon became necessary for him to abandon the idea of factuality in his creative writing.

Indeed the idea of factual reference is altogether rejected in Gao's next story published. The 1981 novella "*Youzhi gezi jiao hongchunr* [A pigeon called Red Beak] is his third published fiction. It begins with self-referential remarks on the narration of the story:

> This is not a story told with traditional narrative techniques, although like other stories it is also about men's fate ... There are six characters in this story ... The events are all true. However, those who have experienced pains do not expect to see reality to be told in its entirety in fiction. Therefore, reality in life is edited and altered before it becomes fiction. (Gao 1981b: 205)

Reality in another sense has emerged. It is a kind of literary reality in which true life is compressed and generalised, edited and altered, in other words, represented in literary texts. According to this, the claim of these stories to be "true events" should be interpreted as references made to similar events that happened instead of a report on one particular event. The story claims to reflect life in general rather than one particular person's life. A division is drawn between reality and fiction. Fiction does not equal reality, it is an edited and altered vision of it represented in writing. In "Stars" the narration is justified by the factuality of the story, while in "Pigeon", the fictionality is acknowledged, and even emphasised, in order to facilitate the narrative flow of the various episodes. Once reality in literature is defined this way, writers are given much freer poetic license to construct their vision of reality.

Like "Stars", "Pigeon" also tells the story of the sufferings inflicted upon innocent people in the Cultural Revolution. The main characters are six people who were friends in their young days. They all lose their career opportunities, their joy of youth and some even lose their lives in the Cultural Revolution. The whole piece is divided into short sections, each consisting of a monologue by one of the six characters or "the narrator". These monologues are sometimes in colloquium with, and sometimes independent of, each other, each giving information about certain events from the perspective of the narrator or character. Since the story is fictitious, the narrator can assume omniscience. This omniscient narrator also functions as a catalyst to fuse different episodes narrated in the voices of the various characters. He fills in gaps in the narration, relating things that other characters are not in a position to "know". His remarks on certain events are juxtaposed with narration in other characters' voices, creating comments on the latter. He also introduces the story to the reader and defines the boundary of the narrative. He even comments on the nature of the story and describes it as a story "about men's fate" and as "a book about geniuses who die young" (Gao 1981b: 205). This figure of the narrator functions to map out a unified "reality" by inventing and fusing the characters' perspectives, in the same way that a complete picture is created by arranging the pieces of a jigsaw puzzle in a specific pattern.

The fictitious nature of the story is further underlined by a discussion of the idea of fate between the narrator and the characters. Characters that are supposed to be dead at that point of the narrative also participate in the discussion. The narrator fully acknowledges the impossibility of this situation at the end of the episode:

> I beg my readers' pardon. I was just carried away. I shouldn't have let the living converse with the dead. (Gao 1981b: 232)

Such authorial intrusion in the guise of "narrator" is frequent, either providing information to achieve a continuous flow of narrative, or commenting on the situation as narrated in the voices of the various characters. It constantly reminds the reader of the fictional nature of the story. Although some remarks made in both the narrator's or the characters' voices are sentimental in tone and clearly demonstrative of an intention to arouse readers' sympathy for the characters, the overall tone is redeemed by the overtly structuralising section titles such as "Cockerel's Words", "The Narrator's Conversation with the Characters", or "Kuaikuai, Cockerel, Zhengfan and Xiaomei's Common Recollection", thus foregrounding the artificiality in the narration and succeeding in creating a distance, which discourages the kind of emotional indulgence commonly found in scar literature.

Suspense is also destroyed right at the beginning of the novella by the announcement of the death of Xianling and Kuaikuai, in order to disturb the reader's habitual expectation in the reading process. There is neither vicarious excitement to be had in predicting whether the characters will survive the Cultural Revolution and be rehabilitated, nor rejoicing with their final victory after accompanying them through the bad times. Prior knowledge of the ending frustrates the reader's desire to experience the characters' adventure with them and forces the reader to observe the way the story is told. It is worth noting that the act of narration is presented as a conscious action in both "Stars" and "Pigeon", although it serves different purposes respectively. Such an awareness later becomes a consistent feature in the repertoire of Gao's writings. In "Stars" it highlights the existence of a source of the story and promotes a sense of factuality, whereas in "Pigeon" it celebrates fictionality by demonstrating the narrative capacity of the artistic imagination. This view is very close to the one suggested in his call for Modernism in *A Preliminary Exploration*.

"Pigeon" has also departed from the excessively straightforward didactic style of scar literature in respect of its characterisation. As the plot is developed, the characters are described from more varied perspectives. They are more interesting than the absolute, ethical, rather cardboard heroes in most works of scar literature. Monotonous political sermonising such as that found in "Stars" is eschewed. Condemnation of the Gang of Four is treated as a vehicle for expressing the characters' emotions, rather than the didactic purpose of the piece. The subjective dimension of the protagonists' experience in the Cultural Revolution, rather than the evaluation of the Cultural Revolution as a political event, is the story's focus of attention. The central theme is not to identify the Cultural Revolution as the source of all evil, but to express disgust with politics over which the characters, who represent the ordinary people, have no control. This theme is greatly elaborated in Gao's plays written at a later time. The characters of this novella are treated on a more human scale. They are portrayed with many more facets than the merely political. For example, Cockerel's disillusionment with political gang struggle is not only manifested in his censure of the Gang of Four, it also leads him to reflect that his self-righteousness and heroic posturing was the cause of Xiaoling's death. His blind short-lived commitment to political campaigns is to be paid for by self-reproach. Kuaikuai has taken a different path from Cockerel and tries to stay away from politics, but he finds no escape. He loses his position at work, and eventually loses his life. These are serious charges against the political authorities, but the focus is on the inter-personal relationship among the characters and on their emotions. This leads the novella further away from the Party doctrine that literature should be didactic and should aim at "exposing darkness" [*jielu hei'an*] in order to attain the ultimate purpose of serving the nation and promoting an air of optimism under the new leadership.

Narrative Perspectives

Experimentation with narrative perspective is in full swing in Gao's short stories after "Pigeon". "Reality" is taken in a strictly limited sense. It is restricted to the perspective from which the story is told. There is no further attempt to construct a unified world from an objective point of view. "*Ni yiding yao huozhe*" [You must stay alive] published in 1980 is written from a third person viewpoint. Its use of omniscient remarks from the transparent voice of a narrator is within common literary conventions, yet the narration still identifies totally with the perspective of the protagonist "he", who is undergoing labour reform in a cadre school. The story begins with "he" coming out from a "cow shed" after an ideology instruction meeting, worrying about his lover and her problems which she tells him about in a letter that has just reached him that afternoon. This is followed by an episode in which he goes for a swim in the river and tries to think over matters privately, but his thoughts are interrupted firstly by the young female teacher in the commune school who has come to hide away and cry among the bushes, then by a fellow-worker from the labour camp who comes to catch fish in the river. The narration concentrates on "his" action. His relationship with his fellow team members in the labour camp is a harmonious one. There is considerable tension between this friendly atmosphere and his heart heavy with worries for his lover. Next, his plan to telephone his lover is forestalled by his responsibility to take care of an old team member who has fallen ill. After taking the old man to the hospital in the middle of the night, he learns that telecommunications with his lover's region have been cut. At the end of the story, he goes to the post office and sends her a letter with the short message "You *must* stay alive".

Since the story is told from his point of view, nothing beyond his knowledge is included in the narrative. The external world is seen through his eyes. The story is dominated by the fluctuation of his emotion. Much is written in what William Tay, in commenting on Wang Meng's short stories of around the same period, called "narrated monologue" (Tay 1984: 9), or "discourse in free indirect form" (Tay 1984: 7) in linguistic terms. A single unified perspective is maintained by narrating in the voice of "he". There is no attempt to create an external reality in order to establish an objective view on the events. The focus of the story allows the plot to be dominated by the psychological reality of the protagonist. What is rejected here is the idea that the situation can be known in its entirety. In fact, the absence of this absolute objective reality, in other words, "his" lack of knowledge of "her" situation, is exactly what creates the tension in the story. All dramatic effects are generated by "his" lack of knowledge of "her" situation. Therefore the story is as much about the limited personal perspective and the unattainable nature of reality in its entirety to individuals, as it is about life during the Cultural Revolution.

In no other of Gao's fictions since "You Must Stay Alive" is a unified reality constructed by fusing characters' perspectives. What is found, on the contrary, is an attempt to create literary narrative effects by skilful manipulation of narrative perspectives. His story "*Ershiwu nian hou*" [Twenty-five years later] published at the end of 1982 is a successful piece of work in which humour and irony are created by such manipulation. It achieves great rhetorical impact in creating surprise at the end. In this story, the theme of post-Cultural Revolution reunion is given an ironic treatment. Sentimental depiction of meeting between old friends or lovers after the Cultural Revolution is an especially popular theme in post-Cultural Revolution literature. Classic examples are Gu Hua's novel *Furongzhen* (1981; translated into English as *A Small Town Called Hibiscus* by Gladys Yang, 1983), which was so popular that it was later turned into a film, and Xie Jin's film *Tianyunshan chuanqi* [*The Legend of Tianyun Mountain*]. Gao Xingjian's own short stories "*Pengyou*" [Friends] (1981) and "*Huadou*" [A girl named Huadou] (1984[2]) are also developed on this theme with a much more deliberate treatment. In many of these stories when old friends meet up after the Cultural Revolution, those who have stayed faithful to each other now comfort each other by lamenting their youth and wasted opportunities together, whilst those who have abandoned or betrayed one another feel ashamed of themselves and suffer remorse for life.

Initially, "Twenty-five Years Later" seems to conform to this motif. It depicts a short episode in which "he" goes to visit a girl he knew twenty-five years ago, who spoke up for him in a political instruction meeting in which his political stance was criticised. He believed it was her romantic feelings for him that gave her the courage to protect him. Since then he has not seen her but the impression she made on him has helped him to maintain confidence in human nature, and therefore helped him to survive subsequent purges and condemnation. Twenty-five years later he finds out where she is and pays her a visit, in order to thank her and apologise for the problems it must have caused her to have spoken up for him. The narration of this meeting takes his perspective, and she behaves in a polite but rather distant way. They chat for about ten minutes without saying anything concrete. This seems natural and reasonable for him, hence for the reader, since he attibutes the cause of this feeling of unfamiliarity between them to the different lives they have lived in the intervening twenty-five years. However, his illusion is shattered at the end when they say goodbye and she gets his name wrong. Her unavowed affection for him that was killed off in its premature stage because of social instability has never really existed except in his imagination. The story represents a mockery of the clichés about tragedies caused by the Cultural Revolution. At the same time it teases the reader's expectation of an emotional impact in the ending of this kind of story. It can be read as a criticism of both the creation and the reception of literature based on this theme. At the end of the story, he contentedly returns to the village he has settled in with presents he buys for his wife and son, since now he realises that the only regret he has had in his pre-marriage years was based on pure fantasy.

Around 1982 and 1983, Gao's fiction displayed a growing obsession with experiments with narrative voices. The focus of his stories is always on the act of narration rather than on the dramatic events. This is also a period in which the attention to narration itself is accompanied by a corresponding abandonment of grand themes such as national politics and social development. Instead this group of stories is typically concerned with humble but interesting episodes of daily life, which are best narrated in a variety of voices from ordinary people from different backgrounds. These fictional works demonstrate innovative manipulations of narrative voice to achieve special literary effects. These stories are also given flesh and blood by the close proximity of the dramatic events described to the readers' everyday experience. Therefore, the overall effect is usually a strong synthesis of form and content. In my opinion they are the most appealing group of works that Gao Xingjian has produced to date.

One of the devices Gao employs in this period is the assumption of a fictive audience in order to foreground the act of narrating. "*Xiejiang he tade nü'er*" [The shoemaker and his daughter] (1983), "*Lushang*" [On the road] (1982) and "*Yuan'en si*" (1983, translated into English as "The Temple" by Mabel Lee, 2004) all demonstrate this approach. In "Shoemaker", the narrator "I" is one of the two village women who discover the corpse of a drowned girl while they wash clothes in the river early in the morning, and subsequently recounts the story. The text has achieved an idiomatic style of the casual colloquial dialect which the author envisages his narrator would use. This is also true in "On the Road", in which a driver who has lived in Tibet for eighteen years reports the death of a cadre from the city on a night journey. This story has also succeeded in imitating the speech of people of similar social backgrounds. One might argue that there is nothing novel about this rhetorical concept, since this is a very common tool of characterisation in fiction writing; and in the 1950s the veteran May Fourth writer Lao She had already pointed out the importance of "characterisation of speech" [*yuyan xingge hua*] (Lao She 1963/1991: XVI: 46), and systematically discussed the relationship between the background of characters and their styles of speech.

But in Gao's stories, the motive of employing this device is not a purely rhetorical one, nor is it simply for the sake of interesting characterisation. In "Shoemaker", the flow of the narrator's speech has created an unusual structure for the narrative. Her account is intermittently punctuated by interrogatory remarks. To quote some examples:

> This old bastard really isn't kosher. Beating her up for no reason! Of course she is his daughter, isn't she? (Gao1983a/1989: 96)

> Why beat her up? Rice burnt, coming outside for a chat after dark ... (Gao 1983a/1989: 97)

> How did she die? She died just like that. Sister Zhang and I both saw her on the riverbank. Bad guys? Don't know if there are any around. Oh, you're asking about the old shoemaker? He isn't a bad fellow, wouldn't do those things. (Gao 1983a/1989: 99)

The overall tone resembles a dialogue rather than a monologue. The story ends with the revelation that this is a statement she is making to the investigation team from the city. Some of those interrogative remarks are her repetition of the investigator's questions, while others are her communicative remarks to her listeners, who include the investigator and probably other people from the village. She starts by narrating the discovery of the corpse, often being distracted to relate fragmentary episodes of the dead girl's family life and comments on the girl's relationship with her family. The description of the deaths of the daughter and the father only occupies two short paragraphs. The suppression of dramatic action is deliberate since the emotions in the story are created by the narrator's highly personal and subjective tone. The narration is not only a means to convey the plot. Instead of being a transparent carrier, it is the focus and determines the structure of the story. The story ultimately is not about the deaths of the shoemaker and his daughter, but about how the narrator reflects on the events and organises her reflections, in other words, the story is about the narration itself. Similarly, "On the Road" is about a driver's exchange with his passenger telling the latter about the death of a cadre from the city. The account this driver ("I") gives of the event is strongly coloured by the way he feels about the dead man. The frequent complaints that he makes about city folks in the course of his account foreground the subjective position taken by the narrator.

The narration in "The Temple" resembles a speech by one of the participants of a conversation which takes place among a group of people, probably family members or close friends, as the fictive audience "you" in the plural form [nimen] are from time to time referred to as "our closest friends who have shared our sorrow" (Gao 1983c/1989: 149). The narrator "I" relates to his audience his trip with his new bride to Yuan'en Temple. A singular form "you" [*ni*] is also used to refer to his wife Fangfang, indicating her presence in the conversation. At several points he addresses his remarks directly to "you", suggesting interruptions have just been made by her to censure his revealing details of their intimacy. For example:

> At last we have our own home. I have got you [*ni*]. You [*ni*] have got me. Fangfang, I know what you [*ni*] are going to say — no sense of decorum! What's wrong with that? We want to share our happiness with everybody. We have had enough worries. We have also given you [*nimen*] much trouble and you [*nimen*] have been worried about us. What can we repay you [*nimen*] with? Just a few wedding sweets, or some wedding cigarettes? We should repay you [*nimen*] with our happiness. I haven't said anything wrong, have I? (Gao 1983c/1989: 146)

"We" stands for "I" and Fangfang who have recently got married. Shifting of second person form of adressees between the singular and plural forms of "you" referring to Fangfang and the listeners respectively suggests the presence of their family or friends. "I" seems to get carried away in talking about their happy marriage while Fangfang, out of shyness, has interrupted his narration. The following paragraph makes this more obvious:

> I took her in my arms and gave her a kiss. Hey, what's wrong with that? Fine, she won't let me say it. Let's get back to Yuan'en Temple. (Gao 1983c/ 1989: 148)

His narration is constantly checked by her comments on what it is proper to say, especially regarding private details of their relationship. The event and its narration are not one and the same thing. The narration is only a version of the event after editing and ellipses, and certainly embroidered with elaboration and exaggeration. What is illustrated here is how narration shapes the perception of events for its audience, not how events shape narration.

This split between event and narration is further elaborated in "*Chehuo*" (1985, translated into English as "The Accident" by Mabel Lee, 2004) by showing the relation between events and their artistic representation. The opening remark "This was how it happened" introduces an objective account of an accident in which a man was killed because he spent his last moment releasing the carry-cot attached to his bicycle to save his son instead of turning the direction of the bicycle to save himself when he crashes into a bus. The story first gives an account of this accident, then the account is contrasted by comments made by some bystanders:

"What? An accident? Anybody under the wheel?"
"Father and son. One dead."
"Who died?"
"The old man did."
"What about the son?" "Alive and well."
"What a son! Why didn't he care for his old man?"
"It was the father who pushed the son out of the way."
"Each generation is going from bad to worse. What a thankless son!"
"Don't bullshit unless you understand what happened."
"Who's bullshitting?"
"I'm not here to argue with you."
"So the kid has been taken away!"
"Was there a kid as well?" (Gao 1985d/1989: 230–231)

This is of course a radical case of misinterpretation brought about by bad representation, but what it illustrates is that this representation of the accident has engendered varying responses from bystanders, each differing according to the personal interests and associations of the speaker. In other words, it has generated different meanings among the listeners, who are all potential (re)narrators of the incident. This is reminiscent of Brecht's use of conflicting perspectives in accident narration to illustrate his ideas on distancing (*Verfremdung*) — a very Modernist concept. After the "objective" narration of the accident and the subsequent scenes of discussion in the street, there is an appendix where the narrator speculates on the chances of avoiding the accident, for example: "if he had been less hesitant" and "if he had left home one minute earlier or later" (Gao 1985d/1989: 235). These are possibilities that do not exist, but they suggest a potential philosophical debate. Then the narrator goes on to point out that there can be many alternative accounts of the event. It can be presented as a straight-forward news report, or made into a piece of creative literature by "supplementing it with the writer's imagination to make up a touching story" (Gao 1985d/1989: 235). All these suggestions lead to the conclusion that the relationship between an event and its narration is unstable. However, at the very end of the story the narrator declares what he has written is "the narrative of how the accident happened" (Gao 1985d/1989: 235), implying his is the true version, thus privileging one account — his own "objective" one — of an event. This creates a contradiction: the theme of the story is that narrations are merely representational; yet its concluding remark confirms one narration as objective. It sets up the narrator's own version as the transparent control account in order to indicate that other versions are misinterpretations, inaccurate reports and representations, for either literary or philosophical purposes. This contradicts the scepticism about the possibility of unbiased narration, which is clearly suggested in other parts of the story, and which is very much evident in his earlier works such as "The Temple".

Despite such inconsistency, this group of stories effectively brings out two points: the unreliability and instability of narration in mirroring reality, and the endless possibilities of recounting an event. Such a reflection on the nature of narrative is a political as well as a literary response to these stories' context of production. It does not only challenge the romantic and optimistic pictures painted in scar literature about the new social order (as in "Twenty-five Years Later"), but also expresses scepticism about the authority of any narration, and thus any discourse, including political ones, as the bearer of truth. This strips literature of its power to act as political propaganda and should be read as an attempt to release literature from its grand nation-building narrative function. This also explains why the events in these stories are closely related to the daily life of people in the street. The emphasis on the private dimension distances literature from the grandiose vision of social rehabilitation and patriotic discourses. Their closeness to life results in showing up the falseness of such grand discourses. The Modernist meta-narrative in these stories challenges, in its own way, the established hierarchy in which the State is privileged over the individual.

In Gao's 1986 story "*Gei wolaoye mai yugan*" (translated into English as "Buying a Fishing Rod for my Grandfather" by Mabel Lee, 2004), the experiment in fictional narrative is even more radical. The boundary between the material world and the dream-world of the protagonist is blurred. The narrator buys a fishing rod and brings it home without any idea of what to do with it. Its only function is as a homage to his deceased grandfather who loved fishing and hunting. Worried that his son might break it if he keeps it at home, he decides to take it back to his hometown. This is immediately followed by an episode in which he asks his way around, because he no longer recognises the place he grew up in. As his surroundings become increasingly strange, the narration gradually turns into expressionistic images, arranged in the form of stream of consciousness, of the reminiscence he has of his grandfather and his childhood. Grandfather is consistently associated with discontinuous images of the ancient city of Loulan, of Persian and Han cultures, and ruins of palaces and cities; in this way a connection between Grandfather and lost cultures and life styles is established. Then all of a sudden, there is an abrupt intrusion of modern images such as Maradona, the Argentine football team and the World Cup. At this point the story reveals that the trip the narrator takes to his hometown is really a dream. The allusion to football originates from fragments of the TV broadcast of the 1986 World Cup that he hears in his sleep and which seep into his mind in his semiconscious state just before he wakes up.

The readers have no idea where the dream starts. What happens in his dream has no correlation with what happens in the material world at the time of his dreaming. Representation of external reality is entirely eschewed; instead the story is based on what goes on in the protagonist's mind. In this case, his dream articulates the way he feels about his life in the past and his present way of living. It is not a means to communicate his material situation, but a representation of his perception of his own life, or as Erich Kahler puts it, a "subjectivisation of the world" (Kahler 1970 / Winton 1987: 6). It is not surprising since Gao's other stories written in the same period have already intimated a disbelief, though inconsistent, in the legitimacy of narrative as the representation of a unified world. In this last story in Gao's repertoire written in China, logical explanatory language has given way to a more expressionistic style, which is better suited to representing the protagonist's consciousness. To adopt the title Kahler uses for his study, this constitutes "*Die Verinnerung des Erzählens*" (*The Inward Turn of Narrative*), a term which Malcolm Bradbury and John Fletcher later echoed, referring to the "introverted novel" (Bradbury and Fletcher 1976: 394–416). The significance of "Buying a Fishing Rod for my Grandfather" lies in its emphasis on the protagonist's dream-reality. This seems to have been inspired by Freud's postulation that in dreams what is repressed returns and seeks expression. What is repressed is articulated by the images of ruins of ancient civilisations of the lost city of Loulan and of Persia. These images express a desire for alternatives to the dominant Han Confucian culture. This aspiration was shared with many dissidents at the same time and crystallised into the "movement of searching for cultural roots".[3] Through this association with the "movement of searching for cultural roots", the story has tapped into the discourse of nationalism. This is very different from the author's previous fictions in which the mundane life is privileged over nationalist perspectives.

This body of works shows a change from a relatively conservative approach to full-blown experimentalism, a development analogous to that in Gao's theoretical writing on Modernism. Different aspects and techniques of Modernist literature are experimented with in these stories, and Gao's own advocacy for Modernism is put into practice in his creative works. The lack of critical attention does not change the fact these stories are well-crafted and stylish, and represent a significant stage towards the success of Gao's translation of the Modernist writing paradigm into the Chinese polysystem. Advocacy is now advanced and extended into application in these stories with impressive results, which have not in my view bettered in Gao's subsequent creative output to date.

4

Plays 1982–1985:
Modernism Transferred

Transfer of Paradigm

Chapter Two has illustrated how Gao's early essays introduce Modernism into the Chinese literary polysystem as an alternative mode to the outdated and dogmatic Maoist Socialist Realism. Chapter Three analyses how Gao has made the Modernist self-awareness of narrative as representation the theme of his short stories. This Chapter will show that the formal structure of Gao's early plays are essentially Modernist. In other words, the paradigm of Modernism is translated into these plays.

I am using the word translation here in the way J. Hillis Miller does to describe the spread of critical theory from one culture to another. He uses the Biblical story of the Moabite Ruth's assimilation into Israel as an analogy to the translation of critical theory, and suggests that like critical theory, Ruth is translated and transformed as she moves from Moab to Israel (Miller 1996: 219). He asserts that no theoretical paradigm is thought up in a vacuum. It is always generated out of a context in which a certain phenomenon calls for explanation. There are many different reasons for theories to be translated and the needs that prompt such translation are always different in each case. That is why each time a theory is translated, a different method is called for. But the most important point is that when theories are brought across borders, whether read beyond its original context by another culture, or even in the same language by another discipline, they are often "disfigured, deformed, 'translated'", just as Bottom in *A Midsummer Night's Dream* is "translated" (Miller 1996: 222). A great deal of reformulation is necessary to "turn the alien theory into something that can be understood, transformed and assimilated in the new place" (Miller 1996: 219):

> Theory, when it is translated or transported, when it crosses a border, comes bringing the culture of its originator with it. Quite extraordinary feats of translation are necessary to disentangle a given theoretical formulation from its linguistic and cultural roots. (Miller 1996: 210–211)

Miller's point is easy to understand. Sometimes a philosophical idea or an ethical concept conveyed in a story can only be understood by another culture if the idea or concept is set within another story idiomatic to the target culture. In this kind of situation, the translation/transformation of a theory across borders is always an act of "turning it into new forms of itself" (Miller 1996: 210). This process should at the end arrive at assimilation, which would give the theory a new lease of life in the target culture. He also finds the transmission of literary theory not unlike the transmission of Western technology in the non-Western world, except that "it [theory] may be more dangerous" because it is "not just one more tool of industrialization but a bringer of an even more profound cultural change" (Miller 1996: 211). Miller sees theory as a very powerful entity. For him theories do not convey information, they form ways of seeing:

> Theory's openness to translation is a result of the fact that a theory, in spite of appearances, is a performative, not a cognitive, use of language … Works of theory are nevertheless potent speech acts. A theory is a way of doing things with words, naming facilitating (or sometimes inhibiting) acts of reading. (Miller 1996: 223)

This also holds true for Modernism. Although it is not exactly a theory, it functions as one. It is a writing paradigm with which a way of seeing and comprehending what constitutes reality is constructed through the depiction of the characters' relationship with their environment. Some Modernist writings resemble literary-psychological exercises, others metaphysical inquiries. Psychological and philosophical insights are formulated in language, often with plots and settings, such as in fictions or drama, in order to analyse the material, psychological and metaphysical conditions of human beings. Every image of human life constructed in a Modernist work is an instance of philosophical deliberation. Modernism also, to borrow Miller's description of theory's function, "facilitates, or sometimes inhibits acts of reading" human conditions. In this way, Modernist writing is also performative in the Austinian sense, and in the same way that theory is to Miller. The transmission of the Modernist writing paradigm out of its Western European original context necessarily involves transformations. One famous "new form of itself" is Columbian Magical Realism represented by Gabriel García Márquez's works. It successfully blends the native Latin American magical tradition with the Modernist fictional narrative. Likewise, Gao Xingjian's plays written in the early 1980s show successful acculturation of a Modernist theatrical paradigm, that is, how European Modernist dramatists construct their views on the human condition, into the Chinese polysystem. Transformation and "disfiguration" are necessary to the process, given that the circumstances in the Chinese target culture were widely divergent from those of the European cultures.

The Chinese Dramatic System

For one thing, the existing dominant dramatic conventions were very different in China from its European counterpart. In China, *huaju* [speech drama], as opposed to *xiqu*, the traditional sung theatre of stylised music and movement, has a relatively short history. In the entire twentieth century realism has been privileged as the prototype of progressive theatre, and has been married to the promotion of political ideology since the form's inception in China. This is simply the result of circumstances attendant on its introduction to China: it was first introduced by humanists among overseas students, such as Hu Shih, Lu Jingruo and Ouyang Yuqian, and was used as an expression of dissent against the established social hierarchy. At this stage, Ibsen was the major influence on the Chinese dramatists. Realism was closely associated with the voice speaking for the oppressed. Statistics show that out of the 387 plays translated into Chinese between the years 1908 and 1938, realist plays constituted the second most popular group after translated Shakespeare plays (Sun 1994: 31). In the 1930s some Chinese left-wing dramatists found themselves much inspired by the Japanese Socialist Kurahara, who denounced the Realism of Flaubert and Ibsen as bourgeois and petit-bourgeois, and declared that the authors' class consciousness should be the prior concern of Realist literature, and Dialectical Materialism should be an important structural element. Based on his ideas, Chinese left-wing dramatists developed their own brand of Proletarian Realism and later Socialist Realism with strong Maoist associations. Realist drama was pushed even further towards a utilitarian mode and was expected to function as political propaganda. In fact, between the 1930s and 1950s, *huaju*, acted out in the naturalistic style, was the main device the Chinese Communist Party used to fulfil the functions of immediate propaganda, either against Japanese aggression or in support of the Communist revolution. After the Cultural Revolution, the development of theatre ran parallel to that of literature. Socialist Realism continued to be dominant in the Chinese theatre, embracing the new social atmosphere of rehabilitation and extolling a different group of heroes who were victimised in the Cultural Revolution. Some of these examples are Sha Yexin's *Chen Yi shizhang* [Mayor Chen Yi], Wang Deying's *Peng dajiangjun* [The Great General Peng] and Bai Hua's *Shuguang* [Dawn]. These plays adhere closely to the principles of the monodimensional structure and perspective of Socialist literature laid down in Mao's 1942 "Talks at the Yan'an Conference on Literature and Art". The theatre was confined in a way similar to scar literature. However, this kind of theatre could not represent the sense of disillusion with the slow pace of social change felt by many, and in any case such opposition to the prevailing authority was not on the agenda of Socialist Realism. Consequently theatre audiences declined rapidly. There was a drastic drop in box office receipts in the early 1980s. This reflected a disjuncture between Socialist Realist drama and the need and interest of the time. Alternative modes of dramatic expression were to emerge very soon.

A number of plays attempted to break new ground. Sha Yexin's 1979 *Jiaru woshi zhende* (translated into English as *The Imposter* by Daniel Kane, 1983) drew extensive attention, for the creative use of the spatial relation between the stage and the auditorium, and especially for the social criticism it fired at the new social order. It gave its critics and audience a good shock with its prologue when its main protagonist entered the auditorium as a VIP sitting in the front row and was then arrested by police entering also through the auditorium. The audience did not know this was staged, but were told that the arrest was to do with fraud committed by the man, assuming the false identity of the son of a high-ranked official and taking advantage of corresponding privileges. As the man was taken out of the theatre, he asked aloud what would happen if he really was what he faked and challenged the inequality between the politically privileged class and the ordinary people. As the dramatic action started on stage and the same actor enacted the story before his arrest, the audience realised what had happened in the auditorium was part of the play. This theatre treatment was very powerful. In the prologue, the audience witnessing the arrest became part of the dramatic action. This is an effective way to create for them a strong sense of participation and to arouse strong emotions in them. Moreover, the audience were first convinced of the authenticity of the situation in the prologue, and thus the criticism it offered subsequently acquired an extraordinary force of veracity.

Gao Xingjian's *Juedui xinhao* (1982, translated into English as *Alarm Signal* by Shiao-Ling S. Yu, 1996) and *Chezhan* (1983, translated into English as *The Bus-stop* by Geremie Barmé, 1984; *Bus Stop* by Carla Kirkwood, 1995, *The Bus Stop* by Shiao-Ling Yu, 1996; *Bus Stop: A Lyrical Comedy on Life in One Act* by Kimberly Besio, 1998) are both typical and atypical of their contemporary dramatic norms. Both respond directly to the new social order, but it is their formal kinship with European Modernist drama rather than nineteenth-century Realism that differentiates them from other scar literature in the dramatic form. The central concept of this group of plays is anti-illusionism.[1] Minimal stage becomes the dominant style. Elaborate scenography which attempts to convince the audience of a real physical background is eschewed. Since there is no reference to real life, there is also no need to follow the logic of daily life outside the theatre. *Alarm*

Signal is about a group of train passengers anticipating a train robbery. The play emphasises the psychological process of its characters. It successfully cultivates a claustrophobic atmosphere which arises not only from the setting of the small train carriage, but also from the numerous psychological spaces of the characters jostling in the same common external space. This is indicated by the use of lighting and sound that constructs a contrast between the exterior world around the characters and an interior one within each of them. Set in such a claustrophobic environment as a train carriage, the conflict among the characters becomes intensified. The changes in the psychological state of each one of them are important because they trigger the dramatic actions.

Internal monologues and dialogues are used to dramatise this. Interior monologues are rather straightforward and done in a way similar to conventional soliloquies, also with the help of atmospheric spot-lights highlighting the speaker's face and simultaneously blackening the rest of the stage. Interior dialogues are slightly more complicated. There are two kinds of interior dialogue — first, the dialogue between two or more characters imagined or recollected by one of them; second, the communication by body language between two or more characters, but dramatised as "internal speeches" to be spoken. Smooth transition between realistic scenes and interior speeches is facilitated by the lighting and sound effects. External and internal space are collapsed into one. Meanwhile, in *Bus Stop*, time on stage is different from time measured in our daily life. The play is structured around the non-realistic plot of a group of people waiting for ten years at a bus-stop. Ten years elapse in the course of several lines of speeches. Reality in the theatre consists of representation by the actors and other theatrical means such as props, lighting and sound. The plot is not restricted by the logic of space and time in real life. Both *Alarm Signal* and *Bus Stop* display conceptions of drama that are basically Modernist.

Many critics have discussed in detail the Modernist features in Gao's plays. Some expressed great pleasure in seeing innovations in Chinese theatre, others critiqued them as imitations of Western fashion. Thus the reception was polarised.[2] The drastic response is easy to understand, since the transfer of the Modernist representational framework from its indigenous European context into China is much more than the simple matter of trying out another interesting style. Modernist drama is another paradigm of looking at reality and representation. It had to negotiate with the existing norms in Chinese theatre; and these existing norms, predominantly realistic and pertaining to scar literature in the dramatic form, are the result of the interaction within a complicated network of many cultural and political factors. To negotiate with the existing norms means to negotiate with all these factors; and this is not merely an aesthetic issue.

As discussed in Chapter Two, what made Modernism unacceptable to the authorities was its ideology, which triggered off formal experiments in the first place, and was now embedded in the innovative technical devices of writers such as Gao. These included nineteenth- and twentieth-century ideas on anarchism, nihilism, existentialism, Freudian psychology and so forth. Modernist technical devices elaborate the rejection of unity and faith. Modernist works embrace scepticism and non-conformity. Chinese modernists in the 1930s had already been branded by the left-wing as decadent and anti-social — "the third kind of man" [*di san zhong ren*] (Su 1932: 378–385). In the 1980s the resistance against the transfer of Modernism into China was epitomised by Min Ze's condemnation of it as a "product of the distorted historical development of modern capitalist society" (Min 1984: 41). Modernism, together with Gao Xingjian as its chief promoter, were castigated as elements of "spiritual pollution" in the Twelfth Plenary Session of the Central Committee of the Communist Party of China held in October 1983.[3] Yet Gao's plays written as adaptation of the Modernist paradigm had by then already entered the Chinese literary polysystem and become an integral part of it. These texts bear clear signs of cultural, political and theatrical negotiation with the existing norms.

The Absurd

Bus Stop amazed its audiences with its unconventional use of theatrical symbolism that went directly against the norms of Socialist Realist drama in the Naturalistic style. On account of its plot, which is about a group of people waiting in vain for a bus to the city, the piece is frequently compared to Samuel Beckett's *Waiting for Godot*. In *Bus Stop*, a group of people from different backgrounds wait at the bus stop to go into the city. It turns out that ten years have passed and they are still waiting. There is no scene division in the play, and both the stage setting and the plot are non-realistic. The set is a simple bus stop without any realistic elaboration. There might be resemblances between its mode of expression and that of the Theatre of the Absurd, but the anti-realistic style of each play is backed by very different underlying philosophies. In the definition of the Theatre of the Absurd given by Martin Esslin, who originally coined the term, special emphasis is placed on the "metaphysical anguish at the absurdity of the human condition" it articulates (Esslin 1961/1983: 23–24). The concept "Absurd" is borrowed from Camus' description of the human existence being devoid of purpose in *Le Mythe de Sisyphe* [*The Myth of Sisyphus*] (Camus 1942/ Hamilton 1975). To explain this, Esslin quotes Ionesco:

> Absurd is that which is devoid of purpose .... cut off from his religious, metaphysical and transcendental roots, man is lost; all his actions become senseless, absurd, useless. (Esslin 1961/1983: 23)

The imagery, the unusual stage set, the incomprehensible gestures and language typical of the Absurd drama are not merely theatrical tricks to shock or to please, but in Esslin's own words, it is a form determined by its subject-matter. The Existential view of the world represented in the Theatre of the Absurd is simply incongruent with Realistic theatre that implies logic in the Enlightenment tradition. Its form also differs from the Existentialist theatre of Sartre, which still provides a realistic setting as background for the plot. Esslin sees the Absurd as a more efficient vehicle for expressing the ideas of Existentialism, because it has found an expression that shows the human situation according to this philosophy, rather than discussing it in the kind of logic that the philosophy itself has already rejected (Esslin 1961/1983: 24). Therefore, in applying the term "Absurd" to any literary work, there is always the implication of the metaphysical dislocation between human beings and their situation, as described by Camus: men have lost what they once believed to be the meaning and purpose of their existence, and now they feel totally out of place in the world (Camus 1942 / Hamilton 1975).

Waiting for Godot is one of Esslin's chief examples of Theatre of the Absurd. The two tramps keep waiting, however futile their sojourn may be, because there is no other way out of their purposeless lives. Their tragedy resides in their lack of future prospect. There is no sign that Godot will definitely be coming, and even if he did come, there is no suggestion anywhere in the play as to what changes he might bring to their situation. Even the assumed arrival of Godot does not guarantee salvation. Not only has every day been the same for the tramps up to this point, but every day to come will also be the same.

Waiting for Godot and *Bus Stop* are both allegories, one of what Beckett sees as modern life, the other a microcosm of Chinese reality in the years immediately after the Cultural Revolution. The characters all share an incentive to get to town. Lout[+] wants to get there to buy himself some yogurt, Carpenter wants to start a training class for young trainees, Old Man is going to a chess competition and Glasses is preparing for a university entrance exam. They are people who yearn for an improved and modernised life. They all believe that getting to town can satisfy their hopes. The nature of the waiting is purposeful, the direction in which they are going is certain. This is in stark contrast to the general lack of purpose in the actions in *Waiting for Godot*. Beckett presents us with the Sartrean idea that the teleological assumption of life is ultimately futile. Didi and Gogo's problem is not knowing what to do with life, since there is no meaning to it, and everything done in and for it; but the problem for the people waiting for a ride to town in *Bus Stop* is not having the means to achieve their clear goal. In *Bus Stop*, one of the characters, Silent Man, gives up waiting very soon; he leaves the crowd and starts walking to the city. There is a melody that often accompanies his appearance and actions, thus establishing an association between the melody and him. Later on in the play when the other characters notice that they have waited for ten years in vain, the melody is played again. It creates a contrast between his initiative and their passive waiting. The message of the play is apparent: an affirmation of the initiative to construct a bright modern future by the characters' own efforts, to walk to the city, however slowly, instead of waiting any longer for a bus to take them. If, for the Absurd writers, God is dead, then for the whole of China as represented in the play, God exists in the form of modernisation and literal progress towards the city.

In the world as constructed in *Waiting for Godot*, human relationships are twisted. Didi and Gogo kill time by irritating each other. The relationship between Lucky and Pozzo is sado-masochistic. The old Christian ideal of a loving human relationship no longer applies. But in *Bus Stop*, the agitation and competition to get on the bus felt by the characters in the beginning gradually turns into comradeship as they face the same crisis. There develops a romance between Girl and Glasses, female bonding between Girl and Mother, and a parental concern of Carpenter for Lout. This is a call for unification in the country and for joint efforts to build a brighter future for the whole national community. *Pace* William Tay's view that the play ends where it starts, showing a circular structure as in many examples of Absurd drama (Tay 1990: 112), there is rather a linear development in the plot: exposition-crisis-resolution. But he is correct that the play has a different message from *Godot*. The need for collective efforts to achieve modernisation is definitely implied. The dominant voice in the play is one that calls for initiative from the people to work toward modernisation; the overall tone is one of an optimistic national future.

At the end of the play, the bureaucrat Director Ma calls out to stop everybody from walking on because he needs to tie his shoe-lace. But this should not be read as an indication of inertia. Instead, it acts more like a moment of comic relief at the end and turns the bureaucratic figure into a laughing stock. The inefficiency of this bureaucrat only reinforces the overall message of the play: the bus is not coming, in other words, the "company" is not doing its job. The ten years wasted suggests the ten years of the Cultural Revolution. No doubt the characters experience a shock and find it difficult to accept the loss of time. The subjective psychological impact might even be Kafkaesque, but there is a fundamental difference: for Camus, Esslin and Beckett, the cause for the Absurd existence is metaphysical and the Absurd condition is absolute. But in *Bus Stop*, the cause is political and the Absurd condition is situational. In the transfer of the idea of the Absurd, its content is adapted. Nevertheless, to draw such a difference is not to invoke the idea of authenticity, since transfer is not cloning. Transformations are not only legitimate in Miller's model of transmission, but also necessary and expected. The divergence between Gao's and the European Absurd highlights the different functions and nature of the Absurd in the two contexts. The Absurd is transferred into the Chinese polysystem and acquires a new lease of life. But this Chinese Absurd does not replace the European one; it exists side by side with its European counterpart, in the way that a translation remains adjacent to the "original".

Psychological Reality

Gao's play *Alarm Signal* is also written without scene division. The scenario is a potential train robbery. Blacky,[5] a young train passenger, has arranged to help robbers board the train. Also on the train are his girlfriend Bee and his friend Trumpet. The train conductor, guessing his intention, persuades him to stop the plan in time. Depiction of external reality and the characters' expression of their psychological state in the form of interior monologue alternate to make up the play's main structure. Dramatic actions and soliloquies cut into each other. Characters of the play are depicted as types. Although characters in *Bus Stop* are also presented as types, it is their personality attributes, rather than their social situations as in *Alarm Signal*, that are stereotypical. Blacky is torn apart by the conflict between his good nature and the temptation to commit crimes, but the real cause of his action is unemployment, a problem faced by many young people after the Cultural Revolution. He resists temptation, decides not to comply in the train robbery and proves his worth at the end. Bee, his girlfriend, is timid, honest and harmless, fitting into the ideal traditional young woman. The experienced conductor of the train is a straightforward, cautious and dutiful worker. He reminds the audience of the loyal comrades in Socialist Realist literature of earlier decades. It is this character who finally resolves the problems for the train by preventing the robbery, and for Blacky by taking him on as adopted son so that the latter can take over his job when he retires. His speeches are often didactic in content and in tone, for example,

> Young man, I was your age once. I've crossed more bridges than the roads you've traveled. Don't be so hot-headed and work yourself into a corner .... Our country is experiencing some difficulties these past few years and cannot provide jobs for all of you. You may be out of work for one or two years. But the situation is bound to improve and you won't be without a job your entire life. (Gao 1982a/ 1985c: 48 / Yu 1996: 197)

> Blacky ... You've just become an adult and your life has just begun. You know what you should do. It's up to you to earn your right to live. (Gao 1982a/1985c: 78 / Yu 1996: 227)

No wonder *Alarm Signal* achieved a rapport with the audience. Unemployment was a serious problem faced by many young people in the early

1980s. The favourable ending for all parties in the play must have consoled its audience. The happy resolution consisting of success in both romance and career functions as encouragement to the audience, stressing the message, again in the persona of the conductor that:

> If you want the right to live, you must first bear the responsibility of life. (Gao 1982a/1985c: 79 / Yu 1996: 228)

The moral of the play remains conservative. Individuals must consider the welfare of the community at large and not become consumed by their own problems, because the latter would naturally be taken care of when the former is achieved. Here, the Communist belief in the collective coincides perfectly with the traditional Chinese patriotic hegemony of nation over family. Moreover, the contrast between the dominance of the male characters in the plot and the decorative function of the female character, Bee, also coincides with the social hierarchy of male over female; and the authority of the old over the young reflects the traditional family and the current political hierarchies. These are no doubt safe ideologies to adhere to. They please both the political and the cultural conservatives. Wisdom in the play is passed on from the older generation to the younger. The conductor is undoubtedly the wise older man, who is the representative of the truth, as well as possessing the resources to provide the hero Blacky with a job. The other father figure in the play, although he does not appear on stage, is Blacky's father, Chen Shoushan, whose name alludes to the Confucian virtue of a gentleman adhering to the righteous way. As Kongzi [Confucius] says, "*shou si shan dao*" — adhere to the righteous path till one dies. (*Lunyu* c. 5th century B.C.: 8:13; translated into English as *The Analects of Confucius* by James Legge, 1861–1872) This is no doubt a reminder for Blacky, in the name of the father, at such a critical moment of choosing between right and wrong.

There is, however, no need to be too harshly dismissive of this kind of conservatism. After all, the play is situated within the context of the time. A wholesale ideological subversion of all these structures, even if intended, would have had little chance of getting through censorship and gaining public exposure. The theatre is particularly vulnerable as an institution because the nature of public congregation in the theatre has often caused censorship to be particularly tight. Moreover, in spite of this conservatism, the formal structure of allowing articulation of the characters' inner voices, thus giving vent to the voices of the individual, has given considerable edge to the play.

An intertextual comparison of this psychological aspect in *Alarm Signal* with European Modernist works would serve as an important reference point for the present analysis of these plays as a part of Gao's project of translating Modernism into China. Whether acknowledged by their writers or not, many European

Modernist works are influenced by Freudian psychology. The emphasis given to psychological reality often aims at giving voice to the repressed libido and "anti-social" desires. Luis Buñuel's classic film *Un Chien Andalou*, Wedekind's *Lulu* trilogy for the stage, many Picasso paintings and James Joyce's novels are good examples of this. Yet again, the "psychological approach" in *Alarm Signal* is not exactly identical. In the production of the play by the Beijing People's Art Theatre, special lighting effects such as intense spotlight and voice over in the sound design were employed to create a psychological space for the characters. Their inner voices expressed the positional differences of the various characters rather than their repressed subconscious, and these positional differences are social in nature. The psychological space opened up in European Modernism is transferred onto the Chinese stage, but to address a different problem. A number of things previously excluded in dogmatic Socialist Realism are present in *Alarm Signal*, including doubt and discontent with the new social order, and most important, a personal dimension which also has to be satisfied before harmony can be achieved with the collective. Although the play finally concludes with the preservation of the collective interest, it has already pushed the limit of what is allowed by the norms of the time. In both European Modernism and its adaptation in *Alarm Signal*, what has been repressed in the public domain is given expression by means of "Psychological Realism", although the content, dimension and nature of the repressed are different.

The Polyphonic Structure

In this context it is interesting to note theatre critic Lin Kehuan's reading of Gao's plays as "polyphonic, multi-levelled, polythematic and polytonal" (Lin 1987: 145). There is no doubt that Gao's plays of this period are rich in plots and innovative theatrical devices. Polyphony, however, like other literary concepts transferred from European Modernism, is transformed, applied to serve different ends and endowed with new meanings. A close look at these plays reveals divergence between the function of a polyphonic structure in its original European context and that in Gao's plays. This divergence is the result of cultural negotiation when Gao translates this structure into his own plays.

One of the most important definitions of polyphony in literary studies is proposed by Bakhtin in his early studies of Dostoyevsky's novels. He is concerned with the co-existence of various voices in a work of literature, not only in the technical sense, but also in the ideological sense. Bakhtin defines polyphony as he sees it in Dostoyevsky's novels thus:

> A plurality of independent and unmerged voices and consciousness ... with equal rights and each with its own world, combined but not merged in the unity of the event. (Bakhtin 1929/ Emerson 1985: 6)

Bakhtin observes that the different voices in Dostoyevsky's novels develop in parallel with each other. Together they build up a polylogised structure. Every voice is given an expression not counteracted by one another. Each of these voices receives fair treatment and avoids entering into dialectical argument, so the whole structure will not be "reduced to thesis, antithesis and synthesis" (Bakhtin, 1929/ Emerson 1985: 6).

Being read against this idea of polyphony, Gao's polyphony appears to be more of a technical innovation than content structure. There is always an ideological closure at the end of Gao's plays, a moral of the story to be gleaned by the audience. Although conflict between the individual and the collective is a consistent theme, the solution of the individual problems are always presented as consolidation of the collective, thus reinforcing both a hierarchical superiority of nation over individual and a patriotic desire to unify different elements of society to build a better future. In *Alarm Signal*, Trumpet, Bee and Conductor have all expressed their opinions and expectations for life. Although Bee's ideal of simple life on the grassland, Trumpet's artistic aspiration and even Blacky's discontent with his unemployed state effectively arouse sympathy from the audience, all these voices come into negotiation in the context of the safety of the train passengers. Individual interests are forsaken for the benefit of the greater community. These conflicts gradually build up to a crescendo as the action reaches a climax when the gang of robbers climb aboard the train. Blacky's preoccupation with his personal situation is criticised by the conductor as self-indulgence. The moment when Blacky subscribes to the latter's opinion is the point where the belief in collective interest embodied in the character of the conductor becomes dominant.

Bus Stop also concludes with an ideological closure. The characters share the same hope that the bus, which can accommodate all of them, would come and take them to town, so their respective wishes can all be fulfilled. Instead of their differences, their common interest becomes the focal point. Their different backgrounds and intentions are used more for a decorative purpose, with the result that each is a part of a composite; together they make up a dense texture. Although these voices start from different positions, they all converge at the conclusion that there is no point of waiting and complaining, and that only self-dependence and initiative will bring success. Silent Man is the only one who does not join with the crowd. Not having said a word about the long wait, he gives up waiting altogether and starts walking by himself. Instead of waiting to be taken, he chooses to help himself and sets off for town. The symbolic meaning is explicit. This character is emblematic of the determination to go through hardship to achieve one's goal. In the original production of the play by the Beijing People's Art Theatre in 1982, Lu Xun's mini narrative "*Guoke*" [1925, translated into English as "The Passer-by" by Xianyi and Glady's Yang, 1956] from his collection of prose poetry *Yecao* [*Wild Grass*] was dramatised and played as a prelude. The story depicts a loner who keeps walking to an unknown destination. He keeps on walking in spite of the extreme fatigue and the lack of understanding and sympathy from other people. This character is often interpreted as personification of the progressive national revolutionary. In the 1982 production of *Bus Stop*, the same actor assumed the roles of Passer-by in the prelude and Silent Man in the play. This arrangement asserted a double affirmation of the actions of these two characters. The message of both the play and the production is very clear: among all the characters, it is Silent Man, the patriotic hero, who has made the right choice and taken the necessary action. This is very different from Bakhtin's model in which the relationship between the different points of view, or in his words, sets of consciousness, are presented in parallel and on equal terms. In *Bus Stop*, Silent Man is proven to be right when all the other characters regret not having followed him. The music, which at first accompanies the appearance of Silent Man but then is used when he is gone to suggest the presence of his spirit, is modified into a jolly and even mocking tone to evoke a sense of triumph over the other characters. Thus the play reaches a closure with a monologised moral. Again, having said this, such explanation does not imply a derogatory criticism of this particular play. One has always to take into account what is allowed in the target polysystem at the time of transfer. It is already remarkable that such formal experimentation was actually realised on stage in a situation where formal innovation inevitably bore the connotations of ideological non-conformity. Thus the meaning and function of Polyphony in European literature was negotiated in Gao's translation of it into the Chinese polysysterm.

Yeren (1985, translated into English as *Wild Man* by Bruno Roubicek, 1990) is given a secondary title, that of a "polyphonic modern epic" [*Duoshengbu xiandai shishi ju*]. Each character, or voice, represents a very different scope of experience. Together they make up a complicated and composite picture of different attitudes towards deforestation and ecological protection. The play's plot follows Ecologist's visit to the forest and his encounters with the various characters before he writes his report to recommend designation of the forest as a protected ecological zone. This public dimension of his life makes up the main plot, but there is a sub-plot about his private life. His attention to work is from time to time distracted by reminiscence of his divorced wife living in the city and the romantic feelings he has nurtured in Xiang Mei, a young girl he has met in the village. This sub-plot accentuates his disappointment with the urban value system and increasing identification with the rural one. Other characters occupying different positions complete the composite structure: the non-realistic appearance of Primitive Man represents the voice of the primitive; Old Singer embodies a pre-modern relationship between human and nature which is mutually nurturing rather than disproportionately exploitative; The timber merchants are only interested in quick economic returns regardless of the impact of their trade on the environment. In between the poles of unconditional protection and ruthless exploitation, Team Leader Liang[6] tries to strike a balance between institutionally approved human exploitation and preservation of nature. But most of these positions are criticised in the play. The timber merchants are characterised as being selfish, wicked and greedy. Their characterisation is rather two-dimensional. The effort of Lin, the director of forestry, to sustain the deforestation zone in order to facilitate a livelihood for the villagers in the forest is presented to be lacking in sense because nature is paying too high a price for this. At the end of the play the forest is classified as a protection zone as recommended in the report that Ecologist has sent to the government. His stance on environmental protection prevails, not only over the cynical self-interest of the timber merchants, but also over the compromising approach adopted by Team Leader Liang and Lin. The wish for the next generation to live harmoniously with nature is represented by a little boy running to the downstage area hand in hand with Wild Man in the last scene. Ecologist's intention to protect the forest receives favourable treatment while all other positions are to be suppressed. His singular voice becomes the most important and most correct position overruling all other reasoning. This politically correct closure constitutes great dramatic and ethical pleasure for the audience. Judging from the effectiveness of advocacy for nature preservation, it is certainly a successful work. But the right and wrong are simply so obvious and Ecologist's ethical superiority runs through the entire play almost too easily. The audience will hardly finds the piece intellectually challenging or possessive of dialectical profundity.

Gao's only polyphonic works in the Bakhtinian sense are the four shorts entitled *Xiandai zhezixi* [1984, Sketches of modern *xiqu*], which Gao published as one composite work. *Duoyu* [Taking shelter from the rain] is probably the most illustrative example because it can be compared to the short story Gao wrote based on the same scenario. In the play, the character Old Man, overhearing two young girls' discussion on life and love, responds to each of their points of view, and has to communicate his feelings to the audience through silent action because in character he is trying not to make noises which would alarm them. The girls' conversation provokes him into thoughts, sometimes he agrees with them and other times disagrees. There are three points when his reaction is particularly strong. Firstly, one of the girls remarks on her love of rain because she didn't have to work on rainy days when she worked in a production team in the country. Old Man shakes his head to show disapproval. Later the same girl expresses her admiration for the boldness of walking in the rain to celebrate one's feeling of pleasure. Pain is registered on his face, because the passage of his own youth is highlighted when compared to the young girls' celebration of theirs. Then the girl complains that her grandfather does not understand her, and he shows anger. He is obviously identifying with the opposite side of the generation gap. Their contrasting positions make up the main structure of the play; they encounter each other, nevertheless they remain polarised at the end as at the beginning. The lack of two-way communication protects each of the voices from entering into dialectical argument and from being counteracted. There is no attempt to reconcile the two. The dialogic tension remains unresolved.

Taking Shelter is adapted from Gao's own short story *Yu, xue ji qita* [Rain, snow and other things], written in 1981. Here the dominance of the eavesdropper's consciousness is established at the expense of the dialogic structure preserved in the play. The story is divided into three sections. In the first one the two girls, who are the speakers of the dialogue, are identified as the "sweet voice" and the "clear voice", with quotation marks for the speeches to emphasise the dialogue form. In the second part, the distinction between the speakers is blurred and quotation marks are replaced by dashes. The individual identity of the girls is no longer important. All that is emphasised is the boundary between the eavesdropper's own world and the external stimulus he receives from hearing the conversation. In the last section it is not clear whether the speeches are really made by the girls since they have become totally merged into the eavesdropper's consciousness. They are written in short paragraphs without any speech markers. The form changes as the relationship between the eavesdropper and the text he is listening to changes.

Although Bakhtin holds that polyphony in drama is impossible, the above comparison between *Rain* the short story and *Taking Shelter* the play proves the opposite. For Bakhtin:

> in drama the world must be made from a single piece. Any weakening of this monolithic quality leads to a weakening of dramatic effect. The characters come together dialogically in the unified field of vision of author, director, and audience, against the clearly defined background of a single tiered world. (Bakhtin, 1929/ Emerson 1985: 17)

Bakhtin is concerned with the process of the making of a play, especially in the case of Naturalistic drama, on stage in which all participants and interpretations are guided by the director's vision, and the outcome is the representation of a unified view of the director. However, the theatre has much higher potential in creating complexity. The physical aspects of the theatre, on top of the verbal one, make the audience's reception more pluralistic than the reading of a written text. Any alternative points of view can be expressed and strengthened by the physical presence of the actors. The body language, blocking and on-stage kinesics can work on another level to counteract what is being expressed in words. It is exactly the physical presence of the alternative consciousness that is being exploited in *Taking Shelter* to fulfil the polyphonic potential of the theatre.

As in his short stories, in Gao's plays it is when grand nationalist narrative is abandoned and an interest in individuals' daily lives is assumed that the most interesting moments emerge. But unlike short stories which come to be read by the reader by virtue of an editor's consent to publication, drama reaches its audience only with the audiences' attending the production, and the possibility of production is dependent on financial and censorship realities. Therefore, by conforming to the atmosphere of social rehabilitation of the time, *Bus Stop* and *Alarm Signal* received both the critical and box office popularity that *Taking Shelter* could not have achieved. In fact the latter has never been put on stage in China. Its only productions have taken place abroad.

Apart from *Taking Shelter*, Gao's plays are not really polyphonic in the Bakhtinian sense, but there is perhaps a musical sense in which the idea of "polyphony" can be applied. In music polyphony refers to a composition structure in which different voices perform variations on the same theme. In *Bus Stop*, the characters each have their own purposes for going to town. The basic structure of the play is the orchestration of various consciousnesses of a group of people sharing the same aspiration of going to town. In cases of conflicting interest, there is always counterpoint where they express their differences and the conflict is emphasised before the final resolution. There are times when the characters speak short interior monologues alternately one after another, and at other times several characters speak at the same time as duet, trio or in polyphonic style. The highest number is seven parts speaking alternately or four parts speaking at the same time. Some commentators have criticised this hyper-complicated sound structure, maintaining that the content of these speeches are completely lost in the confusion of voices (Xiao 1984: 126–128). Despite this confusion, this structure has succeeded in creating a simultaneity in the feelings of the characters. There is inevitably a play-off between emotion and reasoning, and the effect of the voices is privileged over clarity of speech. This is the first instance in Gao's plays where the human voice is used as a sound or even a series of musical effects to convey emotions rather than an expository device for verbal reasoning. It will become a recurring feature in his later plays.

Songs and music also function to create a multi-levelled texture in *Bus Stop* and *Wild Man*. As mentioned earlier, the music used for Silent Man in *Bus Stop* establishes a relationship with the action on stage through its varying tones. It constantly creates a comparison between Silent Man's action and other characters' hesitation, and underlines the dramatic antithesis. In *Wild Man*, songs again produce an ironic effect. A happy love song is sung when Ecologist is faced with marriage problems and again when Xiang Mei marries a man she does not love. But the more poignant use of songs is those sung by Old Singer and the primitive dance performed by the Primitive Men. These short episodes are presented in a non-realistic mode, having no logical continuation within the plot but recurring constantly, punctuating the narration of the modern. By means of this device, two very distinctive levels of reality (the primitive and modern civilisations) are successfully juxtaposed, the choice that has to be made between the value of nature and that of civilisation appears urgent.

The Influence of *Xiqu*

The cliché that history often comes full circle is indeed a simplistic view of what actually happens. The second time round is always different, since for example *Don Quixote* can only be *re*-written in the Borges story *Pierre Menard, Author of Don Quixote*. One may prefer to invoke Yeats' image of spiralling historical progression. This latter image is much more suitable to describe the intertextuality between Gao's plays and traditional *xiqu* theatre. Both in the critics' analyses and in Gao's own acknowledgement, the use of song and dance in *Wild Man* is influenced by *xiqu* (Gao 1985b/2001: 161). Modern Chinese theatre follows the *huaju* tradition, and *huaju* itself, as mentioned earlier, is transferred into the Chinese polysystem at the turn of the twentieth century as a more progressive modern form of theatre than the traditional musical theatre of *xiqu*. Early Chinese *huaju* was greatly indebted to European drama, both in form and in content. The early 1980s saw a revival of interest among Chinese dramatists in Western culture which was perceived to be capable of offering alternatives to the State-sanctioned theatrical Realism. But when Chinese playwrights, this time round, looked to the West for a new form of theatre, they found common ground between their own theatrical tradition and a form of contemporary Western theatre. This form had been greatly influenced by Asian theatre after revolutionary transformations initiated by dramatic giants such as Brecht, Artaud and Yeats. In the second half of the century, further steps were taken by Post-Modernist "intercultural" dramatists including Jerszy Grotowski, Ariane Mnouchkine, Eugenio Barba and others. These have inherited the Modernist taste for minimalism and reinforced its eclectic nature by extensively blending in methods of traditional Asian forms, which are basically anti-illusionistic. But the devices these dramatists borrowed from Asia to shock their audience were hardly novel to the Chinese audience, especially *xiqu*-goers; and one must not forget that it remained the most popular entertainment in theatrical form in China until the middle of the twentieth century. Therefore, if one is to revive these devices in contemporary Chinese theatre, they are not necessarily deployed to alienate the audience in the way that Brecht and Grotowski sought to do, but rather to function as highly economical and effective dramatic devices. Early *huaju* masters such as Jiao Juyin (Jiao 1956/1985) and Wang Zuolin (Wang 1962/1990) had already pointed out this direction for the development of Chinese drama in the pre-Communist Revolution era.

But for the experimental Chinese dramatists in the 1980s such as Gao Xingjian, the deployment of traditional *xiqu* devices in drama fulfilled yet one more function. This theatrical trend was predicated on "literature in search of cultural roots". Critical reflections on China's cultural tradition functioned as a critique on contemporary Chinese culture as continuation of traditional values. *Xiqu* techniques in experimental theatre in this period are not only applied for the sake of convenient narration, but serve simultaneously as a reminder of the Chinese past and a critical attitude toward the present, since the content narrated through these techniques display critical rather than conservative tendencies. Therefore, these plays should be read as having integrated elements of the "movement in search of cultural roots". What we see in *Wild Man* is exactly this desire to look to the primitive and to assume it to be an alternative to modern Chinese culture. Its employment of devices from traditional *xiqu* as an alternative to Realism is very much a part of the same impetus. In fact, prior to *Wild Man*, Gao had published a suite of four short sketches to experiment with the deployment of *xiqu* devices in modern theatre. They are published as one single composite work under the title of *Xiandai zhexixi* [Sketches of modern *xiqu*], of which *Duoyu* [Taking shelter from the rain] is one of the sketches. The title of the suite suggests formal kinship with the traditional form, even the intention to function as a modern version of it. Each of these four *Sketches* experiments with one feature of *xiqu*. However, as mentioned earlier, none of these four *Sketches* has been produced in China so far. In 1987, *Taking Shelter from the Rain* was put on in Sweden in Göran Malmqvist's translation and under the direction of Peter Wahlqvist. The only Chinese production, which is also the only full production of all four *Sketches*, was the 1987 Cantonese production in Hong Kong directed by Kiu Po-chung, Yip Ka-lai and Kuk Cho-wai. Although both productions have their own artistic merits, they were produced as modern drama rather than *xiqu*. None of the directors or actors were *xiqu* practitioners. Therefore the potential of these *Sketches* has never been properly explored.

For the benefit of readers who are not familiar with *xiqu*, a short description of this form is perhaps in order. The central theatrical conception of *xiqu* is anti-illusionism. On a *xiqu* stage, nothing is supposed to realistically represent reality. Sets and props are not used to create the illusion of reality. The stage décor is typically an embroidered backdrop, and the floral and fauna patterns that embellish this backdrop carry no symbolic meaning. Situations are commonly indicated through gestures and verbal means including speeches and lyrics, rather than represented by realistic scenery or properties. The stage, stripped of elaborate scenic aids, leaves plenty of room for the actors' exaggerated make-up and highly formalised gestures to produce the dramatic signification on stage. These special dramatic structures result in a highly expressionistic effect. Once these expressive means are accepted as communicative convention and understood by the audience, the theatre becomes endowed with unlimited power of representation. But to make it work, the audience has to participate in this transformation from empty stage to imagined scenography by exercising their mind's eye. In Gao's own exegesis of the methods he employed in *Wild Man*, he observes that it is the "theatricality" [*juchangxing*] that distinguishes an active experience of going to the theatre from a passive one of receiving images from TV or films; the former requires the audience to exercise their intellect and imagination while the latter allows audience to simply receive images packaged for them (Gao 1985b/2001: 162).[7] One example of this kind of dramatic signification in *xiqu* is the famous mimetic action of lifting a door latch and crossing the threshold to suggest opening a door and entering a house. Another example is the highly stylised mime of boarding a boat in the popular and frequently performed *kunqu* (often known as "*kun* opera") sketch *Qiujiang* [Autumn River]. This is done by moving a short distance across the stage in quick but small steps to suggest walking across the plank connecting the boat and the shore, then bending and straightening the knees to create upward and downward movements, suggestive of the motion caused by the waves and the physical reaction of the people on board. By showing the action, the situation is suggested. There is no need for realistic scenery to be built or props to be used. References to things and situations are suggested with manners and gestures, not scenic verisimilitude. As Jiao Juyin points out, in *xiqu* the dramatic quality is constituted by the characters, especially the emotional impact of events on them, rather than by the events (Jiao 1956/1985: 1–3). By the same token, "theatricality", as it is called in Gao's exegesis, should depend on the characters' emotion and action within a particular stage set, not on the stage set itself.

In *xiqu*, lyrics and speeches are the major means to prompt the audience's imagination and to introduce the situation in which the dramatic action is set. It is common for each character to introduce himself and announce what he is going to do at his first appearance in every act. This provides the audience with information on the initial dramatic situation, and prepares them for the subsequent scenes in which they will have to exercise their imagination more vigorously. Equally common is the description, especially in songs, of what the character "sees" without the material presence of the objects. In such cases, the quality of the lyrics is vital because it is the most effective means of arousing the audience's imagination and invoking their emotions. One typical example is in Wang Shifu's *Xixiangji* (c. 1297–1307; translated into English as *The Romance of the Western Chamber* by S. I. Hsuing, 1935). The protagonist Scholar Zhang travels to see the Yangtze River. The beautiful scenery of the river is atmospherically depicted in his aria. As the actor walks round the stage signifying his journey along the river, he explains:

Strolling along, I have arrived at the bank of the Yellow River. Look, what a magnificent sight it is!

He sings:
Where is the special danger from incessant wind and water?
Surely that is the very spot!
This river passes by the States of Qi and Liang, divides those of Qin and Jin and
    serves as a defence of Yan.
The foam of the waves, white as snow, reaches the heavens,
And looks like the autumn clouds that roll in the sky.
The floating bridges, kept together by ropes of bamboo,
Look like black dragons crouching on the waves.
From east to west it passes through nine regions,
And from north to south a hundred streams flow into it.
What does the pace of the home-coming junks recall? It is like that of an arrow
    shot from a bow!
The river resembles the Milky Way, tumbling out of the ninth heaven,
Its source is so high that it seems to be beyond the clouds.
It maintains its course unchanged until it falls into the Eastern Sea.
It enriches the many thousand flowers of Lo-yang,
And fertilizes the innumerable acres of Liang Yuan.
Would that I could embark on a raft and sail to the confines of the sun and
    moon. (Wang c. 1297–1307 / Hsuing 1935: 7)

Such a scene is impossible to create on a naturalistic stage. But in a *xiqu*, the sense of beauty can be easily evoked with the actor singing the aria as he moves on stage. Every step he makes seems to suggest and open up fresh scenery to the audience. The audience's imagination is inspired by the actor's singing and acting, which describes the landscape and shows the character's emotional response to the situation. The scenario is defined simply by the actor naming what there "is" that the audience cannot physically see. When he says there are mountains there are mountains; if he says there are rivers there are rivers.

Another scene in *The Romance of the Western Chamber* also superbly makes use of speeches to set up the dramatic situation. It is the scene in which Cui Yingying and Scholar Zhang recite poetry to each other from their respective positions inside and outside Cui's chamber. The scene is performed without any physical barrier between the two performers, but the actions of the protagonists preceding this scene indicate that Cui is inside her bed-chamber while Zhang is taking a walk in the garden. The two players arrive at centre stage standing side by side. The ambiguous existence of the wall creates an ironic reference to the sexual segregation they are subjected to. It infuses the scene with a sense of humour and jollity. This is closely echoed in Gao's *Taking Shelter from the Rain*. The whole piece shows the response from an old man overhearing a conversation of two young girls. As in the scene in *Romance* described above, the acting area for *Taking Shelter* is understood to be split into two parts with imaginary barriers in-between. Visual communication between the two parties is supposed to be blocked. However audio communication alone is sufficient in providing all the dramatic elements. There are only several bags of cement piled up to suggest a construction site in which the old man and the two girls are sheltering from the rain and where the old man subsequently overhears their conversation:

> Evening. A construction site with shelter on a road. Only a few bags of cement piled up on stage are required. No need for strict designation of territories in acting areas. The situation is conveyed through the acting. (Gao 1984a/1985c: 145)

Not wanting to disturb them and being tempted to listen to their conversation, the old man prevents himself from making a noise and keeps himself well hidden in a position where the girls cannot see him. Irony is created between the aural voyeurism of his eavesdropping and the lack of stage properties to physically separate the two parties. This in turn highlights the response provoked in the old man by the girls' conversation, which constitutes the dramatic conflict of the whole play.

The same imaginary splitting of the stage also makes up the overall structure in another of the four short sketches, *Kabala shankou* [*The Pass at Kabala Mountain*]. But the space represented by the conceptually divided stage is much more extensive. It stretches both the audience's imagination and the capacity of this kind of stage signification. The stage is split into two acting areas. They represent two spaces, one in the air and one on the ground. Half of the stage stands for the inside of a plane flying over Kabala Mountain while the other half represents the same spot but 8km below on ground level. The stage is completely empty, and each of the halves is lit up when action takes place there. The only suggestion of scenery is the silhouette of mountains on one side of the stage and a spotlight in an oblong shape to suggest a window in an aeroplane on the other side. Explanation of situation is achieved by a Brechtian type narration but the narrator is neither a singer/narrator as in *The Caucasian Chalk Circle* nor a character involved in the story as in *The Good Person of Szechuan*. Instead, the actors exit their characters and assume the narratorial task. For example, at the beginning of the play, the actors define the stage space and name it thus:

— This is a pass at Kabala Mountain.
— Between the valleys of Kabala Mountain.
— An expressway built between two spurs at the height of 5300 m.
(Gao 1984a/1985c: 172–173)

The actors need to assume and drop characters instantly at various points in the play. This creates a sense of alienation, as in Gao's narrative fiction, constantly reminding the receptors of the fictional nature of the characters, their identity and the entire story, hence of the dramatic narrative itself.[8]

The other two sketches in the suite, *Xinglu nan* [Tough walk] and *Mufangzhe* [Imitator], are experiments on the dramatic potential of actors' movements. The two protagonists in *Imitator* are named This Person and Shadow. They perform the same gesture simultaneously to achieve a mirroring effect. This requires intensive training and practice on the part of the actors. The material absence of a mirror also helps to create the illusion whereby This Person mistakes Shadow for another person instead of realising that it is his own reflection. *Tough Walk* elaborates the psychological state of indecision to set off with highly stylised movements. The sketch makes use of four *chou* type of characters in *xiqu*, often translated as "clowns". They do not assume characterisation, which would have endowed them with specific background and identity. Instead, they represent stereotypes. One of these four clowns is a *xiaochou* [minor clown]. He is usually someone of low social status. The second one is a *fangjinchou* [hatted clown]. He wears a square hat and is often a scholar without any practical sense of life. The third one is a *wuchou* [acrobatic clown]. He wears short top and trousers and performs agile acrobatic skills. He is usually someone with physical strength but no intelligence. The last one is a *laochou* [old clown]. He is a meek and fragile old man. Since none of them has a definite identity, they give different reactions to the situation according to the category of personality the corresponding types of roles often typically represent. By using types rather than individuals as characters, the play intends to experiment on the dramatic capacity of the categorisation of roles in *xiqu*, or *hangdang* [lines of professional role]. The clowns are each placed on a wooden pedestal performing stylised actions to express their feelings, and their psychological and physical states. Each considers taking off and leaving the stage but never manages to make the move. The dramatic effects arise not from actual actions, since there aren't any, but from the tension generated as to whether their potential actions are to be fulfilled, as well as from the four respective contrasting states of the characters expressed in their discussion on whether to make the move. In putting the four clowns together and stripping the dramatic situations of a plot, this sketch shows that any situation in comparison, contrast or simply juxtaposition can arouse dramatic conflicts. This is the same idea as demonstrated in *Taking Shelter*. Both plays show that drama might not necessarily be generated by a plot. Contrasting positions in any given situation, as shown by the actors' highly dramatic acting, may be adequate in motivating dramatic performance. Nevertheless *Taking Shelter* still adheres to a hypothetical situation and characters, whereas *Tough Walk* is an even more radical experiment in reduction.

All these four sketches are limited to situations of either short duration or involving simple spatial relations. *Wild Man* is a much more ambitious attempt.

It entails a more extensive setting. It puts the signification system of *xiqu* to a harsh test. The play is set in a huge tract of time and space, as stated in the stage directions: "From seven or eight thousand years ago to the present; in cities and rural mountainous regions" (Gao 1985b/2001: 9). Such an extensive background is impossible to represent on the Naturalistic stage, since, as with Scholar Zhang's representation of the Yangtze River in *The Romance of the Western Chamber*, this scenery is impossible to construct realistically on stage. To make representation possible, scenery and properties are kept to a minimum. Small hand props, such as a bunch of keys for the inn keeper and a tea cup for the clerical officer, are wittily used to capture certain characteristics of the characters, actions or situations. The stage is basically empty with the occasional use of a bed or a table which can be easily carried by stage hands or actors themselves. Scenery is conveyed through acting or with the help of sound effects. Actions are clearly delineated in the script, for example,

> Sound of flowing stream. Xiang Mei jumps from one boulder to another. Half running, half jumping along the stream like a frightened deer. (Gao 1985b/ 2001: 114)

Although actors in *Wild Man* are not required to adopt gestures formalised into a pattern as in *xiqu* performance, they adopt the same method of signification in which stage setting is suggested through gestures rather than presented with tangible properties. It works particularly well in a play set against a background and situation of such complexity. The scene changes from an office to an inn, then a village hut, followed by a rainforest, then the bedroom of a house in a city. Next comes a grassland and a flowing stream, with the insertion at various points of Primitive Men dancing in the wilderness, and Old Singer singing about pre-historic times, both belonging to an era thousands of years ago. The mythical sense in the play, as well as the complexity of the scenery, is beyond the scope of representation of Naturalistic theatre. The choice of dramatic methods to suit the theme, appropriate to both the desire to search for cultural roots and the practical need for representation, is impressive. Not surprisingly the play has won enormous popularity among critics and audiences.

Wild Man was published in the second issue of the literary journal *Shiyue* [*October*] in 1985. In the same year, in fact a month earlier, Gao had a short play entitled *Dubai* [Monologue] published in the theatre journal *Xin juben* [New playscript]. The play is the monologue of an actor commenting on his own entrance and exit in the context of various characters and dramatic situations. Stage instructions indicate an empty stage with lighting changes to create moods and to designate acting areas. One of these dramatic situations is the actor pretending to come through a door by miming actions of opening a door in front of him and crossing the threshold. The overall theatrical conception alludes to the convention of *xiqu*. This meta-theatrical piece reveals *xiqu* as the governing principle of Gao's experimentation in this period.

A 1980s Chinese Modernist Structure of Feeling

By this stage, Modernism had firmly established itself in the Chinese polysystem through the many experiments writers had instituted and the discussions critics had launched. It is fair to say that in the process of Modernism's acculturation, Gao's body of works published before 1985 acted as a major agent of transfer, first by diegesis, then by mimesis. The introductory essays and *Preliminary Exploration* give an account of Modernism in a language that is not only linguistically but also culturally and politically comprehensible to its Chinese receptors. By stating that some of the methods of Modernism are universal and further legitimising it by relating them to Chinese literary masters such as Lu Xun, preparation is done for this foreign paradigm to enter the Chinese polysystem. On the practical level, such diegesis also prepares readers to receive Modernist writings, possibly in their original languages, but more probably in their Chinese translations. In Gao's creative works of fiction and drama the Modernist paradigm is directly translated into Chinese writing, recomposed with local themes and scenarios already in existence in the Chinese polysystem. In this act of translation/ transfer, the source is never a single text, but a network of texts that share the same structure of feeling. "Structure of feeling" is Raymond Williams' seminal concept. It states that in drama, and literature by extension, any formal innovation that stabilises and enters the mainstream has to be substantiated by the feelings generated by the experience of life in that community at that time. The form is not separate from its subject matter, but form and content stand as a unified structure that organises and articulates the feelings substantiating the work (Williams 1952: 19). In Gao's translation of Modernism, the product is not a document or a showcase of certain great European works. Instead, these acts of translation are performative instances when the European Modernist structure of feelings is transferred to the Chinese context in order to articulate a different structure of feelings. The two modernisms are analogous to each other, rather than homogeneous.

The content of the new structure is complex. On the material level, the post-Cultural Revolution modern life style in the urban areas was changing people's conception of time, space, speed and distance, in much the same situation postmodern societies find themselves in. The rigid temporal and spatial sense inherited in Naturalistic Realism was becoming much less necessary. But more important was the presence of an overwhelming impulse of anti-Naturalism and anti-Realism among the generation of writers who started writing after the Cultural

Revolution, firstly because of their discontent with the ideological control and political victimisation that had been associated with the hegemony of State-sanctioned Realism; and secondly on account of their scepticism toward the truthfulness of representational reality after their experience of the Cultural Revolution. Once European Modernism was translated into a post-Cultural Revolution Chinese Modernism, it became an extremely productive literary paradigm, moving increasingly towards the centre of the Chinese literary polysystem. In the mid-1980s Modernist writings, including Mo Yan's *Honggaoliang jiazu* (1984, translation into English as *Red Sorghum* by Howard Goldblatt, 1993) and other examples, proliferated and gained both critical and popular acclaim. In Even-Zohar's theory, a successful transfer is achieved when the transferred entity has become an integral part of the indigenous repertoire; that means not only is the transferred entity domesticated in the target culture, but also the need for it is generated (Even-Zohar 1997: 359). This is exactly what happened with Modernism in 1980s China, and Gao's translation project of the Modernist paradigm, in both diegetic and mimetic modes, played an important role in Modernism's successful transfer.

Part 3

The Translated Man

.

5

Soul Mountain 1982–1990:
From Modernism to Eclecticism

The novel *Lingshan* [1990; translated into English as *Soul Mountain* by Mabel Lee, 2000] represents the most important turning point in Gao's writing career. There are two reasons to support this claim. First, after the success of his translation project of Modernism, Gao departs from high Modernism and makes an attempt at translating the Postmodernist writing paradigm in this novel. Second, it is with this novel that Gao receives recognition from the "West" and a pathway is open for his works to enter the canon of "World Literature".

Indeed, in the Swedish Academy's statement justifying their award to Gao, *Soul Mountain* is given a prominent place. One can reasonably assume that it was on the strength of this novel that the author was awarded the prize. This has put the novel in the spot-light and made it Gao's best known work. Before the award he was much better known as a playwright than as a novelist. The first edition of the novel was published by *Lianjing*, one of the major Taiwanese literary publishers, in 1990 after Gao had been living away from China for several years. But the writing of the novel had started long before. According to Gao, it was in 1982 that the idea of the novel was conceived and he started working on it (Mabel Lee 2000: viii). Therefore a contextual analysis on this novel needs to consider not only the circumstances of its publication, but also those of its conception and development.

The Quest for Soul Mountain and the Search for Cultural Roots

One outstanding feature of the novel is the dominance of the spirit of the "search for cultural roots", as in his play *Wild Man* and in "Buying a Fishing Rod for My

Grandfather ", the last of his short stories published in China. The novel extends to around 300,000 words and the plot is highly complex.[1] There is a total of eighty-one chapters, each one a self-contained episode. Some episodes are directly related to the ones before and after them, others are not. The general narrative follows a journey taken by the protagonist "I" to the less developed regions in Southern China in search of a mountain called *Lingshan*, or "Soul Mountain". As a way to pass time, "I" makes up fragments of adventures experienced by an imagined self, also on a journey to look for Soul Mountain. The cultures he sees and people he meets prompt him to metaphysical reflections on the nature of existence. The details of these two parallel journeys make up very different textures of narrative; one is more realistic and the other almost surreal, but both are dominated by abundant descriptions of ethnic variety afforded by different places and customs.

In a large number of "fictions in search of cultural roots" written in the 1980s, the protagonists travel spatially to less developed areas. In some cases they encounter ethnic minorities; in other cases, they revisit the remote areas in which they spent the Cultural Revolution years. Such a journey also implies travelling in time because the life styles of these places remind the protagonists of alternative ways of life before urban development took over. If the plots are stripped of their details, one can see an archetypal structure in these stories: a modern subject confronts a less modernised world and the customs and values of this world. He identifies this world with his own way of life in the past. Confronting this other/old way of life prompts him to reflect on the tradition of his culture. These stories always conclude with the protagonists obtaining a different or a new awareness of their cultural identity. Among the many articles written on these stories, Fang Keqiang's structuralist analysis offers useful insights. He summarises this common theme as a kind of "semi-primitivism", akin to the return to the primitive of twentieth century European primitivism, echoing Rousseau's conception of the "noble savage", and manifested in numerous works of art such as D. H. Lawrence's fiction and Paul Gauguin's paintings of Tahitian women. Fang summarises the "deep structure" of these stories thus:

City-dwellers or intellectuals feeling discontented with urban life
Leaving the urban for the primitive
Affair with primitive female
Discontent with primitive female
Leaving the primitive and returning to the city

In Fang's model, the "roots-searchers" are always either city-dwellers or intellectuals educated in big cities. Their search for roots is a romantic spiritual adventure brought about by their critical response toward urban life. They are idealists who feel discontented with the pressure and alienation caused by modernisation, but not with the material aspects of modern life. They leave the modernised society but have not left behind the values they have acquired in these societies, so they can never resolve to identify with either one of the two ways of life. They come to the "primitive" communities as outsiders and finally have to leave as outsiders (Fang 1989: 64–69).

This description of fiction in search of cultural roots is surprisingly apt for the structure of *Soul Mountain*. "I" travels to less urbanised regions along the Yangtze River. He is inspired by what he sees and experiences to reflect on the tradition of his culture. This foregrounds the individual's Chinese cultural identity. However, there is a crucial difference between *Soul Mountain* and other fictions in search of cultural roots. In the copious works grouped under this category, the protagonists' "cultural roots" provide the theme and focus of the stories, but in *Soul Mountain*, they are the cultural anchorage for the most central theme of metaphysical reflection on existence. The ultimate concern of the novel is metaphysical rather than national or cultural. Whether this metaphysical reflection is of profound philosophical value is a question to be examined later on in the present chapter. For the present purpose of illustrating the difference between *Soul Mountain* and other fictions in search of cultural roots, I will cite a few straightforward examples of fictions in search of cultural roots below.

Zhang Chengzhi's "*Beifang de he*" (1984; translated into English as "Rivers of the North" in *Selected Stories by Zhang Chengzhi*, Xianyi and Gladys Yang eds., 1999) is a story about a geologist who gives everything to his study of the rivers in North China. The power of the waters he adores (which is a symbol for the life-force of Chinese culture) acts as the inspiration for his determination and consistency in his work. The identification of the nation with the "mountains and rivers of the land of the ancestors" [*zuguo heshan*] in patriotic discourse accounts in large part for his obsession with the geology of China. The extensive territories and antiquity of the rivers are figuratively elaborated by the discovery near the rivers of fragments of ancient coloured pottery. The emphasis on the rivers' antiquity and their broad extension of tributaries and distributaries contributes to the grand idea of the nation and national history. In this story, the protagonist is moved by this grand idea and it becomes the driving force behind his devotion to geological work. The national-cultural collective embodied by the geographical landscape is represented as the source of life force for the individual, like roots are to a plant.

In some fictions in search of cultural roots, the voice of the modern subject is not embodied in any protagonist, but is present in the authorial perspective. Stories of life in rural areas are depicted from a critical point of view representing the value system of the modernised world. One example is Han Shaogong's "*Ba ba ba*" [1985; translated into English as "Pa Pa Pa" by Martha Cheung, 1992]. It provides an allegorical reading of China. It tells the story of a mentally retarded young man named Bingsai, whose only two responses to every external stimulus, "Pa, Pa, Pa" and "mother-f—", are the parody of the Chinese attitudes toward anything that is foreign: either excessively obsequious or cynically contemptuous. Wang Anyi's "*Xiao bao zhuang*" [1982; translated into English as *Baotown* by Martha Avery, 1989] criticises the traditional codes of behaviour [*li*] as being dated and meaningless. The protagonist Laozha, like Bingsai, is almost mute and not in a position to make himself understood. His worth in the community is determined by the judgment of his fellow villagers who represent the ethical context in the world he lives in. The individual's life is contextualised within the convention of the collective.

Jia Pingwa's "*Shangzhou xilie*" [The Shangzhou series] provides other examples. This group of stories depicts characters who are torn apart by public values and private feelings. "*Mangling yitiao gou*" [A valley in Snake Range] tells the story about an old doctor who finds out that the fox he saved kills people in the village. This act of kindness prompted by his professional instinct turns out to do harm to his kinsmen. His personal feelings towards the animal cannot be reconciled with his responsibility for the collective welfare of the village. In utter desperation he commits suicide. In "*Liujia xiongdi*" [The Liu brothers] the protagonist Jiali indulges in two mutually contradictory reactions concerning his bandit brother's death. He celebrates his brother's death in public and cries privately at the graveyard. On the one hand he follows the folk practice of keeping peach blossom branches at the grave to subdue his brother's ghost spirit, so that the latter cannot haunt the village. On the other hand, he tries to perpetuate his brother's blood line by getting a girl to marry the latter's son. His actions prompted by the concern for collective welfare and those by brotherly love are carried out alternatively.

Stories in the Shangzhou series share two distinctive features. One is an abundant description of the landscape and customs of rural China. This sets the context for the protagonists' thoughts and actions. The traditional Chinese rural life and ethics leave little room for individuality and idiosyncracy. Second, although all these stories emphasise conflicts between the collective and the individual, they all end in reconciliation through the individual's conformity with the collective. In "A Valley in Snake Range", a tablet inscribed with the old doctor's story is erected. In "The Liu Brothers", when Jiali becomes an old man, he also erects a tablet bearing the inscription "no human beings should behave like Jialie [his bandit brother]" in the village. In "*Heilongkou*" [Black Dragon Pass], another story in the series, an old man laments the days wasted during the Cultural Revolution and wishes things would improve for the next generation. Reconciliation is achieved through the recognition of one's virtues by the collective in the old doctor's case; in Liu Jiali's case, through condemning his brother who has harmed the collective, and thus identifying with them; and in "Black Dragon

Pass", suppressing the resentment toward personal suffering and wishing the collective a brighter future. The collective in these stories often succeeds in achieving an ultimate unity that includes everyone in the village, but at the expense of repressed counter elements such as Jiali's brotherly affection, the old doctor's life after saving the fox, and the personal well-being of the old man in "Black Dragon Pass". Jia Pingwa puts subjective feelings in opposition to collective stability and laments the loss of the individual within the context of the traditional rural Chinese cultural setting.

In all these examples of fiction in search of cultural roots, the protagonists' choices represent the desire for reconciliation of the individual with Chinese history and culture, the latter being represented by the value system upheld and lived by the collective community. It shows a basically outward-tending development of the individual identity. The ego is being socialised. But this is not the case in *Soul Mountain*. The protagonist in *Soul Mountain* goes in the opposite direction. He undertakes a similar journey to remote areas; this journey also implies a visit to the past since these places are less advanced and modernised than his city of origin. Instead of being socialised and reconciled with the collective, he feels increasing alienated from the places and people he meets, and experiences a typical existential angst. The gradual withdrawal from his environment is constructed through a tripartite reality structure of the protagonist's consciousness.

Tripartite Reality Structure

As mentioned at the beginning of this chapter, the overall story-line follows two parallel journeys. The narrative at times takes a first-person perspective, and at other times a second-person perspective. In several chapters it also assumes a third person viewpoint. Chapter 1 of the novel begins with a journey without a fixed itinerary taken by "you". On the way "you" hears about a place called Soul Mountain, and decides to look for it. Then "you" meets "she" and they keep each other company for a time, during which they tell each other stories. But the narration of this journey is interrupted constantly with episodes of another trip taken by "I" and his feelings and reflections during the trip. The initial chapters alternate between these two plots with very few disruptions. The places "you" and "I" go to most of the time correspond to each other in their descriptions. Later it is revealed in Chapter 52 that "you" is in fact a creation in "I"'s mind to mitigate the loneliness of the journey, and "you"'s journey is a story "I" makes up to entertain himself. "He" in later chapters performs a similar function to "you". "She" is also a creation of the mind based on "I"'s experience and knowledge of women, in other words, a stereotypical woman figure for "I". Some of these episodes are descriptions of the journey, some are dreams, legends and stories the personage makes up, some are simply descriptions of imagery generated by the protagonist's feelings and emotions, whilst some chapters are metafictional explanations for this novel and for writing in general. One can take this last category as comments made by the protagonist "I", who is a writer; or as authorial presence injected into the narrative.

Such a narrative results in a structure made up of three levels of reality. The basic level is the trip taken by "I", by which all other elements are inspired and generated. The description of this trip is supposed to be based on the author's journey along the catchment areas of the Yangtze River in 1982, paid for with money given to him by a publisher who commissioned him to write a novel (Mabel Lee 2000: viii). Although many details in the novel appear to be based on what the author saw during this real trip, and the metafictional element in the novel coincides with his attitude towards fiction writing as expressed in his theoretical writings, there is no need to read the novel as "reliable" autobiography or to assume the "I" as representing the author himself, because such a reading would not clarify understanding of this novel, which is tightly-structured and forms an enclosure of its own. Speculation beyond the text itself is not necessary, except perhaps in connection with biographical studies on the author. In fact, emphasising the potential autobiographical elements in this novel risks the same kind of confusion caused by the explosion of Gao's personality following the Nobel Prize award. After all, the object of literary criticism is the literary text, despite the fact that biographical details often provide useful materials to help comprehension. Nevertheless, an over-emphasis on the latter would do more harm than good in the case of *Soul Mountain*.

The second level of reality in the novel is that of the imagination, generated by what "I" sees and does in the "external world". These episodes, as mentioned before, consist of a corresponding trip taken by an imaginary "you", and other subjective experiences, including memory, dream, imagination and emotion. The narrative makes it very clear that mental and psychological experience is taken to be as "real" as, if not more so than, "external" experience. At various points, the novel's preferred definition of reality is hinted at. Once it is described thus:

> The reality of life does not equal the appearance of life. (Gao 1990b: 13)

Obviously, the novel does not confine "reality" to actions and events. Memories, dreams, and the plot of an imaginary journey together make up a psychological reality that contributes to at least one-third of the novel's description. This parallel structure of the real and the imaginary reminds one of the influence of Modernism on Gao's works. But the two realities in *Soul Mountain* are intertwined in a more complicated manner. The imaginary journey and the dreams function as a process of self-reflection, and self-reflection is indeed the very aim of "I"'s real journey, as the proclaimed aim of this journey is to look for "Soul

Mountain". But the imaginary reality is only realised by the protagonist's act of writing as a writer. His comments on writing therefore make up the third level of reality, which functions on the meta-narrative level. At the same time, this theme of writing is dependent on the theme of spiritual quest, since it is only with an understanding of "I"'s desire to look for Soul Mountain that the act of writing acquires its intensity. The overall structure of the novel could therefore be aptly described as the two plots about the real and the imaginary journeys alternating within the narrator's self-aware long monologue. In fact "a monologue of the narrator" is exactly how Gao Xingjian himself described the novel in a talk he gave in 1991 entitled "Wenxue yu xuanxue: guanyu Lingshan" [translated into English as "Literature and Metaphysics — about Soul Mountain" by Mabel Lee, 2007].

One might argue that this is hardly a special feature of this particular novel, since all narratives written from the first person point of view are by their very nature the narrator's monologue. Yet readers cannot fail to discern the overwhelming meta-narrative tendency in the narrator's voice, and this tendency is precisely what Gao has experimented with in this novel and in his previous short stories. The function of this meta-narrative voice in Soul Mountain does not attempt to construct a chronology or logic of the events as authorial presence often does in many other novels. Instead, it develops a theme of its own and becomes increasingly prominent in the last chapters of the novel. In the talk "Literature and Metaphysics", Gao made the point that the "monologue" is an attempt to imitate the process of thinking of the narrator, and therefore, the episodes are not in chronological order and the narration jumps back and forth between reality, dreams, memories and imagination. This attempt is to disrupt narrative linearity similar to the technique of stream of consciousness, which is a direct imitation of discrete human thoughts (Gao 1991b/1992c: 211). Then Gao adds a further spin to his explanation: he calls his monologue "a stream of language" [yuyanliu] rather than a stream of consciousness [yishiliu] (Gao, 1991b/1992c: 211), since, according to his argument, the consciousness of the narrator is but a construction of language. If interpreted this way, the first two levels of reality (the real and the imaginary trips) converge into the third one (the meta-narrative), and the latter becomes dominant in the overall structure of the novel.

Both stream of consciousness and Gao's "stream of language" attempt to create the impression of random human thought. But Soul Mountain is not very successful in this respect, since the intimate connection of the real and the imaginary journeys requires the two layers of reality to be read in an interwoven manner. Moreover, it is not difficult at all to follow the two interposed plots as the readers progress through the chapters. As a result, the overall continuity of the plot is not interrupted. The fragments read in rather an organised way, as opposed to a random one.

In this connection it is worth comparing the "stream of language" in *Soul Mountain* with the dream sequence in his "Buying a Fishing Rod for My Grandfather". In the latter the protagonist's dream content is much less neat and complete. The images of ancient ruins of Loulan and Persia are fragmented and disconnected. The only connection is the theme of antiquity they share. This is more akin to stream of consciousness as defined by William James, a pioneer in the study of Psychology in the late nineteenth century. He describes it as a continuous flow of consciousness within which subjects of concern move freely from one to another, thus dividing concentration into segments. As he puts it in the often quoted paragraph:

> Consciousness, then, does not appear to itself chopped up in bits... it is nothing jointed; it flows. A "river" or a "stream" is the metaphor by which it is most naturally described. *In talking of it hereafter, let us call it the stream of thought, of consciousness, or of subjective life.* (James 1952: I: 155; emphasis in original)

Modernist writers are very much influenced by such innovative interpretation of the human mind. Fragmentation plays an especially important role in any attempt to imitate the operation of subjective reality for Modernists, because it is this very property that foregrounds the Freudian chaos in man's repressed soul, and draws a dividing line between their newly defined reality as opposed to the organised and rationalised reality of classic Realism embracing Enlightenment ideals. Marinetti's description of verbal articulation of the human consciousness as a kind of "*immaginazione senza fili*", or "imagination without threads" expressed in "*parole in libertà*", "words in freedom", is most representative of the Modernist position. This new poetic he formulates refers to:

> ... the absolute freedom of images or analogies, expressed with unhampered words and with no connecting strings of syntax and with no punctuation. ...

> With words-in-freedom we will have: CONDENSED METAPHORS. TELEGRAPHIC IMAGES. MAXIMUM VIBRATIONS. NODES OF THOUGHT. CLOSED OR OPEN FANS OF MOVEMENT ... (Marinetti 1913 / Brain et al 1973: 99–100; emphasis in original)

Such description is much more appropriate for the dream sequence in "Buying a Fishing Rod for My Grandfather" than for *Soul Mountain*. Although the chapters in the novel are not always directly consistent with the ones immediately before and after them, they unfailingly contribute to the construction of the two inter-relating plots. Even the non-interrelating short stories "you" and "she" tell each other contribute to an ultimately consistent pattern. The non-chronological arrangement of events has not conveyed a sense of "imagination without threads", nor has the narration achieved a linear structure similar to human thoughts. The text's ambition to structure the novel as a long interior monologue of the narrator in imitation of the way his mind works fails, exactly because it is too consistently fragmented in a calculative manner. Within this well-structured master-narrative flow, the text has taken care to include a number of paragraphs in the form of stream of consciousness, which no doubt capture the fragmentation of mental reality of particular moments. However, this organised fragmentation clearly demarcated into a tripartite reality only results in a sense of constructed arbitrariness. Moreover, the events narrated in the episodes that represent imaginary reality are often complete. This results in a self-subsistent world of the imagination. This inner world stands as an alternative to, rather than part of, the same complex reality that Modernists try to capture.

Meta-narrative: The Third Level of Reality

Much of Gao's early fiction questions the truth value of narrations of events that are taken for granted. In *Soul Mountain* this scepticism is further developed to negate any possibility for any narrative functioning as the bearer of truth, since narratives are nothing but language. One example is found in Chapter 15. "You" arrives at a village and claims that "your" ancestors are from there, so "you" is allowed to enter the ancestral temple and read the family genealogy. Although taken as the formal record of the history of the clan, the whole thing is simply a reconstruction according to the memory of three brothers in the family after the original copies were destroyed in the campaigns against feudalism. Therefore, even this formal version of history can have no claim to accuracy. Another example is found in Chapter 34 when "you" and "she" enter into an argument. "She" accuses "you" of telling tales and "you" accuses "she" of telling the truth in the stories "she" claims to be fictional. "She" has told a few stories about young girls initiated into sex and claims that they are simply stories she makes up. "You" suggests that these are actual events that happened to her but she is too ashamed to admit it. It is often assumed that a narrator's intention is to convince others of the story's factuality, but there is no reason why it cannot be the other way round. Both episodes cited here echo statements already made in Gao's previous short stories on the dubious reliability of narration.

The most striking feature of the novel is its frequent use of stories "you" and "she" tell each other. Instead of communicating through reasoning, discussion and explanation of emotions, they make up stories about places and people they see in their journey. Some of these stories are longer and make up short episodes of events, while others are merely descriptions of places and people. The couple's views on relationship and other matters in life are communicated to each other through telling these stories. In later chapters, the narrator "I", his alter egos "you" and "he" continue to tell episodic stories and describe dreams and mental images they have. All these contribute to a proliferation of images in the novel, which constitute an attempt to privilege expression through imagery over rational description and explanation. This idea can also be traced back to reflections on language and logic among European philosophers. In their study on the Enlightenment, Adorno and Horkheimer propose that reasoning has become a specific form of reasoning, a discourse secured by the operation of the linguistic system. The process of reasoning is no more than translating matters into reasoning's (thus language's) own system. This is a process in which unfamiliar or non-conceptualised reality can be lost in the translation (Adorno and Horkheimer 1944 / Cumming 1986). With its pre-dominant imagery, *Soul Mountain* participates in discourse which aims to challenge the supremacy of rational diegetic language.

But the scepticism about language in *Soul Mountain* does not stop here. As mentioned earlier, instead of referring to the intended imitation of thought underpinning the basic structure of the novel as a stream of consciousness, Gao calls it a stream of language. To foreground language is to imply a differentiation between it and consciousness, in other words, a split between language and thought. This idea is even more radical than the Modernist scepticism toward Realism expressed in Gao's own early fiction. In *Soul Mountain* there are comments challenging language's capacity to represent what is "intended" to be conveyed. So the scepticism is not only directed at a certain mode of language use, but at language itself. This issue is explicitly referred to as early as Chapter 2 of the novel when the narrator talks about his feeling of the moment:

> The only thing real is myself sitting near this fire in this smoke-blacked house, watching the flame bouncing inside his eyes. The only thing real is myself. The only thing real is my feeling at this moment. It is impossible to communicate it to another person. (Gao 1990b: 18)

The split cuts deep into the fundamental difference between human experience recognised by the senses and language as a system with its own rules of signification. Another example is a remark in Chapter 54:

> ... in the end all you can achieve are memories, hazy, intangible, dreamlike memories which are impossible to articulate. When you try to relate them, there are only sentences, the dregs left from the filter of linguistic structure. (Gao 1990b: 357 / Lee 2000: 329)

In *Soul Mountain*, the author is not as dead as Barthes would claim him to be. His frustration with articulation and communication implies the presence of a phenomenological intending subject who bears the truth of an experience that language fails to represent. This view on language is upheld by many

Postsstructuralists. Philosophers of language from Saussure to Derrida have debunked a direct correlation between language and reality by isolating meaning from sign. Seeing language as a symbolic system which works inasmuch as it only refers to rather than equals reality, Cassirer describes human cognition as being "imprisoned in its own creations". He then explains that this human's "own creations" are no other things but "the words of language" (Cassirer 1923 / Manheim 1961: I: 113). This philosophical view on language is taken up by numerous philosophers including Paul de Man and many others. They are convinced that language has dictated perception. Human thoughts are pigeonholed into existing lexical and grammatical rules. Derrida's ultimate separation of *logos* and meaning, formulated in the idea of *différance*, has become the central theory of Poststructuralist linguistics, and the heart and soul of Postmodernist writing. In spite of this problem of language, it remains the main means of communication. The result is the impossibility of perfect communication between human beings, leading inexorably to the isolation of the individual.

There are a number of remarks in *Soul Mountain* directly echoing these philosophies, complaining that a large part of human experience is not translatable into language. This kind of comment is often made at the end of a narrated memory or an interpolated anecdote introduced by one of the characters. Sometimes these stories explode into surrealist images, sometimes they take the form of unpunctuated utterances. They often frustrate the attempt for subjective reality to be logically communicated to another person. Linguistic communication that depends on a fixed grammatical and lexical system is taken as an inadequate means to convey subjective reality, which is not defined by language. This is why, although "you" and "she" have tried to communicate through telling each other stories, which is actually a means of expressing feelings and emotions, they still fail to reach each other and finally end up parting on bad terms. In fact this question of language's (in)capability to convey reality is an issue so frequently brought up in the narrative that it dominates the meta-narrative, the third level of reality in the novel. It is a level on which the text is aware of itself, a reality beyond both the external and psychological realities of the narrative.

The novel also deliberately creates ambiguity in the sequence of events in order to challenge language's capability to convey meaning and experience. Unlike in Indo-European languages, there are no temporal or mood inflections in Chinese verbs, and the time-frame of actions is not expressed through tenses. Chronology of events is often conveyed with the use of conjunctions, connectives or other lexical items that function as temporal markers, or is simply conveyed by the order in which actions and events are accounted. There are neither conditional nor hypothetical tenses in Chinese. These moods are expressed also by the use of lexical markers. Therefore confusion and ambiguity can be much more subtly created in Chinese than in Indo-European languages where tenses and mood markers are built into the morphology and are essentially present in the sentence. This property of the Chinese language is fully exploited in *Soul Mountain* to create an almost mythical unreality similar to many works of Columbian Magical Realism. One of the most obvious examples is Chapter 41. The chapter opens with two points of time in comparison: when "I" arrives at a village and two years before when "he" died. Since there are no markers for tenses and singularity/plurality in Chinese verbs, a word-for-word translation of the sentence would read something like:

> When I *arrive* here, two years ago he already *die*. He at that time *is* the last shaman among these hundreds of stockades in this area... (Gao 1990b: 251; my emphasis)

The narrative point is set at the time when "I" arrives at the village. In the next clause, by fronting the temporal-theme "two years ago", the narrative point is shifted backward. It then continues to be shifted further back as the rest of that chapter describes the last sacrificial ritual the old man performs before his death. Unconstrained by the relatively rigid framework of tense sequences of Indo-European languages, two successive quick shifts of the narrative presence are achieved within the first three sentences of this chapter. The more realistic present of "I" going through the journey to Soul Mountain is blended into the legendary past and the mythic world of the old shaman's folk religion. This clever manipulation of Chinese grammar and its resulting unusual literary effect draw attention to the meta-narrative fact of the act of writing. In this case, language does not necessarily make things clear. On the contrary, it confuses.

This challenge to language as an effective means of conveying meaning and communication becomes a recurrent theme in Gao's later writing. In this connection, one might recall his play *Duihua yu fanjie* (1993, translated into English as *Dialogue and Rebuttal* by Gilbert Fong, 1999), in which there is an attempt to abandon linguistic dialectics. The play is divided into two acts. The first act depicts a man and a woman having a quarrel in a flat. She is desperate to express her feelings and discontent with their relationship. Lines are often broken and things are left half said. Communication becomes broken down. In the second act, she has killed him and committed suicide. The two heads still remain in the flat arguing. The same pattern of conversation takes place. She finds herself worse off as they are now dead and not able to leave the flat. They will remain in the same situation until their bodies are found by other people. The less-than-perfect communication in the conversation is the only dramatic action. According to the endnotes of the play, the lines are written to imitate the questions and answers in the *gong'an* (also as Koan) of Chinese *Chan*, or Zen, sect (Gao 1993e: 84). *Gong'an* are stories with dialogues told by Zen masters recorded in scripts. Since one of the principles of Zen says that "the way to spiritual enlightenment cannot be taught by language", [*bu li wenzi*], explanation of spiritual enlightenment with language is impossible. Spiritual enlightenment is not a philosophical concept, but a mental, psychological and physical state. So masters often talk about certain things or scenes in life that resemble the state of spiritual enlightenment. They often convey a certain atmosphere and sensitivity similar to the property of montage of scenarios or objects on films or in some classical Chinese poetry. This is very similar to the sensory effect the imagery creates in the brief stories that the characters in *Soul Mountain* tell each other when they try to express their emotions. Such a device is much more successful in *Soul Mountain* than in *Dialogue*. In the former, ethnic objects and customs accumulate and sediment into an opulent aesthetics, which would be difficult if not impossible to create with diegetic language. In the play *Dialogue*, the broken dialogues merely repeat philosophical clichés and lack both sensitivity and subtlety.

However, the scepticism about language in *Soul Mountain* is soon contradicted as the narrative proceeds. In Chapter 51 of the novel, the act of narrating is suddenly endowed with the power to organise experience and to make meaning out of it:

> I am perpetually searching for meaning, but what in fact is meaning? … I can only search for the self of the I who is small and insignificant like a grain of sand. I may as well write a book on the human self without worrying whether it will be published. But then of what consequence is it whether one book more, or one book less, is written? … (Gao 1990b: 337–338 / Lee 2000: 308)

The narrator's avowed intention in writing this novel is to look for a meaning for the experience acquired from the journey. Narration becomes not only an organisation of thought, but a process through which meaning is delineated. Meaning is not generated by experience, but is defined by narration. The relationship between meaning and experience is not direct. Narration acts as a stabiliser to establish a nexus between the two. This comment comes as a surprise because by using narration to attribute a meaning to experience, the novel celebrates the power of language. As the agent to define meaning for the character's experience from the journey, language plays a more active, and even positive, role than it appears to do in the narrator's other remarks elsewhere in the novel about writing being the "dregs left from the filter of linguistic structures" that frustrates any attempt to convey experience (Gao 1990b: 357 / Lee 2000: 329). The site of meaning is shifted from experience to narration. Language is now a necessary process of making meaning rather than an impotent shadow of meaning that has already existed in experience prior to it. The novel does not show a consistent attitude toward the nature of language. Instead, it combines a collection of ideas which can be traced back to philosophies of language proposed by various philosophers.

This makes it difficult to decide on what the overall view on language is behind this contradictory configuration. If the author is really utterly pessimistic about language and believes that it cannot translate experience into communicable terms, then we need to ask: what is the point of writing this novel? Gao Xingjian is definitely not the only writer who is caught up in the dilemma of writing about the meaninglessness of writing. In fact this is a recurrent theme in many Postmodernist writings. Among Gao's fellow exiled Chinese writers, the poet Duoduo wrote about the paradox of language in his poem "*Meiyou*" (1992; translated into English as *There is No* by Gregory B. Lee, 1993) at about the same time that the first edition of the novel was published. The poem is basically not about anything. It depicts several beginnings of processes including that of the rusting of iron and of sand being blown in the air. But successive descriptions are interrupted by the next one. None of these processes is allowed to proceed toward any sort of completion. In his analysis of this poem, Gregory B. Lee summarises this paradox thus:

> Language self-consciously tells of its own disappearance, only to be recreated in the telling of its own destruction. The poem itself as it moves down through vertical time constructs a hopeful riposte to its own horizontal narrative of negation. (Lee 1996: 254–255)

Such a paradox is shared by both this poem and *Soul Mountain*. The idea that language is not an adequate medium to communicate human thoughts is communicated through the writing of the novel. By the very act of writing, the author implicitly reinscribes language's ability to communicate, although this notion is at the same time rejected in the content of the novel. The problem of language becomes reified, something to be written about. It becomes an issue incorporated into the range of themes written in a language of conventional usage. This third level of reality, that is the meta-narrative level of the novel, talks about the thinking about language, rather than attempting to tackle the paradox of such thinking. This explains why, on the one hand, narration of subjective experience is invalidated as no more than "dregs left from the filter of linguistic structures" (Gao 1990b: 357 / Lee 2000: 329), and on the other hand, the narrator narrates in order to attempt self-analysis.

Bildungsroman vs Postmodernist Novel

The narrator's negative comments on language create for the novel a major epistemological crisis. Language, the only tool the narrator aspires to use to define and delineate experience, is refuted by the meta-narrative level of the text. In fact the structure of the novel is elaborately constructed in order to make it distinct from classic Realist novels, in which events are all connected with each other and a conclusion can be drawn at the end. "I" in *Soul Mountain* cannot construct meaning from his experience. Therefore, instead of a conclusion that serves as the final *denouement* that assigns meaning to the details in previous chapters, a sweeping epistemological rejection brings the long novel to a close:

> The fact of the matter is I comprehend nothing, I understand nothing. This is how it is. (Gao 1990b: 563 / Lee 2000: 506)

This remark is in sharp contrast to the kind of religious optimism that embraces faith in a wise loving purpose, known or unknown, that governs human affairs. In the West, the uncertainty regarding the meaning of life produces an atheism associated with French Existentialist and Postmodernist thinking. This is diametrically opposed to the Christian belief that assumes the existence of God who has an overview of life and ensures a teleology that anchors every single moment to an eternal and transcendental meaning. It is indeed these different philosophies that denote the polarised difference between a *Bildungsroman* and a Postmodernist novel. The former, as Bakhtin states, is about "the image of man in the process of becoming" (Bakhtin 1938 / Emerson, Holquist and McGee 1986: 19). He classifies *Bildungsroman* into five categories according to the extent of spatial and temporal changes experienced by the heroes. All five categories consist of the common central feature of the emergence of the hero's personality as a result of experience. A development of plot which results in the hero's achievement of wisdom is necessary. The ending involves a conclusion to the hero's adventures. It is the point where all previous episodes reveal their meanings. This structure conforms to a teleological view of the world, one that Postmodernists reject. Robbe-Grillet calls this desire to control the world "by assuming for it a meaning" no more than "an illusory simplification". He rejects the "impulse of each episode toward a conclusion" (Robbe-Grillet 1963 / Howard 1965: 23–39). The worlds created in his novels are unstable, incoherent, discontinuous and indecipherable. His novels depict a wealth of appearances of objects and events without assigning them coherent meanings in the narratives. He maintains that reality is not hidden behind appearance; there is no reason to assume a "meaning" beyond the appearance of objects and events. What he writes about is "here and now", not an assumed "there and then" beyond the appearance of life where "meaning" is supposed to be present (Robbe-Grillet 1963 / Howard 1965: 23–39).

There are numerous episodes in *Soul Mountain* that are redolent of just such a Postmodernist position. In Chapter 30, "I" arrives at a mountainous region in which poisonous snakes are common. At the end of this long episode describing how the village people come to terms with the danger and adopt various measures to protect their lives, "I" sees a naked woman bathing in a stream. The narrator states that there is no connection between this scene and the details provided about snakes. The concluding remark of this chapter reinforces the absence of necessary link between episodes:

> Below the highway, a young girl is bathing naked at the water's edge. When she sees vehicles drive past on the highway, she stands there like a white egret, moving only her neck to stare. In the strong noon sun, the sunlight on the water is dazzling. Of course all this has nothing much to do with *qi* snakes. (Gao 1990b: 182 / Lee 2000: 171)

On the surface, the text states that there is no relation between the snakes and the woman. Nevertheless this statement is contradicted by the correlation between the two entities. The concepts of snake and woman have been inherently linked in knowledge in the Christian world ever since they were brought together in *The Bible*, where human beings are depicted to have forfeited eternal paradise. The association between the two has later become a part of universal consciousness since Europe's colonisation of Asia, South America, Africa and Australia. The woman in this episode is not any woman, although transported to a modern setting of a stream below a highway, but an innocent one bathing in a stream without feeling ashamed of her naked body. This female figure representing pre-original sin woman and the poisonous snake together suggest an allusion to the downfall of mankind in *The Bible*. The loss of eternal life implies that there is an eternity somewhere beyond the reach of human beings. But in the above quotation, the deliberate denial of the connection between the two refutes the myth of transcendental existence. In short, it denies the existence of God, and by implication teleology.

Another episode in Chapter 76 also deals with the theme of transcendental meaning. "He" asks the way to Soul Mountain from a figure of a wise old man who tells him that Soul Mountain is always on the other side of the river, no matter which shore one is on. This can be read in two ways. First, the possibility of an end to the quest, of anticipating a transcendental meaning beyond the journey itself, which is also a metaphor of the narrative itself, is denied. If there is no ultimate transcendental meaning of experience to justify life, then it must be taken as it is; the meaning of it then relates to this present life, not the other assumed life after death. A possible second reading is cultural. The concept of "the other side of the river" can be related to the Buddhist concept of "the other shore" [*bi'an*] from the *Heart Sutra*. It is a metaphor for *Nirvana*, and is indeed used as the title of Gao's last play written in China. When a person has achieved Nirvana, s/he is in the Buddhist state of spiritual enlightenment and his/her consciousness transcends the mundane world. In this state, the subject achieves ultimate union with the universe and "meaning" becomes irrelevant. If both the possibility to find Realist transcendental meaning and that of achieving the Buddhist state where meaning is irrelevant are negated, every kind of quest will be futile.

It has been mentioned above that there is hardly any immediate consequential relation between the various events in the novel. This is consistent with the Postmodernist philosophy in negating transcendental meaning in the deliberate fragmentation of narrative events. Each chapter is about the individual's experience, material or psychological, in one place or at one time. At various points, the individual gets lost in mountains, falls over a cliff, or loses his way in fog at the end of some chapters. The successive events described however present new places and new experiences, unlike conventional plots which require resolutions for their events. Since there is no emphasis or climax at the unfolding of any mystery nor any enlightenment at the end to justify previous events, every point of the narrative is read and interpreted in its own right, not as one of the many elements which contribute to the ultimate revelation of some enigma. Each episode and each mini-story told by "you" and "she" demands an equal degree of significance. Each unit is a moment of reality. This deliberate fragmentation of episodes and modes as the basic structure of the novel has functioned to promote a palpable sense of inconsequence in individual experiences. It is in turn also matched by the application of diverse linguistic styles used in the novel to avoid emotional consistency. The range of linguistic styles is extensive, each conveying the individual's emotion at one particular moment. Chapter 1 of the novel begins with a detailed depiction of the scenery and of people's life in a town:

> People are getting off the bus or walking past, men humping sacks and women carrying babies. A crowd of youths, unhampered by sacks or baskets, have their hands free. They take sunflower seeds out of their pockets, toss them one at a time into their mouths and spit out the shells. With a loud crack the kernels are expertly eaten. To be leisurely and carefree is endemic to the place. They are locals and life has made them like this, they have been here for many generations and you wouldn't need to go looking anywhere else for them. (Gao 1990b: 1 / Lee 2000: 1)

The tranquil and humble, yet lively, small town life reminds the reader of Shen Congwen's portrayal of West Hunan or Wang Zenqi's stories about the Big Marsh, both renowned for the self-contained serenity of the villages described. Such an opening tempts readers to expect a similar style throughout, or even a classic fiction in search of cultural roots in which the customs and life-style of the described villages and towns provide the focal point and occupy a major part of the novel. But this style does not persist for many chapters, and the impression of tranquility and the casual is very soon supplanted by other emotions. The narrator's anxiety over his spiritual journey in general and "your" anxiety over his relationship with "she", whom he has met on the journey, becomes dominant, and scenery and people are no longer represented as serene. Such changes in moods are conveyed through other linguistic styles. For example, Chapter 15 finishes with a long paragraph expressing disturbing ideas in the form of non-coherent prose. "You" asks the way to Soul Mountain from an old woman whose answer is neither coherent nor consistent. This paragraph is followed by a reflection on the incident. The questions in his mind are as incoherent as the old woman's answer. The contrast in style with the previous quote is sharp:

> Is there a stone bridge? No stone bridge? Follow the creek in? ... Once you understand in your heart you will find it as soon as you look for it? The important thing is to be sincere of heart? ... If I don't say that, what should I say? If I don't say that, is it because I shouldn't say it or because I can't say it? ... (Gao 1990b: 98-99 / Lee 2000: 93)

Apart from disrupting patterns of logical reasoning, incoherence is also used in the novel to convey dream sequences. The entire Chapter 23 is written in one long paragraph in imitation of the form of a dream. The linguistic structure adopted resembles the sequence of a strange reverie in which details are unfolded or sometimes repeated in an incomprehensible manner:

> You say you saw a black sea rising, its flat surface slowly, inexorably, towering up. When it was upon you, the horizon between the sky and the sea was squeezed to nothing and the black sea occupied the whole of your vision. She says you were asleep pressed against her breasts. You say you felt her breasts swelling, like a black tide, a surging tide ... Afterwards, on the beach, after the tide finally subsided, there remained only an endless stretch, flat and covered with fine sand ... You say you saw the bodies of human-like sea animals or animal-like humans, black, sleek bodies with a sheen like black satin yet like moist fur ... (Gao 1990b: 147–149 / Lee 2000: 137–139)

The sequence displays classic features of stream of consciousness of the Modernist novel as observed in James Joyce's *Finnegan's Wake*, to cite one among many examples. But neither does such a Modernist style become consistent and dominant in the rest of the novel. There are many other variations. The brief stories "you" and "she" tell each other about the legends of places they have visited are very similar to the format of traditional Chinese regional annals. Some chapters are made up of folk legends or stories, and the styles of different types of oral literature or classical fiction are adopted. One example of this is in Chapter 36. The whole chapter consists of sixteen paragraphs. Except for the first one, they all start with the verb "*shuo*", a traditional story-telling device meaning "it is said that ..." employed by folk entertainers and conserved in prompt-books and subsequently maintained in the novels based on them such as *Shuihu zhuan* (c. 14th century A.D.; translated into English as *All Men Are Brothers* by Pearl S. Buck, 1933; and as *Outlaws of the Marsh* by Sidney Shapiro, 1981).

There are other styles of Chinese literary tradition adopted and adapted in *Soul Mountain*. In Chapter 63, "I" stays in a temple and is overwhelmed by the serenity and sublimity of the place and the philosophy that is attached to such a lifestyle. The narrative immediately adopts a different style to represent the beauty of this serene atmosphere:

> The flying eaves curling upwards are lines of pure simplicity and the majestic forests on the mountain behind soundlessly sway in the night breeze. Suddenly the myriad things turn silent and the sound of pure pipes can be heard, serene and flowing, then abruptly vanishing. Then, beyond the gates of the temple complex, the noisy surging of the river under the stone bridge and the soughing of the night wind all seem to be flowing from my heart. (Gao 1990b: 445 / Lee 2000: 403)

A number of paragraphs in this chapter reveal the same acute sensitivity to sights and sounds and a strong empathy for the environment, redolent of the style of the classical Chinese poetry expressing Buddhist and Taoist philosophies by poets such as Ruan Ji, Wang Wei and Su Shi. The chapter's lavish application of stock images from traditional poetry such as "flying eaves" [*feiyan yangqi*] and "the myriad things turn[ing] silent" [*wanlai juji*] are deliberate allusions to invite connection between the novel and that particular poetic tradition. Those poems usually represent a world filled with the sight, sound and scent of nature in which the poets forget about the difficulties and competitive circumstances they encounter in human society and achieve harmony with nature. Like those poets who sought contentment in nature and spiritual refuge in Buddhist and Taoist philosophies, the narrator "I" also acquires peace of mind in the temple. "I" is absorbed in the atmosphere of such a place and easily forgets about his angst in the quest for Soul Mountain. Perhaps this is exactly a moment of enlightenment which "I" has been seeking, but is unaware of when it occurs. Therefore, the poetic style is not merely employed for aesthetic reasons. The Buddhist and Taoist philosophies and their association with a peaceful and worry-free life, both embodied in such a style, are of thematic importance.

But this short-lived restfulness soon vanishes. Chapter 64, coming immediately after the temple episode, describes a meeting between "you" and "her". The focus of the chapter is on the sexual desire and action of the two characters. The earthly in this chapter follows on from the spiritual in the previous chapter to establish a contrast. In Chapter 65 "I" declares that "I" does not belong to the peace and beauty that was experienced in the temple. The protagonist's anxieties become more and more emphasised in successive chapters. In Chapter 68 they reach a climax of disturbed images:

Then your soul exits from your body. All you see is thousands of toads facing the sky with their big mouths wide open. Then they become little headless people thrusting their arms in the direction of the sky and shouting desperately: Give me my head back! Give me my head back! Give me my head back! Give me back my head! Give me back my head! Give my head me back ... Give back me my head! My head give me back! My back give me head! Me give my head back ... (Gao 1990b: 489)

It is true that there is a great variety of moods in the novel, each accompanied by corresponding changes of linguistic usage. Yet despite such fragmentation, the reality represented in each of the episodes is very unambiguous. No matter how much the narrator may give vent to his frustration at the failure to represent subjective reality through language, a momentary reality (either external, psychological, or dream-like) is elaborated in these numerous episodes in diverse styles. This is fundamentally different from Postmodernist fictions, as exemplified in Robbe-Grillet's depiction of an unlocatable reality. In a Robbe-Grillet novel, any type of conclusion is conspicuously absent, due to the unstable reality in his changing description of objects as narrative time goes by. There is no attempt to evoke any sense of realism. The unstable reality cannot be fixed and mapped on the chronology of events to produce meaning. Whereas in *Soul Mountain*, the failure of the narrator's quest for meaning is ultimately rewarded with the knowledge that there is no transcendental meaning to be found in the universe. One is almost tempted to conclude that the message of the novel is that each moment in life should be taken and understood for its own sake, just as individual episodes are presented in their own right. In fact, the overall aesthetic of the novel is largely accumulated through the scattered episodes. When the novel is read in this way, the consistent fragmentation cannot justifiably be interpreted as a haphazard phenomenon, whereby episodes are not interrelated. On the contrary, it is a well-planned pattern within a tightly constructed plot, which leads to its final paradoxical conclusion that refutes a conclusion. In other words, *Soul Mountain* has displayed the typical feature of a classical *Bildungsroman*, instead of that of a postmodern novel, to which its meta-fictional elements aspire. It reveals itself as a *Bildungsroman* in which the protagonist gains an infallible knowledge about life and reality, that is, the absence of an ultimate meaning to justify previous events by the end of his spiritual quest. Such a structure implies an omniscient position in the process of writing. From this position, the ultimate narrator, the author himself, is able to oversee the protagonist's fragmented reality and assign to it an ultimate unified meaning. In short, the text demonstrates a teleological structure. It is a novel about the writing of a postmodern novel without itself being one.

Crisis of the *Avant-garde* vs the Subject as a Site of Cultural Transfer

No doubt there is a contradiction in *Soul Mountain* between its Postmodernist aspirations and its overall narrative structure as a *Bildungsroman*. There are at least two possible readings of this situation. One is to read *Soul Mountain* as typical of works trapped in the crisis of the avant-garde, in which avant-gardeness has become a reified ambition rather than an ideological force, a tradition rather than an innovation. This reading can be supported by the above analysis that the carefully constructed formal artifact lacks a corresponding ideology to justify the necessity of such a form. In other words the Postmodernist elements become superfluous. In his analysis of the avant-garde in the visual arts, Raymond Williams spells out the cynicism of such reification:

> ... certain techniques which were once experimental and actual shocks and affronts have become the working conventions of a widely distributed commercial art, dominated from a few cultural centres, while many of the original works have passed directly into international corporate trade. This is not to say that Futurism, or any other of the avant-garde movements, has found its literal future. The rhetoric may still be of endless innovation. But instead of revolt there is the planned trading of spectacle, itself significantly mobile and, at least on the surface, deliberately disorientating. (Williams 1994: 62)

Viewed this way, the innovation in *Soul Mountain* seems little more than a hollow gesture to maintain the appearance of an avant-garde novel, which is in fact consumed just like any other literary spectacle. Surely "avant-gardeness" of this complexion has no power to subvert. Instead, it conforms to the literary market's demand for spectacles of the "avant-garde". In Willliams' words, it is a text of "the New Conformist" (Williams 1994: 62).

The second possible reading of the novel is more sympathetic. The writing of the novel is dated at the end of the text as being from summer 1982 to September 1989. This period spans a long period during which both the literary climate of China and the author's life underwent tremendous changes. Different literary influences might have left traces in the narrative of the novel. To start with, 1982 was a time when fictions in search of cultural roots were at their height. The novel's impulse to write about the historical and anthropological entities of the Chinese minorities is definitely informed by this root-searching sentiment. As far as literary effects are concerned, these entities are recounted with substantial and fascinating content and in colourful detail. They mitigate the harshness and coldness of the deliberately architectured structure. In fact, the abundant use of imagery, created in the mini-stories told by the characters and written in a variety of styles akin to different traditional Chinese literary genres, results in a strong sense of continuity. A distinctive ethnic aesthetic is accumulated in the description of the objects, people and places of these minority cultures, enhanced by precise lexis that invokes imagination of these cultures, and in the literary expressions and narrative templates reminiscent of classical Chinese literature and folk story-telling. The profusion of these elements in the novel creates a flavour consistent with the style of literature in search of cultural roots of the same period.

The spirit of the movement in search of cultural roots, however, is not merely to return to old traditions, but to promote an awareness of the relationship between modern life and old traditions, since advocators of the movement believe that a great deal of the values upheld in Chinese culture at present, and especially the obscure ones, are related to traditional Chinese lives and habits. The main tenet of the movement is therefore a historicisation of contemporary life. One can argue that in *Soul Mountain*, the Modernist attacks on narrative and the Postmodernist scepticism toward language, experience and meaning do not posit the real conviction of the text, but represent treatises on Western philosophies that have seeped into the consciousness of the modern subject in the character of the narrator. Along this line of argument, one might even venture to conclude that the novel has constructed a Chinese subject with historical depth, yet subjected to the influence of modern Western thinking in his reflection on his cultural history and identity. Thus it provides a variation from the straight-forward pattern to be found in many works in search of cultural roots, in which China is depicted as an enclosed system and the assumed qualities of the Chinese people are highly essentialised and generalised. If read this way, the novel can be viewed as revealing the subjectivity of the narrator as the site where cultures meet and different ideologies enter into negotiation. This reading will lead to the conclusion that the novel demonstrates how cultural transfer takes place in a subject; or put simply, it is about the "translated man",[2] one whose life is constantly exposed to different cultures and whose subjectivity is heavily inscribed with the traces of cultural negotiations and transfers.

6

Plays 1986–1990:
Portraying the Individual

It is open to debate whether *Soul Mountain* is an utter failure in translating the Postmodernist writing paradigm, or an ingenious construction of the subjectivity of a "translated man". But an eclectic subjectivity is indeed a good reflection of the increasingly complicated life of the Chinese urbanites. The unhappy memory of many people caused by the bad experience and personal suffering inflicted on them in the name of the people during the Cultural Revolution was met with the post-Cultural Revolution open-door policy, which triggered on the unstoppable influx of ideologies embedded and implied in the material commodities imported into the Chinese mainland. The more simplistic patriotism and loyalty to the Party, which had by the early 1980s lost its credibility with the people, was confronted with new challenges from a growing spirit of individualism. The latter promoted the goal of accumulating wealth on a personal basis in a social system increasingly approximating to capitalist consumerism.

Certainly from 1986 onward, Gao Xingjian's plays displayed an increasingly distinctive emphasis on the split between the individual self and the collective, and this marks a strong shift from his early plays in which stress is put on the individual as a component in the overall composition of the masses. In his later works, the wish to fit into the collective and to contribute to the collective welfare is replaced by a confrontational relationship between the individual and the collective. The concern for the well-being of the individual turns into fierce criticism and interrogation of the Communist ideology of collectivism and the more traditional Chinese practice of demanding the individual's conformity to community ethical codes. In Gao's own essay entitled "*Geren de shengyin*" (1993; translated into English as "The Voice of the Individual" by Lena Aspfors and

Torbjorn Lodén, 1995; and also as "The Voice of the Individual" by Mabel Lee, 2007[1]) he observed two new trends in the construction of identity for the Chinese intellectual individual in the post-Cultural Revolution era. One of these projects the image of the "victim of history" rather than the "national hero". The other aspires with great intensity to assert the right to individual freedom of way of life and thought. This latter trend necessarily entails liberation of the individual from state control and, thus could be interpreted as a kind of politics. But the important thing is that "this line of thought no longer sees the freedom of the individual as intimately linked up with the fate of the state and the nation" (Gao 1993a: 117 / Aspfors and Lodén 1995: 77). Obviously this post-Cultural Revolution demand for personal freedom is different from the May Fourth discourse of personal emancipation in which individual liberation and national liberation, both from traditional "feudalism" [*fengjian zhuyi*] and material backwardness, are seen as one and the same thing. The corollary of Gao's observation is an intrinsic individuality: the demand for personal freedom and the individual's quality of life is no longer justified by its intimate link with the fate of the nation, but is valued entirely for its own worth. This is very much in tune with the individualism of the Western liberal humanist tradition. But this does not yet describe the full picture of Gao's individualism since in his plays written after 1986, the liberal humanist individualism is engaged in all kinds of interplay with a host of other sentiments and ideologies including nationalism, nihilism and even Buddhist philosophy. The subjectivities of the individuals portrayed in those plays are therefore also inscribed with the traces of conflicting and varying cultural and ideological influences. The following sections in this chapter examine the portrayal of the individuals in this group of plays.

The Individual as a Loner

Bi'an (1986b; translated as *The Other Side* by Jo Riley, 1997; and as *The Other Shore* by Gilbert Fong, 1999) is a play about the relationship between the individual and the collective. Although there is no division into acts and scenes, as the almost empty stage and the minimal use of props makes it technically unnecessary, the play actually consists of two parts. There is an introductory section on human relationships in general that acts as an exposition to introduce the theme and to facilitate the reception of the audience to the play's mode of expression, which is a less linguistic and more visually expressionistic form; and this is followed by a story about an individual negotiating his relationship with the collective. At the beginning of the play, that is, in the introductory section, the abstract notion of human relationships is translated into visible signs by the use of a piece of rope, which is manipulated by the actors who hold both ends and pull it into different shapes and degrees of tautness to represent different kinds of relationships. For instance, a forceful pulling on one side signifies dominance of one party in the relationship. Then the pulling develops into a competition of force, in which a winner and a loser are involved.

The use of a piece of rope is economical, visually expressive and highly symbolic. It also highlights the distance between the two ends of it. A Self and an Other are presented as the necessary elements for the existence of a relationship:

> Before that I was I, and you were you, but the rope has bound us together and now it's you and me. (Gao 1986b: 239 / Riley 1997: 154)

"You" and "I" are put in distinctive positions as two absolute entities. The existence of the Self and the Other is assumed to precede the existence of a relationship. Both Self and Other are taken to be stable and the dichotomy natural. However, this is not necessarily the only way to perceive identity. In marked contrast to this is Bakhtin's idea of the dialogic definition of the Self and the Other, in which the consciousness of the Self is constituted by its relationship towards "a thou": "I must find myself in another by finding another in myself" (Bakhtin 1963 / Emerson 1985: 287). This Self and the Other are formative of one another during their interaction. The Self is defined in the exchange of his "own speech" and the "alien" speech of the other (Bakhtin 1963 / Emerson 1985: 287). In the process of reacting to the other, a boundary for the "I" is defined. In Bahktin's model, relationship is a pre-requisite for the existence of the Self and the Other. What this comparison highlights is the assumption in *The Other Shore* of an unconditional essential presence of a Self which is differentiated by a boundary from all other people. This assumption sustains the binary opposition of a Self and an Other. Interestingly enough, the avowed intention of Gao's later writing is to eliminate this Self.

In *The Other Shore*, the Other is the masses. The "thou" takes a plural form. As soon as a Self and an Other are fixed on to the two ends of a relationship, the Other is immediately qualified as all other people beside the singular Self. This is achieved by increasing the number of actors and the number of imaginary ropes amongst all of them. It results in everyone being linked to more than one person directly (holding on to the same rope) or indirectly (holding on to the same rope with someone who is also holding on to another person's rope). A web-like complex is formed in which each actor's position is related to all other actors. To each member, the "you" is a plural one. The Other is the whole collective. This is a web in which any intersecting point, representing an individual, can be a starting point in tracing the linkage. So every individual becomes the centre of his own world while all other individuals are taken as the collective Other:

> For example, you circle around me, taking me as your axis. Now you are my satellite. If you won't want to revolve around me, I can turn on the spot and make believe that everyone is really turning around me. Is it you or are you revolving around me? Or are we both turning on the spot, or ... (Gao 1986b: 239 / Riley 1997: 154)

This binarism between the individual and the collective becomes the starting point of the play's theme. When the story in the play begins, a group of people cross a river to the opposite shore where life is supposed to begin again. There is no sense of individuals until Woman teaches them the words "I" and "you". At this point the individual Man becomes conscious of himself being an individual self, separated from the rest of the masses. Epistemological acts here are represented as a series of introductions to vocabulary. The female figure Woman who teaches them about life is indicative of the primitive female figure Nüwa, the mother of mankind in Chinese mythology. However, in the play she has not given birth to them, but has turned them from innocence to knowledge, through the process of teaching them the use of language for naming and thus defining their experience. How the world is viewed is thus governed by the definition and logic available in language, in other words, the lexis and grammar. This reminds one of Cassirer's view that men are "imprisoned" in language, their own creation (Cassirer 1923 / Manheim 1961: I: 113), a philosophy that has been taken up also in *Soul Mountain*. Then among the crowd, the language that has been learnt gradually becomes used for the expression of malicious thoughts. Rumours and curses are created, leading to the eventual killing of Woman. Language here is given the power to replace and take over experience and decide the crowd's action. Again, it is redolent of the inaccuracy of language in representing truth already explored by Gao in his previous fictions, and elaborated later in *Soul Mountain*. This idea is highlighted in the performance of the play by the explicit attempt to play up extra-linguistic elements as an alternative to linguistic communication.[2]

One of these extra-linguistic elements is the elaborate use of mime-like gestures and movements to convey situations and scenarios. The audience is being sensitised to non-verbal means of communication, which helps to alienate them from their habitual logic dominated by syntactical structure in the language system. Instead, the actors attempt to engage the visual and aural senses of the audience, in order to appeal to their immediate sensory responses. It is stressed in the playwright's note that this play requires the actors to give up the kind of acting that is built on linguistic dialectics and logical thinking. Instead, they should be sensual and spontaneous (Gao 1986b: 251 / Riley 1997: 153). The actors' presence and the variation in their physical attributes are taken to be their main acting tools. Such emphasis on the actors' bodies is further enhanced by the minimal use of props, costumes and other stage properties. Their bodies remain the only instrument for communication with the audience. The acting itself is the centre of attention. The actors' body language, as opposed to their speeches, has to assume responsibility for the expression and the aesthetics, in order to combat the inaccuracy of linguistic communication suggested by the playwright. Most critics note this minimalism in Gao's plays of this period as heavily influenced by the Western minimalist theatre of dramatists such as Peter Brook. Indeed the playwright himself also acknowledges such influence. But there is another aspect of this minimalism that is pertinent to the present discussion of the portrayal of the individual in this group of works: to strip the actor of any props and tools is to decontextualise him and alienate him from all possible acting conventions that such props might be associated with. This nakedness foregrounds the physical state of the actor as he is. The actor aspires to be a detached individual, one that is in tune with the idea of the post-Cultural Revolution intellectual later portrayed in the playwright's 1993 essay quoted at the beginning of this chapter.

The split between the individual and the collective in this play first takes place after the murder of Woman. His disapproval of the murder and condemnation of the masses as being ungrateful together function to highlight his own virtue. Such a difference is further cultivated in subsequent episodes, the most elaborate of which is the scene with Card-player. It constructs an even more negative image of the masses. Black and white cards are flashed in front of the group. These cards are bold symbols for true and false, right and wrong. When a card is flashed, they cannot, or do not, say what it is. Their opinions are subordinated to the authority of Card-player who perverts black and white. Those who lose the game are stuck with awkward looking pieces of paper on their faces. But collective pressure, like authority, dominates their judgment. As more and more people lose their game, the disgrace of having pieces of paper stuck on faces becomes not only acceptable, but so much the norm that no one wants to be "excluded", and thus inclusion becomes the main goal. The crowd is represented as a group without free will, a group that submits to authority. The individual Man is again put at the other end of the scale. His original insistence on what he sees on the card regardless of the collective's consensus, his reluctance to assume the responsibility they have imposed on him to lead the way later in the story, and at the same time his strong desire for Girl (which is represented as his alternative interest against the above-mentioned responsibility for the collective, in other words, the personal domain opposite to the public one) all combine to suggest his yearning for individual autonomy.

As the play proceeds, the lines uttered by the characters become increasingly incoherent, both within the same speech, and in terms of the logical connection among different characters' speeches. The failure of linguistic communication further isolates Man from the collective. He is trapped within his own "truths" which are not shared by others. These truths include the murder of the innocent Woman and his knowledge that the whole pack of cards does not contain a single black one. His concept of truth cannot prevail against the opinions expressed by others. The individual becomes an absolute loner who is facing a world defined, and from his point of view, perverted, by words. The collective and the individual are not only put into binary opposition as drastically different, they are also depicted as being threatening to each other. In fact, one of the play's strongest indictments of collective pressure is its power to repress individuality in order to preserve the *status quo*. Man is persecuted for holding different opinions. He cannot even leave the scene maintaining his own point of view. There is no other alternative for him but to submit to the collective. At the end he collapses with the crowd abandoning him and dancing in a grotesque manner around Card-player, the new authority. Another character described as Mad Woman is also outcast from the collective. This character functions as a foil to Man. Her alleged promiscuity threatens the collective with its suggestion of non-conformity. As a result she is punished and labelled "mad".

Unlike many works of Socialist literature approved by the doctrines of the Chinese Communist Party, in which the hero belongs to, or lives for, and sometimes even dies for, the masses, Man's relationship with the collective is far from an amicable one. The following speech is very telling of this antagonism:

> Why are you pestering me? I need peace and quiet, I need to be alone, I don't want a crowd of people staring at me, I don't need you and you don't need me. What you need is a leader to show you the way, but as soon as you have found a way, or think you have, you run away like frightened rabbits, and desert him without so much as another look. Like throwing off a pair of worn-out shoes. (Gao 1986b: 243 / Riley 1997: 164)

The negative image of the masses and the positive heroic yet tragic one of the individual (tragic since he cannot exercise his individual autonomy) becomes a recurrent motif in Gao's plays written after *The Other Shore*. One might conclude that the hero's situation among the masses, which exercise strict political control over him, is highly allegorical of the situation of individual autonomy in Communist China, in which the ideological preference for the collective has justified the sacrifice of individual autonomy. But it is worth noting that in the model constructed in this play, the duality is established between the individual and the masses, instead of between the individual and the state authority. Such a construct is even more obvious in the play *Shanhaijing zhuan* [Stories in the Books of Mountains and Seas] and assumes justification in ancient Chinese mythology.

The Individual as Hero

The material of Gao's 1993 play *Shanhaijing zhuan* [Stories in the Books of Mountains and Seas] is taken from the ancient *Shanhaijing* (c. 475 B.C.– 24 A.D.; translated into English as *The Classic of Mountains and Seas* by Anne Birrell, 2000). The ancient text is a compilation of stories and myths of heroes and rulers, and descriptions of geographical and agricultural details. Scholars of different periods have regarded it variously as a book of mythology, geology, or fiction. The modern scholar Yuan Ke in his various studies concludes that it is a record of history, geography, politics and religions, written according to the primitive people's understanding of these matters (Yuan 1982, 1988, 1996). Therefore, it is a book of tremendous anthropological value; and this is a view widely accepted among scholars in the field.

Gao's play *Stories* seems to have adopted Yuan Ke's understanding of the books. It traces a narrative line out of the various events in the original books and constructs these events as an epic account of politics among various tribes in primitive times. It starts with the myth of Nüwa creating human beings at the very beginning of the world. This is followed by tribal events. The mythic figures are organised as four political parties, led by Di Jun in the east, Yan Di in the south, Xiwangmu in the west, and Huang Di in the north. Act 1 deals with the internal affairs in Di Jun's court. Acts 2 and 3 tell the story of the warfare between Huang Di and Yan Di's armies. This war finally brings about the establishment and dominance of Huang Di's regime in what becomes China. His race is believed to be the ancestors of the Han race. This chronological arrangement gives the play and the mythical events a sense of historical continuity. It betrays a strong desire to narrate a primitive history for the Chinese nation. It is without doubt a play about the beginning of China, a story about the ancient ancestors. Among them are the ancestors of the Han race and other minority races. On the surface this seems to have put the Han race on an equal level with warlords of other tribes, which is a highly popular position since the enthusiastic promotion of minority cultures by writers of literature in search of cultural roots in the mid 1980s. However, the play finishes with a court scene, after Huang Di has assumed the power to rule heaven and earth, where he assigns ruling power on different matters and territories to his own warriors and descendents. This politically stabilising process being used as a conclusion to the play centralises the position of the Han regime and marginalises other ethnic groups. The ideology revealed conforms to the political, cultural and economic hierarchy maintained by the Han race in modern China. The representation of a stabilised and unified territory under Huang Di's rule satisfies the ideological desire for a sense of national integrity in the play's modern audience. One might argue that the play's negative portrayal of the tribal leaders including Huang Di attempts to ironise the national unity at the end of the play, but any ironic effect is ultimately overwhelmed by the neat nationalist conclusion. If indeed an ironic effect is intended, it is too feeble and has failed to make a sufficiently strong impact.

There is a potentially subversive line in the plot. The current of national events is underlined by another current of an individual's fate. The main plot focussing on political affairs intertwines with the story of Hou Yi throughout the play. Di Jun's ten suns (sons) appear all together in the sky. They are casting too much heat on Earth. The people living on Earth plead with Hou Yi, one of the minor gods, to help them before they all die of the heat and drought. He takes pity on them and with his divine skill in archery, he shoots down nine suns. But for that, he is rejected by the heavens and loses his immortality. Yet he finds mortal existence not good enough for his august person and cannot settle on Earth. He is finally killed by the masses for whom he has sacrificed his immortality. Thus two groups of activities are established in the plot. The manoeuvres and wars of the gods and the final victory of Huang Di belong to the realm of the power game. Hou Yi's actions and his subsequent experience in the mortal world belong to the domain of the common people's life. But this domain is represented in the play as completely irrelevant to the politicking among the powerful. Politics is therefore a cynical struggle of power without any genuine ideological and humanist substance.

Equally cynical is the relationship of the hero with the collective. It is not only inharmonious, but also one of exploitation and betrayal. The plot of a hero who cares for the people and has made a great contribution to their welfare being deserted and purged by them in return has a very familiar ring to readers of scar literature. The lone hero Man in *The Other Shore* demonstrates a love-hate complex for the collective as he builds a forest of human figures around himself that eventually wears him out. Similarly, Hou Yi desires recognition from the masses. He mourns his lost immortality but is still content with his heroic deed of shooting down the suns for the people. It is only when he is confronted with his murderers that he realises that they have not been grateful for the sacrifice he has made for them. Unlike Man's tragedy which is predicated on the impossibility of individual autonomy, Hou Yi's tragedy, like the heroic victims of the Cultural Revolution as represented in scar literature, is his lack of recognition by the masses. The rounded characterisation and positive image of Hou Yi as compared with the negative image of the authorities (the cunning Huang Di, the farcical Di Jun, the ruthless Xiwangmu and the frail Yan Di) privilege the unrecognised yet heroic figure over those with authority. However, the desire of the hero to be embraced by the masses leads to the impression that his latter rejection of them is motivated by resentment.

Both Man and Hou Yi embody virtues. Man is appreciative of the good deeds Woman has done to him and other people. Hou Yi is willing to sacrifice his immortality to secure the welfare of other people. Man is honest and righteous; Hou Yi is brave and chivalrous. These virtues stand in contrast to the many vices attributed to the crowd. The upright image of the heroes and the negative one of the crowd are put in sharp contrast. Our identification with moral supremacy immediately causes us to reject such crowds. When Man collapses with the crowd abandoning him and dancing in a grotesque manner around Card-player, our habitual identification again is for the individual who appears noble and our instinct is to reject the crowd. The divergence in the moral standard between this individual hero and the crowd puts the two in irreconcilable binary opposition. The crowd is represented as the mob. Again, this is not the only possible view on the masses, and again, for example, a very different approach is adopted by Bakhtin. Speaking of the crowd in a carnival, Bakhtin regards it as a new life force that provides an opportunity for change in the existing social and communal order. For him, the carnival of *Corpus Christi* celebrates death and revival. It is the "breaking point in the cycle of nature or in the life of the society of man" (Bakhtin 1965 / Iswolsky 1984: 9). The grotesque body of the crowd, for example as shown in paintings of Carnivals such as Bruegel's *Carnival and Lent* (1559) in which the artist seems to be celebrating the lame, the deformed and the ugly by bringing them to occupy a large area in the foreground, is to Bakhtin an alternative order as opposed to the bourgeois social hierarchy dominated by nobles and aristocracy who value the beautiful, the "good", the neat, and of course, the ordered. The significance of such a crowd is its potential for political power to subvert the *status quo* with the alternative order in which the people manifest themselves. The carnivalesque crowd in the market place is empowered by their collectivity as the people as a whole "organised in their own way, the way of the people", "outside and contrary to all existing forms of the coercive socio-economic and political organisation" (Bakhtin,1965 / Iswolsky 1984: 255). It is subversive in nature. It is a form of power resisting the social order as organised by the authority.

The crowd in both *The Other Shore* and *Stories in the Books of Mountains and Seas*, although represented as grotesque, and more importantly, possessive of political force, is conservative and conforms to the established order. In fact they even eradicate any threat to the *status quo*. Neither do the individual heroes display any incentive to upset the ruling authorities, being more interested in protecting personal space in *The Other Shore*, and most preoccupied with his own immortality in *Stories*. Therefore, the conflicts between the individuals and the collective are not a function of their different political or ideological stances. The heroes are privileged over the masses, because the former possess virtues and honour, while the latter lack them. The superiority of the individual heroes over the masses is *a priori*. He *is* simply superior. The line between Man and the rest of the people is drawn when he denounces the ungrateful murder of Woman, not because of his distaste for the idea of collectivity. The hero's moral superiority is even more obvious in Hou Yi's relationship with the people. Hou Yi's characterisation is a celebration of the classic Chinese virtues of benevolence [*ren*] and bravery [*yong*]. The desire for individual autonomy can also be interpreted as a desire to act as Kongzi [Confucius] teaches a gentleman should act: "When right principles of government prevail in the empire, he will show himself; when they are prostrated, he will keep concealed" [*tian xia you dao ze jian, wu dao ze yin*] (*Lunyu*, 8:13 / Legge 1893/1991: 131). The mentality assigned to the character Hou Yi is consistently supported by classic Confucian morality. Whether consciously deployed in the play or not, it is revealed in its attachment to traditional Chinese philosophy and codes of behaviour. The tragedies of both Man and Hou Yi are not the result of a lack of individual autonomy, but of the heroes remaining unrecognised and abandoned. What is challenged in the play is not the idea of collectivity, but a collectivity not arranged in the hierarchical order of virtues.

In the playwright's endnotes on the production of *Stories*, it is recommended that forms of folk entertainments including masks, dance, puppets, acrobatics and magic be used to create an atmosphere similar to that of a temple fair in religious festivals (Gao 1993b: 106-107). Such a folk culture is the legacy of two earlier practices. First, the emphasis on the inclusion in the play's overall structure of a variety of entertainment forms to create the atmosphere of fun-fair should be attributed to the inspiration of "a hundred entertainments" [*baixi*], a mixture of athletics, tricks, dance, music and drama, a practice that was already recorded in the Han Dynasty. According to the poem *Xijing fu* (107 A.D.; translated into English as "Western Metropolis Rhapsody" by David R. Knechtegs, 1982) by Zhang Heng of the Han Dynasty, a "hundred entertainments" includes dragon dance, chorus singing, wrestling, a story plot, somersaults, juggling swords, highwire-walking and other tricks (Zhang 107 / Knechtegs 1982: 227–235). Secondly, the characterisation of the mythical figures through the use of masks, costumes and stylised movements is influenced by *nuo* religious drama, a combination of rituals and drama performed by priests among early settlers scattered mainly in villages in south-western China. The earliest record of descriptions of *nuo* performance is found in the book *Zhou li: Xia guan: Fangxiangshi* (Zhou Rites: Summer Officials: Fangxiangshi c. 475 B.C.– 221 B.C.). It is about a priest having his:

> head covered with bear skin,
> face bearing a copper mask with four eyes,
> body wearing a black top and red lower garment.
> hands holding a shield and a spear. (*Zhou li*, c. 475 B.C.– 221 B.C./1987: 2493)

These theatrical devices are popular with Modernist dramatists who seek to establish an alienating effect opposing the Naturalistic illusionism that imitates the appearance of real life. The promotion of traditional Asian theatre by European dramatists such as Brecht and Artaud also links the use of Asian ancient dramatic devices with the avant-garde and the esoteric. But in this case, telling ancient stories through theatrical forms related to folk cultures is an act of uncovering tradition and showing pride in historical Chinese popular culture. It is also an act of celebrating the historical presence of the Chinese people as a collective. The text's intention might have been prioritising popular culture (of the people) over official culture (approved by the court and the learned). Such a positive perspective on the people, however, contradicts the depiction of the crowd as mob in *The Other Shore*. In the play *Stories* itself, there is minimal focus on the people. Their existence depends on their being beneficiaries of Hou Yi's heroic deeds and sacrifice. Toward the end of the play, it is a mortal man who kills him (playwright's) when he regrets having done what he has, but there is no reason given for this murder. *Stories* is essentially a play about gods, kings and nobles. It is not about the masses. Their presence simply facilitates the story of the nobles, but if the playwright's dramas are to be viewed as a body of work, one would expect some kind of consistency in regard to major issues, including the texts' stance towards the collective and the masses. The celebration of the carnivalesque temple fair indeed contradicts the representation of the people as mob not only in *Stories*, but also in *The Other Shore* and a number of subsequent plays. It creates an internal inconsistency within the text itself, and also within Gao's repertoire. Moreover, to place the story of Hou Yi, the story of a lone individual's inharmonious relationship with the collective, within this framework of Chinese history and culture enhances the nationalist dimension of the theme. Unlike many of his early fictions that are about momentary episodes based on daily trifles, this play departs from the personal domain, which occupies a marginal situation in post-Mao Chinese literature, and approaches closer to the mainstream narrative. It stresses individuality in relation to the political aspects of life, as shown in the prolific scar literature, literature of cultural reflection and literature in search of cultural roots. Although each text grouped under these categories and Gao's play *Stories* might be differently inflected, they all come under the grand banner of nationalist literature.

The Individual as Woman

The motif of the confrontation between the individual and the collective occurs again in *Mingcheng* [Nether City] (1989[3]). The play was commissioned for a dance drama production in Hong Kong and published in a Taiwan woman's magazine *Nüxingren* [Female people]. It tells the story of a woman driven to her death as a result of her husband's whimsical test of fidelity. She is denied the chance to plead her own cause and is finally condemned eternally under the systems of both the mortals and immortals. What makes this play particularly worth noting is the manifestation of the loner motif in the person of a woman.

The story about Zhuangzi's test on his wife in *Nether City* goes back a long way. The character of jealous husband assumes the identity of the Daoist philosopher Zhuangzi (c. 369 B.C.–286 B.C.), but this is no more than a simplistic and crude fantasy on the part of the ancient populace on the possibility of Zhuangzi transforming himself into other identities, and such imagination is inspired by one of the philosopher's own fables of turning into a butterfly in a dream.[4] The story of Zhuangzi tesing his wife was first collected in the anthology of *Jingu qiguan* [Marvelous stories of ancient and modern times] edited by Baoweng Laoren (c.1544–1644). It is said that on his way home, Zhuangzi sees a woman fanning the mud on her husband's grave, because according to customs, a woman is allowed to remarry once her deceased husband's grave is dry. Wanting to find out whether his own wife, Tian, is more chaste than this woman, Zhuangzi fakes death, then transforms himself into the Prince of Chu and tries to seduce his widowed wife at his own funeral. She falls into the trap and on their wedding, "the Prince of Chu" falls very ill. He tells her that only eating the brains of a family member could cure him. In her panic she decides to get the brains of her newly-deceased husband which she thinks should not have dried up yet. She hacks the coffin open and Zhuangzi jumps out from the coffin to reveal her lack of chastity. At the same time he also appears as "the Prince of Chu" to prove her guilt. As a result she kills herself out of shame.

The most famous stage dramatisation of this story is the *kunqu* [Kunqu opera] *Hudie meng* [The butterfly dream]. The tragedy of Tian is presented almost as a comedy. After her suicide, Zhuangzi expresses neither regret nor sorrow. The tone in which he speaks about her death is judgmental and completely lacking in sympathy. Both the story in *Marvelous Stories* and the *kunqu* piece take Zhuangzi's point of view, in terms of both narrative flow and moral stance. This is in fact not surprising in classical Chinese literature, since the majority of works were written by male literati who benefited from the male-centred morality of the period.

Nether City is by no means the first play in which this male point of view appears to be challenged. Early in the Yuan Dynasty, Shi Junbao (1279–1368) already represented such a test of female chastity as selfish and inconsiderate in his *xiqu*, *Qiu Hu Xiqi* [translated into English as *Qiu Hu Tries to Seduce His Own Wife* by William Dolby, 1978], also known as *Sangyuan hui* [Meeting in the mulberry field]. The original story in Liu Xiang's *Lie'nü zhuan* (c. 78 B.C.; translated as *The Traditions of Exemplary Women* by Anna Behnke Kinney, 2002] is about Qiu Hu seducing a woman, who turns out to be his wife, in the mulberry field on his way home after twenty years' absence. The chaste woman refuses him and commits suicide when his identity is revealed, because she cannot bear the idea of her husband's breaking the accepted boundary of decent behaviour by seducing a stranger in a field. This story bears a striking similarity to Zhuangzi's test on his wife. Although the two women react differently to seduction, they both meet tragic ends. It seems to be an invidious situation for women. In the first case, she has to die for her own loss of honour; in the second, she has to die for her husband's loss of honour. The latter appears to be condemning Qiu Hu's behaviour and praising her chastity. But the price is paid by her with her life. An act of utter self-destruction of the female character is necessary for the male character to learn a lesson. The female narrative point of view does not bring about a reverse of the tale's ideology. In fact, the story centering on her has confirmed a male-centred morality, since her conviction and action reinforce it.

But in Shi Junbao's adaptation of the story, he has Qiu Hu vaguely recognising his wife but seducing her to test her chastity. When his identity is revealed, she angrily blames him for risking her reputation and life (since she would have to kill herself had she proved herself unfaithful). The play ends with Qiu Hu acknowledging his inconsiderate behaviour and being forgiven by his wife. Compared with the other works of the same theme, Shi's version is no doubt less straightforward in its masculine orientation. However, Qui Hu's wife has only acquired her right to live and a right to speak up against her husband's trickery because she has refused his courtship in the mulberry field. She has proved herself to have adhered to the female code of behaviour required by the male-dominated ruling class.

In Gao Xingjian's adaptation of the story about Zhuangzi's wife into *Nether City*, there is also a shift of the narrative point of view from the position of Zhuangzi to that of Tian. Tian is of course depicted as the victim of Zhuangzi's selfish game, or the play would not have been published in a woman's magazine. Unlike the earlier versions, the play does not end with Tian's death. It continues beyond her death, and extends the plot to the underworld, where she is put on trial by the ultimate authority of the nether court, and this part of the story is in fact the most significant part of the play, as indicated by the choice of its title. There is still no sympathy for her in the underworld. Scenes of her being kicked off a bridge by the nether guards to join other wandering souls, of her being insulted in the corrupt court of the underworld, and of her being tortured follow in quick succession. Her oppressive forces are identified as the collectively acknowledged authority, the male and corrupt officials.

When Tian tries to defend herself in the nether court, the judge issues the order to cut off her tongue. She is deprived of her right to speak and is silenced forever. In fact, silence is the most important element in Tian's characterisation. Apart from the few speeches she speaks at her first appearances, she basically has no other speeches, except a few exclamations of "*bu*", meaning "no". The image is constructed of a repressed female in a patriarchal society who has no voice for self-expression. It is also a comment on the original story in *Marvelous Stories* and the famous *kunqu* version, in which Tian's subjectivity is completely neglected. To compensate for the deliberate lack of verbal expression by Tian, there is ample scope in the script for a more expressionistic nonverbal communication. Emotions of all kinds are conveyed through the dancer's movements. Since this play is tailor-made for the American Chinese choreographer Jiang Qing, choreography has replaced verbal language and is used as the main communicative device for the character. This accords very well with the tendency elsewhere in Gao's repertoire to reject spoken language and rational logic regulated by the rules of language.

What relates this play closely to the others discussed in this chapter is the depiction of Tian as a loner. Similar to Man and Hou Yi, she is a social outcast, one who is rejected by the masses. This rejection has drawn a boundary between the masses and Tian, making them the Other for one another. But the female identity prompts this loner figure to be depicted differently from the others — she is silent and passive. This arbitrary connection between the woman and the silent and passive prompts two questions. First, are women seen to be essentially silent and passive? If so, this would be a very conservative and dated understanding of the feminist position. Such essentialisation disregards the complexity and divergence of women's situations. It neither clarifies nor helps with the subject matter of the play. Second, if the play is not specifically feminist, what is it about? Where is its relevance? One reading is that the silent and passive woman symbolises all individuals who are suffering in silence.

In her study of the representation of women in modern Chinese fiction, Yue Ming-bao adopts Roxane Witke's position, namely that the prolific works of the May Fourth period about the inequalities to which women are subjected, in fact, indicates something more general than women's liberation. The interest in women's issues is used to raise a banner for progressive thinking against the conservative power which has played such a strong part in the implementation and practice of social inequalities. The issue of "woman" is raised not for the sake of women. Instead, women become a metaphor for the oppressed. Yue concludes that women's issues are used "as a political stratagem for advancing China's nation-building program" (Yue 1993: 51). China in the 1980s saw a similar interest in women's issues, also utilised as a political stratagem. There are numerous works that try to defend women who are condemned as "sluts" in classical literature or in the folk tradition. The most popular one was *Pan Jinlian*, a blend of *chuanju* [Sichuan opera] and modern drama written by the *chuanju* playwright Wei Minglun in 1986. The licentious woman Pan Jinlian who conspires with her lover to murder her husband is depicted as a victim of arranged marriage under the slave system and a courageous woman who sacrifices everything for love. Appearing with Pan on stage are a divorced woman of the 1980s, the first Chinese empress Wu Zetian, Jia Baoyu of *Hongloumeng* [ca. 1754; translated into English as *The Story of the*

Stone by David Hawkes and John Minford, 1973; as *A Dream of Red Mansion* by Xianyi and Gladys Yang, 1978] and Anna Karenina, together discussing the inequalities and discrimination women have experienced and witnessed, and expressing a sense of empathy with Pan. An extensive attack is launched on the old morality by analysing these historical and fictional cases. These characters become a joint force for a powerful attack on conservatism. The play became a big hit in the 1980s. Moreover, its innovative form also frees the play and the artistic representation of the character Pan Jinlian from the strict operatic convention. These factors work together and foreground it ahead of other works of the same women-oriented genre.

Like the May Fourth writers who use the concern over women's issues to position themselves in opposition to conservative power, there was also a trend among many writers in the 1980s to write works similar to *Pan Jinlian*. They sought to express sympathy for the traditionally condemned woman as a gesture firstly to rethink traditional morality, and secondly as a symbol for appeal on behalf of the persecuted, and by extension of those victims of previous political persecutions. In the case of *Nether City*, the inequalities confronted by Tian in a world dominated by men is used as a metonymic trope for the inequalities generally faced by powerless individuals who do not conform to social codes and values but who are suppressed by the state authority. But this kind of utilisation of women's issues is problematic. The first thing to be called into question in this play is the metonym of women and the mute oppressed. This metonym is built on the identification of the powerless with femininity. In other words, what is free and potent is natural, and belongs to the masculine domain; while what is restricted and helpless is perverted, and belongs to the feminine domain. This perversion is measured against the "natural". In de Beauvoir's words:

> She is defined and differentiated with reference to men and not he with reference to her; she is the incidental, the inessential as opposed to the essential. He is the Subject, he is the Absolute — she is the Other. (De Beauvoir 1947 / Parshley 1987: 21)

Instead of protesting against women being pushed into a marginal position, the metonym of women for the Other confirms the position of women as the Other. The marginal position in which women are put is taken as a natural given and as the basis for the metonym. Women are summarised as a concept of the unfavourable Other, seen through the eyes of the Absolute, the male. As Judith Butler points out, such a construction summarises "woman" as the oppressed in a heterosexual society, and in turn enhances these features as the qualifying factor to be "woman". This is an approach contradictory to the principles of feminism, and causing a crisis for feminism. She asks:

Perhaps the problem is more serious. Is the construction of the category of women as a coherent and stable subject an unwitting regulation and reification of gender relations? And is not such a reification precisely contrary to feminist aims? (Butler 1990: 5)

The narrative of *Nether City* conforms to the male-centred construction of the "natural" male and the "perverted" female. Although on one level, it carries a general humanist intent of revealing the suffering of the mute, on another level, the seemingly subversive play only serves to reinscribe and reinforce the hierarchy of the male over the female. One can only conclude that either such a metonym works against its purpose, or that it reveals a lazy conformity to a basically misogynist trope for the sake of convenience.

The Individual as Elite

In all these three plays, the image of the individual self is constructed against a collective other. But there are three fundamental problems with this binary opposition. First, the constructed binary opposition between the individual and the masses is purely arbitrary. There is no reason to justify such an absolute antagonism between the two, except perhaps in terms of a sense of paranoia. Secondly, in these plays the masses are depicted as a unity, a collective within which there is no individual consciousness. The fact that individuals constitute the masses, which means that there is the potential for considerable differences among the masses, is totally neglected. The form of crowd in these plays is like the chorus in Greek tragedy. A unity of voice is assumed to represent social convention, and also communal morality, or the lack of it. Such an assumption is lacking in justification and is a gross over-simplification of reality. Thirdly and related to the previous point, the image of the virtuous individual and the malicious crowd is not a non-judgmental binary opposition. It is a hierarchy composed of an intelligent individual endowed with the capacity for free-thought at the top and the unworthy subjugated crowd beneath him. On the surface the plays seem to be upholding individual autonomy, but this autonomy of the "chosen" individual is at the expense of all other people who are represented as a unified collective with no recognition of their own rights to be identified as individuals. Therefore, to valorise the lone hero's individual autonomy, that of each member in the masses is suppressed. Obviously what the plays advance is not everybody's individual autonomy, but only that of the elite loner at the top of the hierarchy constructed in the plays. If the struggle for an individual's autonomy has to be achieved through the suppression of that of the rest of his fellows, the principle governing such autonomy is ideologically suspect and elitist by its very nature. What is represented is hardly the desire for individual autonomy, but merely a power struggle, for dominance, of a particular individual in his community.

What is revealed is, again, a sense of paranoia, of not being recognised as the elite member of society, of the morbid fear of submersion in the crowd. If a biographical approach is adopted, one might conclude that the author's own experience in the 1970s and the first half of 1980s may well be the source of such a feeling. The purges and persecution to which he was subjected in the various political campaigns, and the resultant needs of constant justification of his theoretical and creative writings have produced a strong desire to be safe from other people (the Other and the potential persecutors), and to be untouched. There is consequently a "need" to be "correct" and to be "superior". Even if one is not able to escape persecution, the feeling of occupying the moral highground still acts as a form of consolation to the ego. If read this way, the romantic lone heroes in these plays who are intended to be represented as idealists single-mindedly fighting for individual autonomy are only victims of paranoia, in the aftermath of political attacks. This would surely arouse sympathy. But if this is the case, such a representation of the individual and the masses will only be valid to an exclusive situation, particular to a certain group of people in China at a given time. It can have no claim of universality. Unfortunately, the setting of the plays in the context of myths and legends means that they are abstracted from the particular situation that has generated the writer's particular paranoia. Of course, such a reading can only remain speculative. The correlation between biographical details and the works is something that literary studies cannot prove. One can therefore only take them on the textual level and conclude that they are informed by a blatant elitism. What surfaces in these plays is a tendentious position which constructs the elitist lone individual as the victim of a lack of autonomy and power. This series of plays thus reveals a stagnation, a self-indulgence in the self-image of being the oppressed, of being the talent unrecognised, and even of being the hero abandoned. An illusion is constructed that to merely raise a lone voice already constitutes subversion since it manifests the presence of the oppressed. However, merely to reinscribe the situation without further interrogation and to make such a reinscription as the means and the end of the text has the contrary effect of turning this reiteration into a celebration of the position of the oppressed, and creating an environment in which the condition of oppression, not the attempt to overturn oppression, infuses the text with a superficial subversiveness.

The Individual as a Non-political Being

The Other Shore is the last of Gao's play written in China. It was, however, never put on stage in China because of political pressure. *Nether City* was commissioned by the Hong Kong Dance Company and staged in the then British colony. Gao left China in 1987, and in 1988 he was granted residence in France. But instead of displaying less relevance to China, more often than not Chinese culture occupies a central position in the works written immediately after the playwright took up abode abroad. This is true for both *Nether City* and *Stories in the Books of Mountains and Seas*. In 1989, the June Fourth Tian'anmen Massacre aroused an intense and emotional response among the Chinese. Massacre appeared as an important theme in artistic and literary creation among overseas Chinese while it became taboo on the Mainland. To refer to only a few of these works, the famous Taiwanese choreographer Lin Huaimin's epic dance on Chinese history *Jiuge* [*Nine Songs*] finishes with a scene of massacre, emotionally portrayed with loud noises of gunfire and a powerful following spotlight on the dancers on stage. Various poems appeared in the short-lived magazine published in North America *Guangchang* [The Square] are one of the earliest outlets for channelling the shock and anger felt by the poets. The highly acclaimed Mainland poet Zheng Min also included a series of poems titled "*Xinzhong de shengyin*" [Voice from the heart] in her collection *Zaochen, wo zai yuli caihua* [Morning, I gather flowers in the rain] published in Hong Kong. The proliferation of works dealing with the massacre in other artistic and cultural sectors such as photography, paintings, pop songs, street theatre and videos also contributed to a general atmosphere of strong nationalism and patriotism, although the object of identification is the abstract idea of "China" with a historic and cultural content, rather than the incumbent government.

It was within such a highly charged social context that Gao's play *Taowang* (1990, translated into English as *Fugitives* by Gregory B. Lee, 1993; as *Escape* by Gilbert Fong, 2007) was written. In this play a confrontation was constructed of individual autonomy against not only certain political ideologies but also all political affairs. The play's main theme is to draw a line between active nationalist support for the democratic movement and a total retreat from politics, and to argue about the futility of the former which in consequence justifies the latter. It attempts to uphold a position devoid of a nationalist perspective. The background of the play is the night of the June Fourth Massacre. Although it is not overtly stated, the sound of gunfire, the constant allusion to the democratic movement, killing in the "Square", and the characters' description of the streets all point to it. There are only three characters in the play, Young Man, Middle-aged Man and Young Woman. They are all running for their lives, but they represent two different attitudes in their relationship with state politics. The background of the 1989 democratic movement foregrounds this theme, since the movement itself epitomises nationalism. Young Man runs away from the present totalitarian authority and embraces an alternative political ideology as expressed in the collective action, organised by the masses without Party authorisation. The collective action of protests and fasting, and the extensive support the activists receive in the streets promotes their claim to be the political power that really represents the people, an entity empowered by the Chinese Communist Party and the People's Republic from the very beginning of their establishment.

But this is not what Middle-aged Man identifies himself with. For him, politics is a game played by people with power. Any civilians engaged in it are manipulated, used and played as chess pieces (an image that has already appeared in *The Other Shore*) by the few who monopolise and control everything in the country. He does not identify with the democratic movement. Politics are equated with the manipulation of the collective by the few political leaders in their exchange of power. The metaphor of cards being dealt by others in *The Other Shore* is also repeated here. In one of Middle-aged Man's lines, he talks about the student protest and the democratic movement as the "small card dealt" (Gao 1990a/1995: 29 / Lee 1993: 109) by some political faction. It is redolent of the manipulative authority figure of Card-player in *The Other Shore*. According to this logic, any collective actions are simply reduced to political weapons for deployment by politicians. In this case, the image of the collective is not of the ugly or the vicious, but of the powerless and the manipulated. A binary opposition is established between the individual bodies (which make up the collective) and the state body. The individual bodies are depicted as inadequate in the face of the state body, which, as constituted by the current authority, is protected by state security mechanisms to keep the masses under control. In *The Other Shore*, there is a simpler binary opposition between the individual and the collective. The former is the good and the latter is the evil. Individual autonomy is necessary for preserving one's own virtues and keeping away from the corruption represented by the collective. But in *Fugitives* collectivity is rejected because it is ineffective in organising resistance against the evil state body as it is manipulated by powerful politicians and the operation of state politics. The masses are not so much grotesque, as weak, fragile and powerless. Therefore the collective body fails to fulfil the function of a force generated by and working for the masses. These are the grounds on which the play justifies Middle-aged Man's decision to reject politics.

Parallel to the political line, there is a theme of sexuality in the play. It is used to represent an alternative to the political domain of one's life. It is on the basis of this division that Young Woman is characterised. Her political attitude is ambiguous. She takes part in the protest but is not depicted as being as enthusiastic a demonstrator as Young Man. There are speeches by her about a private life untouched by public politics, but there are none to express sympathy with Middle-aged Man's disillusionment regarding politics. Like the female characters in Gao's early plays such as Bee in *Alarm Signal*, she is represented as sentimental and "feminine". Woman is barred from the domain of politics, even when she is participating in a political movement. She is merely there to represent the non-political and private aspect of life. She is mute in the political debate between the two male characters. The play has designated differentiated domains for men and women in their concerns.

The differences in the three characters' stances, or the three voices, make up the overall structure of the play. The individual consciousnesses of the three characters are juxtaposed in parallel during their soliloquies expressing what is in their minds in the darkness inside the old warehouse in Act 1. Except the implication in Young Woman's speech about a ruined city, symbolising life blighted by totalitarian politics, the image created in her speech is mainly full of warmth and innocence. When she speaks of a serene and beautiful vision of snow falling over the "Square", her speech is interrupted by Young Man's narration of a visually comparable scenario with the leaflets about the curfew that are thrown from helicopters. They alternate with their speeches on walks in the snow and scenes in the "Square". When Young Man speaks of the day of his dream when darkness is over and a grand ceremony for the nation's martyrs is held, Middle-aged Man interrupts and expresses his wish to stay away from all of this. Then the soliloquies resume and the characters continue to take turns to make their speeches.

Characterisation as shown in this episode, as well as in other scenes, is stereotypical of the age and sex groups the characters are chosen to represent. The men are rational and concerned about politics. Young Woman is sensitive and sensual and becomes the object of competition and the basis of jealousy between the two men. Middle-aged Man is calm, wise and disillusioned; while his foil character Young Man is enthusiastic and idealistic. Throughout the play, there is an inclination to privilege what Middle-aged Man represents. He wins every debate, and is also the one who stays on centre stage throughout while Young Man is absent for part of the time. Like Young Woman resembling Bee, the character of Middle-aged Man reminds readers of the train conductor in *Alarm Signal*. It is also worth noting that Middle-aged Man is the one, instead of Young Man, who consummates the sexual relationship with Young Woman. Just like the state of affairs in the animal world, the male who wins the war (of political position and debate in this play) gets the right to mate. The female in the play is completely reified and reduced to a mere object of male desire. The dominant voice in the play is definitely that of Middle-aged Man.

The only significance of Young Woman in the play is the part she plays in her sexual relations with the male characters. As far as individual autonomy is concerned, a split between the private and the public spheres is essential. For most of the 1980s, sex was still treated as something of a taboo in many sectors of the Chinese society, and was excluded from the sphere of public life. To break this taboo symbolises the breaking out of the private voice, of the voice of the individual. It becomes a metaphor for the expression of the individual's autonomy. Gao Xingjian rated Lao Hong's novel *Luowu dai* [The generation of naked dance] highly. The novel concerns the lives of young university students in Beijing after the June Fourth Massacre. Substantial parts of the novel focus on the sexual relations between them. In the preface Gao wrote for the novel, he draws a connection between sexual liberation and social resistance:

> Oppressing the demand for democracy often accelerates the eruption of sexual liberation. Sexual repression was always used by the highly centralised political powers of traditional China as a means of spiritual control. Sexual repression was always present in the form of traditional feudal morality. The young generation's rebellion is also expressed through sexual liberation. (Gao 1992b: 2)

In *Fugitives*, there are moments, especially in Act 2, when the concern about current politics is taken over by the sexual relationship between Young Woman and the two men. If we accept sex as an expression of resistance against state repression, this scene can then be read as a space in the play reserved for the expression of the private, and thus the resistant and subversive. In breaking this social taboo, this private domain is made visible and the autonomy of the individual is given voice. This seems to work for the two male characters, but not for the female one. The representation of sex as Young Woman's only means of expression does not open up effective and significant channels of autonomous expression for her. Instead, it excludes her from other means of expression. Moreover, sex in the play does not serve her purpose, rather it is Middle-aged Man who seeks a means to valorise the private aspect of his life. She is only the accomplice, or even the instrument, for his self-expression.

If the disinclination to participate in politics, understood as public affairs, is seen as a solution to the individual and collective will being appropriated and used by the dominant authorities, it should be recalled that it is a viable strategy, if one at all, only for those whose life is not under the dominance of Chinese political forces. That means someone such as the author himself who is not living in China. In fact, such a "non-political" stance is already revealed to be impossible for people living in China, as Middle-aged Man is trapped in the warehouse, unable to escape. The play raises the question about the masses being used as instruments in the negotiation of power among dominant political parties, which is a perfectly legitimate question. But the only suggested solution it provides is to reject the power struggle, an action not everyone can afford. It is a highly personal choice, first because it only creates a distance between the question and the individual concerned, while providing no solution to the question; secondly it only reflects a personal choice of someone who has the means to remain at a distance such as by emigrating, while such a choice is not available for most people affected by the problem. The position adopted by the play on the Democratic Movement and on politics seems highly personal and inevitably narrow in its scope. It lacks vision at a universal level and relevance to those readers who are really affected by the problem at a more local level, that is, those who are living under the oppressive and manipulative political powers. Thus its frame of reference is strictly limited. In fact, for someone who is absent to suggest to those who have to live and confront the problem that to attempt action is futile and misguided is indeed insensitive. This is another kind of cross-cultural writing. It prompts one to ask: How does a writing subject write about a culture in which that writer is no longer immersed? In other words: of what and in what manner can one speak *in absentia*?

Part 4

Translating the Self

.

7

Fictions and Plays 1990s:
Writing in Exile

Mary Besemeres notices in Edward Said's and André Aciman's descriptions of their lives as immigrants a constant need to articulate meanings generated from their native culture and native language in another cultural and linguistic framework. She describes this process as a cultural self-translation (Besemeres 2003: 32). Interestingly, Gao's works published after he left China in 1987 show a comparable impulse. Some of his plays including *Nether City* and *Stories in the Books of Mountains and Seas* take material from Chinese mythology and folklore. In this way, the "Chineseness" embodied in this material is carried over into these plays, and therefore into their exilic existence. A more conspicuous attempt to translate the self's past in China into his present exilic existence is found in *Yigeren di shengjing* (1999; translated into English as *One Man's Bible* by Mabel Lee, 2002), in which the narrator's past and present are interwoven together throughout the novel.

Time present and time past

One Man's Bible is a companion novel to *Soul Mountain* (Malmqvist 2000). The links between the two are at the same time thematic and structural. Both texts talk about the same scepticism towards language, literature and representation. Comments debunking the power of language to represent experience are equally abundant in the two texts. Both texts depict an individual ill-fitted to the highly politicised life of China. In terms of the time-frame of events, *One Man's Bible* both precedes and follows *Soul Mountain* as the narrative present of the former is set in the 1990s, but it covers the narrator's memory of personal experience in the Cultural Revolution in the 1960s and the 1970s, while *Soul Mountain* describes the narrator's journey and his reflection during the trip, which is set as taking place after the Cultural Revolution in the early 1980s. The more significant link between the two novels lies in their structure. The two long texts share the same basic features of episodic structure and interchange in the use of personal pronouns as the narrating subject, according to the mode of psychological activity he is engaged in. Like *Soul Mountain*, *One Man's Bible* is structured in layers. The narrative present is set in a period within which a number of trips are taken by "you". The places "you" visits include Hong Kong before de-colonisation, Sydney, Stockholm, New York and Barcelona, and the last chapter of the novel ends with him getting ready to board the plane to return to his residence in Paris. The main actions of this layer of narration are dominated by "you" having sex with Caucasian women of different ethnic origins and "you" recalling his personal experience in China during the Cultural Revolution, at first reluctantly at a woman's insistence. But once he has started tapping into his memory, the reminiscence takes on its own momentum and makes up a rich layer of narration of his past experiences.

These events in the past are narrated with an alternative protagonist, "he", and make up a second layer of narrative. "He" is a less intimate and less familiar position than the more personal address "you". Being in the third-person position, the subjectivity of "he" is reified. It can be interpreted as an attempt to draw a distance between the individual at time present and time past. Such an alienation strategy could serve to highlight either an existentialist view of personal history or an estrangement of the exiled individual from his early existence in his home country. In either case, such a structure is consistent with the layered structure in *Soul Mountain* denoting different levels of reality within the realm of subjective experience. In *One Man's Bible*, events in both narrative present and reminiscent past are constantly punctuated with the narrator's direct comments on life, politics and writing. Such an inward turning of the narrative to emphasise memory and psychological "reality" makes up a substantial part of *One Man's Bible* as it does in *Soul Mountain*. But it is more obvious in *One Man's Bible* that these comments are made by "you". Therefore they belong to the first level of reality rather than making up a third level, as the meta-narrative elements in *Soul Mountain* do.

A good summary of the chapters of *One Man's Bible* is provided in Liang Yiqi's study of the novel (Liang 2002: 76–77). It is made up of sixty-one chapters, each containing either an episode of events, or a stream of thoughts as reflection on certain issues sometimes directly and at other times indirectly related to the events narrated in preceding chapters. The recounting of many single events in the narrator's past experience is often completed within individual chapters. Each of these chapters is a fragment of "his" experience in the Cultural Revolution. This structure resembles that of *Soul Mountain*, with an even tighter and cleaner plot line. Although these events do not follow a strictly chronological order, nor is the exposition composed in such a way that an intrigue is constructed or that a dramatic climate is reached, there is an intrinsic continuity among these events, namely, a single individual's life within a period in history. The relationship between the episodes is strong. One event does lead to another, although they can also be read as free-standing episodes. Indeed this induces the readers to trace a chronological and logical order for the events. One can easily tidy up the narrative flow and trace out a main thread that strings together all the episodes. In this way, it is tighter and more focused than the structure of *Soul Mountain* in which there are a great number of legends and local stories of the places the narrator travels to, each having no causal correlation with others. However arbitrary its conceptualisation, *Soul Mountain* is more fragmented in structure. Moreover, linguistic experimentation in *Soul Mountain* is more systematic and consistent, resulting in a literary richness which is absent in *One Man's Bible*. The latter is on the whole a much less exciting work than *Soul Mountain*.

Like many others of Gao's works, this novel does not follow an exposition-development-climax-resolution pattern in its plot. But the absence of a dramatic climax does not necessarily mean that there is no narrative climax. The climax simply does not take the form of dramatic events nor the instant affective intensity attached to events. A narrative climax is developed in the narrator's reminiscences of the past. "Your" companion Margarethe's request that he tell his past gradually turns into a confession that is driven by his own psychological need to unburden himself. This need gradually intensifies into an obsession. The articulation of his memory of the past soon takes over and dominates the narrative from Chapter 17 to Chapter 48. Once "you" has tapped into his memory, his mind becomes increasingly steeped in that "previous life", until in Chapters 44 to 48 a climax is reached where "you" and "he" are both used as the narrating subject, denoting a unification of the narrator's identity at time present and time past. If this outpouring of personal history represents a kind of identity search, then such unification represents the gratification of a psychological need. The tension created by the outpouring only relaxes at Chapter 52 when his memory, as chronologically recalled, reaches the end of the Cultural Revolution when life becomes much calmer. This structure parallels the progression of sexual desire into gratification and relaxation. Towards the end of the novel in Chapter 53, the relationship between the two narrative positions is spelt out:

> You seem to be seeing him against a vast emptiness …Sometimes [he] casts a steadfast gaze on a certain thing, at other times [he] contemplates. There is no telling what [he] is contemplating upon, since he is merely striking a pose, a rather aesthetically pleasing pose. Existence is a pose. One tries to get as comfortable as possible, by stretching the arms, bending the knees, turning back

to look upon his consciousness. Perhaps the pose is his consciousness, it is you in consciousness, in which an ambiguous sense of joy is felt. (Gao 1999: 409)

"He" is an image in "you"'s vision. "His" consciousness is a projection of "yours". "You" as the narrating subject of the present finally achieves identification with himself in the past. The exiled individual who keeps travelling around the world has forged a connection with his own history through recounting/constructing his past. When this is done, he is at peace with himself. In *Soul Mountain*, the value of language as a cognitive and representative tool is put into question. In *One Man's Bible*, although similar comments are made (Gao 1999: 202), the plot and structure of the entire novel does not support such claims, since it is through a narration of the past that the identity of the exiled subject is connected with his past in his home country, and that the individual has found peace with himself. Language and narrative are not in fact as useless as they are proclaimed to be in the novel. On the contrary, the narrative is performative in the Austinian sense. *One Man's Bible* is primarily about a person in exile finding his identity by connecting his present with his past in his homeland through the act of narraton, as "language is the only unbroken link between him and his past" (Gao 1999: 419), and through which a unity of the Self is created. What is being described as a "book of the fugitive" [*taowang shu*] (Gao 1999: 203) is in fact a book of nostalgia. What is proclaimed to be an act of exorcism [Gao 1999: 441] is indeed one that evokes the "ghost", rather than purging it.

Sexuality and Political Repression

One Man's Bible starts with a thematic sentence commenting on the possibility of alternative lives,

> It was not that he did not remember there had been another way of life. When one thought about those things such as the old yellow photographs kept at home which had not been burnt, sadness was evoked. But it was simply so far away that it felt like another lifetime altogether. And indeed it was gone forever. (Gao 1999: 1)

After a short reminiscence in episodic detail of the narrator's childhood before the establishment of Communist China in Chapter 1, Chapter 2 immediately cuts into the scenario of "you" in bed with Margarethe, a German woman of Jewish origin, in what is supposed to be the narrative present. This narrative present is set in Hong Kong, at the time a British colony but soon to revert to China, in other words, shortly before the territory's "handover" on 1 July 1997. "You" and Margarethe met once in Beijing shortly after the Cultural Revolution.

Her then lover brought her to visit him in his apartment where his young lover happened to be visiting him on the same night. The present meeting in Hong Kong is their first encounter after that early one and is a pure coincidence. At first she plays the role of a half-curious-half-jealous lover who makes him tell her about that young girl in his apartment on the night of their first meeting in Beijing. As her obsession with his past life in China grows, she urges him to tell her more, including aspects other than his relationships with women. At first he refuses to disturb the repressed memory. It appears to be a psychological need to leave behind that part of his life, a time that was unbearable to live through and now undesirable to relive, even in reminiscence. However her insistence gradually becomes an agent to break this psychological barrier. He starts to retrieve his memory and confront it. Her insistence, which at first seems to be an irritation, gradually turns into a much more positive force. Once the flood gate is open there is no stopping it. After they have parted and she has returned to Germany, he goes on to recount his life during the Cultural Revolution, and the events he recalls make up the main line of the novel's narrative.

During the Cultural Revolution, "he", the reified self of "your" memory, works in a cultural unit in Beijing. "He" gradually becomes very involved in the political struggles within his unit. "His" involvement is depicted as being necessary and inevitable. "He" is merely trying to protect himself and to survive. But "he" is constantly bothered by his family background because his family was once associated with the capitalist and land-owner classes. "He" is subsequently sent to a cadre school for re-education. In order to avoid ideological attacks which "he" sees coming directly at him, "he" applies to transfer his household registration to a rural area where "he" eventually becomes a village-school teacher and lives until the end of the Cultural Revolution. At that point "he" succeeds for a second time to transfer his household registration, this time back to Beijing. At this point, the narration from "your" point of view continues with the chronology. "You" moves abroad and travels in different cities to produce "your" plays.

But these shifting of positions amidst political events are not the main dramatic events. They lay down the base for the more dramatic events of his relationships with women during those long years. It is the episodes with the women that constitute the more dramatic writing in the novel. "His" first girlfriend at University is only mentioned in passing. During the Hundred Flowers Campaign, she confesses to the Party about some derogatory comments "he" makes to her on a revolutionary novel. This act of betrayal has made a drastic impact on "him". He can no longer trust the female sex with his safety. His second lover is Lin, a colleague a few years older than him and with whom he has his first sexual experience. Lin is from a family of revolutionary background and is already married to a man from a family with an equally favourable background. Her affair with the narrator is a stressful one. They are under constant pressure to keep things extremely private, which is very difficult in a society of surveillance. Personal freedom is curbed by blatant political control. The relationship is eventually broken up by this stress. Their last meeting as lovers takes place on one of the very early days of the Cultural Revolution. Many people already intuit what seems to be coming, yet the extent and concrete form of the storm is still unknown. Lin warns him of a report she heard about his father once possessing a gun. "He" detects fear in her, both of what might come, and of the possible consequence their connection might bring on her were it to be known by other people. For a second time, his lover's loyalty to him cannot withstand political pressure.

Another significant relationship recounted in "your" memory is "his" marriage with a girl "he" meets during a trip to the provincial areas. Her family background is even more politically disadvantaged than "his". The two are stuck in the same room in an inn since there is no other room. A skirmish among different cliques of red guards breaks out in the town on the night of their stay. They are afraid that they might be swept up in blood-shed. When they hear sounds of red guards coming to their door, their shared fear and feelings of helplessness lead to an overwhelming mutual sympathy. At the end the red guards miss their room and leave. That night they express their mutual sympathy through sexual intercourse and when morning comes, they part. As soon as contact is resumed, they get married hastily. But instead of inspiring mutual sympathy, fear tears them apart this time. A few days after their marriage registration, she finds out about the writings that "he" has produced in secret containing views which are regarded as reactionary and which could put them both in very unpleasant circumstances. Her fear for her own safety turns her against "him". She becomes hysterical and accuses "him" of being a "class enemy". This gesture puts her in the exact position of being "his" enemy. "He" is so deeply hurt that the incident has created an unbridgeable split between them. For a third time, a woman's loyalty, that of his wife this time, cannot withstand political pressure. The once comforting trust between the two is broken by political paranoia. This experience reinforces "his" distrust of women. "His" subsequent encounters with female seducers have not developed into sexual or emotional involvement. "He" attributes this to his own lack of courage (Gao 1999: 356). This phenomenon of refraining from sexual behaviour is a symptom of the feeling of helplessness, paranoia and disempowerment brought about by political purges.

The protagonist's sexual activities only resume after the Cultural Revolution. "He" is visited by one of his young female readers who later becomes his lover. "He" is touched by her curiosity for things not allowed by the authorities, and also by her complete trust in him as her literary mentor. But this relationship is not free of stress. A lack of privacy is felt in their meetings. At that point, his divorce has not yet come through. Moreover, because of his undesirable political background, their relationship can cause trouble for both of them. Therefore they have to be very careful not to provoke gossip in the neighbourhood. To add further stress in their relationship, since she is in the army, she is required to preserve her virginity until a certain age which the army authority would deem suitable for marriage. Penetrative sex is not possible until she finally decides to rebel against this regulation. This is the first time a woman puts her relationship with him before what is allowed by the political authority. It is represented as a very significant, empowering and liberating moment for him as it is arranged in the narrative to coincide with an opportunity for him to go abroad.

Although this relationship is his last one in China, it is the first one recounted in the narrative, and in Chapter 2 as the first episode of "your" memory to be recalled at Margarethe's request. Her role as the curious-jealous lover justifies the dominance of sex and relationship in his narration. These events are put in the context of his life during the Cultural Revolution, showing how much, or how little space politics has left for privacy. The narrator also interjects direct comments on language, literature and ways of life into the narrative. Sex, politics and writing merge to form an intertwining structure in "your" narration.

Fredric Jameson in his 1986 article "Third World Literature in the Era of Multinational Capitalism" suggests that all third world literature necessarily entails features of national allegory. He compares the relationship between the private and the public in European literature and its third world counterpart and observes that in the former, there is a split between the private and the public, and the relationship of the two realms is unconscious; whilst in the latter, "psychology, or more specifically, libidinal investment, is to be read in primarily political and social terms" (Jameson 1986: 72). He quotes the example of Lu Xun's *The Diary of a Madman* and demonstrates how the madman's paranoia is of a social and political nature. Jameson's article has aroused fierce debate in the critical arena. Some critics find his reading of the correlation between the public-political and the private-sexual as national allegory brilliant, and his critique on the over-subjective writing of Western literature in the advanced capitalist society timely. But Jameson's potentially patronising tone on what he called "third world literature" has however left many "third world critics" offended. They find the umbrella category of third world literature unjustified, patronising, essentialising, homogenising, and in a nutshell, an act of Othering.[1] While endorsing this criticism on the homogenising intent of Jameson's theory, I find his model of correlation between the private and the public useful in the reading of some works or some aspects of certain works, such as the sexual elements in *One Man's Bible*. Therefore, I will first offer a reading along this line, and then I will explain why this model is particularly apt for the reading of this novel in spite of the above-mentioned problem with the theory.

The relationship between the narrator's sex life and his experience of the Chinese political situation could not be more overt. His sexual activeness fluctuates directly according to his political situation. His political innocence is lost when his first love of his university days betrays him to the Party. His second relationship, which also leads to his first sexual experience, coincides with the first real personal political threat to him. His lover Lin's fear is not a response to the general political climate. It is specifically a response to a record concerning his father's possession of a gun. His relationship with his wife is even more conditioned by political circumstances. Not only does she turn against him out of political hysteria, their bonding is in the first place established out of mutual sympathy as victims of political struggles. They share the same fear and have been equally battered by the Cultural Revolution. In Chapter 36, the narrator receives a letter from her containing these lines, "We of this generation that has been sacrificed do not deserve any other fate" (Gao 1999: 291 / Lee 2002: 287). The letter implies a suicidal tendency by saying it will be the last letter he will receive from her. This has greatly moved the narrator and prompted him to ride to the telecommunication station in the middle of the night and telephone her. But it is impossible to say anything significant on the phone, because he knows that a telephone call at such late hour will definitely arouse suspicion, and therefore he is sure that the operator is listening to their conversation.[2]

This is a typical example of the frustration in his expression of emotions and sexuality. The cause of such frustration is political pressure. What he feels in private is not allowed in public. He has to take care not to let his feelings be known in order not to endanger himself and his partner. The sense of empathy between them is not only induced, but rather produced by the political situation. Their marriage is the result of a yearning for legitimate private space, a reaction to the overwhelming dominance of the public over the private. But upon her discovery of his writings, she feels that the marriage rather than being a sanctuary, puts her in an even more dangerous position. This realisation plunges her into hysteria and she starts to attack him, to disassociate herself from him and to align herself to the position of his oppressors. Her denial of his writing, and by extension his political stance, breaks the political empathy and sympathy that initially bind them together. For the narrator, this incident means more than a single crisis to be dealt with. It has evoked in him old fears of all the betrayals by women he has suffered before. This hasty marriage is meant to be an escape from the public domain, but it is destined to fail, and indeed it does fail once it is confronted with the overpowering reality of the omnipresent political forces which set out to assume complete control of all aspects of people's lives.

The subsequent absence of sexual consummation between him and his seducers after the failure of his marriage is attributed in his own account to cowardice on his part. After the Cultural Revolution, in an encounter with his old friends from a village where he worked as a teacher in a rural school to avoid getting involved in intensive political persecution in Beijing, he finds out that a girl he has refused has got involved in an affair with an old village cadre. The affair has been revealed and the girl renounced by the villagers. He responds to this news with regret and remorse. He speculates on an alternative fate for that girl had he accepted her. His own verdict on himself is that as a political fugitive, he is disempowered and consumed by a feeling of helplessness. He has lost his courage. He has refused the girl because his fear has left him feeling so impoverished that sympathy for others was a luxury he could not afford. His avoidance of sex is in fact one and the same thing as his avoidance of politics. The suspension of his sexual potency is at the same time a symbol and the result of the loss of his political and social potency. It is no coincidence that his reinstatement in the city and his job in the cultural unit are accompanied by a return of his sexual activity. His sexual and political situations are simply the two sides of the same coin.

All these women except Lin, who is a married woman and has sexually initiated him, share the characteristics of being inexperienced and coy in their first encounter with him. This is very different from the Caucasian women "you" is involved with. They include the European-Jewish Margarethe who "you" meets in Hong Kong, the French woman Sylvia in Sydney and Linda who is one-quarter Turkish in New York. These women are sexually aggressive, very open about their bodies. One good example about this openness is how comfortable Margarethe is with her body. Although more than once she says she finds herself fat and does not like her own body, she shows no sign of embarrassment about it. On the contrary she talks a lot about it and has no problem revealing it in front of "you" in full sight. The narrative also draws considerable attention to her body and offers abundant descriptions of it being fleshy and full of life. The shape and size of her breasts and thighs, and the colour and texture of her skin are mentioned repeatedly without much variation in the use of vocabulary and rhetoric. The effect created is neither aesthetic nor erotic. The novel is obsessed with the idea of sexual openness, which is symbolised by the welcoming female body. Such a polemic differentiating between the Chinese and the Western women's attitudes towards sex conforms to the stereotypes of the conservative China and the carefree West. Since sex is so heavily invested with political impulses throughout the text, this binarism also has to be understood in political terms. Freedom is attributed to the life in the West, and repression to that in China.

The descriptions of most of the women in the novel are brief. Characterisation is minimal. They are little more than the objects with which "you" or "he" expresses sexual potency. The only exception is Margarethe. Indeed, it is the depiction of this female character in some depth that has saved the novel from being a simple misogynist text. Margarethe is of Jewish origin, has grown up in

Italy, lived in various places in Europe before she meets "you" in Hong Kong. She holds a job in Germany at the narrative present. She speaks a number of European languages, is a student of Chinese and once lived in Beijing. She is European through and through, but her ethnic roots are not there. She makes a living out of her command of the Chinese language. Yet Chinese culture, although being an alternative to her European life, is still very far from her Hebrew roots. She is obsessed with "your" history because she is obsessed with her own. He needs to forget about his history while she needs to grasp hers. Again, the empathy of the two personas takes on a political and social content, and is expressed through sexual intercourse between them.[3] One dimension that is worth paying attention to in the comparison of these two characters is the different relationship between personal and collective histories in each of these two cases. First, the collective trauma of the European Jews is of an ethnic nature, while his is national. Moreover, "you" has personally lived through the Cultural Revolution, therefore the Chinese collective memory of the Cultural Revolution is also his personal memory. Yet, Margarethe, as a European Jewish descendent born after the Second World War, has not lived through the Holocaust. She has inherited the collective memory of European Jews rather than having lived through that collective history. Interestingly, it is revealed in Chapter 14 that she was sexually harassed by her step-father, and at the young age of 13, she was raped by a painter. The history of her race being ravished is symbolised by her experience of being ravished in her personal history. The two histories are constructed as analogy. The discrepancy between "you" and "Margarethe" created by the different ways they relate to their collective history is bridged by this analogy between Margarethe's being ravished as a woman and the Jewish race being ravished as the racial and cultural Other in Europe. Therefore, Margarethe needs to be read as a representative of her race. Her presence in the novel is the presence of her collective history. She is an icon of the Jewish collective trauma in history reified. It is also worth noting that in the characterisation of Margarethe, coercion takes on a sexual form. Such a construction is consistent with the direct correlation between the protagonist's social and sexual (im)potency. Sylvia is a foil character to both "you" and Margarethe. She is not interested in history at all. His account of his history is boring and tedious for her. She carries no burden of collective history as the Chinese or the Jewish characters do. There is no psychological empathy between Sylvia and "you". There is a lightness in her that "you" finds cute.

In his much contested theory of the national allegorical nature of third world literature, Fredric Jameson suggests that third world writers/intellectuals are much more conscious of the relationship between the personal and the political, and all third world literature can be read as national allegory. In order to arrive at an aesthetic theory of third world literature, he has to take his object as one single category. What he is driving at is actually the role of the intellectual in the society.

The agenda of this theory is obvious. He lauds this social-awareness of the third world intellectuals as a good example of social engagement, which is politically effective and is much needed in the current era of globalisation when coercion takes a much less visible form of cultural and economic domination. Many critics have pointed out that there is one major flaw in this model, namely that both the category and the process of writing in the third world is excessively generalised and simplified. There is yet another theoretical gap. He has not spelt out that this literary phenomenon he calls "national allegory" in the third world is not necessary, but the direct result of political coercion, either by the colonial masters or the post-colonial authorities in some countries. Such coercion often dominates the everyday life of the people. To deal with daily life is also inevitably to deal with politics, as is the case of "you" in *One Man's Bible* during the Cultural Revolution. As a result, political coercion is easier to locate in details of quotidian life.[4] This is why although I reject Jameson's sweeping categorisation of third world literature and the overarching theorising of such literature as national allegory, I find the correlation he draws between the libidinal and the political helpful in my reading of *One Man's Bible*. I stress that I am using this correlation as one reading model that can be suitably applied to this text in particular, without claiming universality for it. I have borne in mind that there are definitely other forces at work in the making of other Chinese literary texts, and that there are definitely plural forces that inform the making of a text.

The correlation Jameson draws between the libidinal and the political does perfectly match the structure of *One Man's Bible*. What is repressed of the protagonist's libido is not simply sex, but also the desire for the expression of one's power. "His" sexual inhibition and frustration is not only a matter of the lack of private space; it is also directly related to the character's being intimidated by the brutal social reality which has left individuals feeling a general sense of helplessness, as explained in "his" own confession. The Cultural Revolution has done much more than invading individuals' private space; it has rendered individuals powerless by making everybody vulnerable, since as a consequence of that political hysteria any unintentional acts or utterances could be interpreted politically and trigger serious consequences, including the person being sent to prison or sent away for "re-education". Even small regional Party units and red guards had enormous power in generating drastic changes and violent intrusions on people's lives. Individuals were largely disempowered. This is why the idea of *potency*, or power, is a key concept in the novel. The reason for "him" to refrain from sexual relations with a number of young women in the village is the lack of courage (Gao 1999: 356), a matter of power rather than space. The only aspect of "your" life outside China depicted in the novel is his sex life. If not having sex represents disempowerment in China, then frequent and carefree sex outside China is a celebration, not of the private, but of power. Power is at the centre of both "your" and "his" sexual relationships. Women are depicted as no more than objects through which "your" potency is expressed. Nevertheless this humanisation and empowerment of one individual is constructed at the expense of these women characters who are being objectivised, thus dehumanised, and disempowered by "his" expression of "his" own "humanity".

What is lacking in this construction is dialectical thinking. Ideas and symbols are locked in fixed positions of signification. China and the West are positioned as a binary model of repression and freedom, politically and sexually at the same time and it would seem interchangeably. The Self cannot relate to the Other without objectivising them. The depiction of Hong Kong in the novel is another good illustration of this. It is represented as a place which is neither China nor the West. As a colony, it is not exactly China but an extension of ("your" meeting with Margarethe in) China. But this colony is soon to be returned to China, so its Westernised qualities have no guarantee. It is represented as a place in transition and for transit. It is where "you" and Margarethe accidentally meet up many years after their first meeting in China but it is only a place they visit rather than live in. Its status is also one in transit. Hong Kong is depicted solely in the image of a colony soon to be retroceded. Its relation to China, the central Mainland, is the only terms by which its identity is defined. "You" takes Margarethe to a dinner with a group of mainland artists living on Lamma, an outlying island of Hong Kong. Lamma Island is reputed to be a place that offers an alternative life style in the crowded city of Hong Kong, with the provision of plentiful open space, good seaviews and beaches. It is inhabited by many young expatriates, mainland artists and dissidents, and also some local yuppies who combine a more international with a Chinese lifestyle. In the second half of Chapter 12, it is on this margin of the marginal city of Hong Kong (from the perspective of the central Mainland) where a conversation takes place among these people of non-Hong Kong origins, who live in a Hong Kong in transit, about freedom in this city under threat as Hong Kong is on the point of being handed over. Each character is thinking where to leave Hong Kong for after 1997. Apart from them, other characters that "you" interacts with in Hong Kong include a businessman from China who has found success in Hong Kong, and is thinking about moving his business to Australia if necessary after the handover. There is also a young female journalist, who is planning to go abroad, and some young theatre workers who are working on a local production of his plays. These locals are marginal characters in the novel. They appear as a flock of extras making up a local landscape in the first one-third of the novel to set the scene for the more colourful descriptions of the passers-by, including "you", Margarethe, the dissident artists on Lama and the Chinese businessman. For these main characters, Hong Kong is a place and a state they find themselves in when waiting for transit. Hong Kong itself is a non-entity, like a boarding ramp. Everybody walks on it and is aware of it on their way to board the plane, but nobody would think about the materials it is made of.

Hong Kong, the local people of Hong Kong and the women in the novel are confined to stereotypical signification. There is no substantiation in the text of their symbolic meanings; rather, this symbolism is taken as the starting point, as their functions and content in the text. Lives are abstracted into signs. The naivety in the depiction of the West as the land of freedom, of Hong Kong as the transitional space and of women as the sexual Other, is the net result of this kind of abstraction. They appear not as what they are or what they do, but as what they are often assumed to symbolise. Such representational strategy refrains from depicting any realities about these people and places. Some critics might argue that all other lines in a novel should serve the flow of the main actions and the main protagonist. My answer to this objection is: this is exactly what a colonialist apologist would say about the novelistic depictions in the works of Rudyard Kipling or Jules Verne. Let us not forget that it is on the same ground against abstraction and essentialism that we reject Jameson's sweeping categorisation of the third world, that feminists and post-colonialists refuse to accept the position of the Other.

From National Allegory to Nihilism

The time-frame of the novel spans over two decades and the events cover the vast geographic, political and cultural spaces of urban and rural China, Hong Kong, Europe and Australia. There is a marked difference between the style of writing for the description of life in China and that outside it. Although "he" is the subject in memory while "you" are supposed to be living the present life, "his" life is depicted with much more concrete and colourful details than that of "yours". A lot more emotions are invested in the recount of life in the past in China. The construction of the protagonist's libidinal drives as being so closely linked with and analogous to "his" social and political position is a particularly successful strategy. The only weakness in this writing strategy is the absence of the women's subjectivity, which almost makes the text misogynist, as discussed in the previous section. Nevertheless, this intimate correlation between "his" libidinal drive and social agency tells how deeply people are damaged by political coercion, and is indubitably very moving. In contrast, "your" bohemian life style of the present is somewhat out of focus, in terms of content and also of literary impact, rather like blurred photographs. The descriptions of environments and actions lack detail and force. In comparison to the clarity, concreteness and solidity of the depictions of Chinese life, the present life reads much less convincing and seems less real. It creates a feeling of uncertainty and even dreaminess in "your" life. The only parts that stand out with emotive substance are the sex scenes. But the consistent Othering of the women in these scenes makes this part of the text problematic rather than attractive, quite apart from the fact that even these scenes come across as repetitive and lacking in literary appeal. It is not the memory that is etiolated, but rather the present.

The entire narrative is interjected with comments expressing a deep scepticism toward social participation, made as authorial comments in the narrative present. Consistently "you" expresses the wish to be left alone, with no trust in any forms of engagement. But this comes as a surprise after the free West is established as the antithesis to the repressive China. The text seems to be embracing this freedom, at least on the surface, as an antidote to the damage that has been done to "him" by the repressive China. One would expect the protagonist to be living happily ever after. But the scepticism toward social participation in general negates the possibility of a happy life. I read such a cynical attitude as a typical symptom of what I recognise as the kind of insidious nihilism that prevails in the globalised world of advanced Capitalism. Of course no person should be living under heavy-handed political control. But anyone with any experience of life in the rich and "free" cities of the urban West would agree that there are corresponding problematics of life there, and recognise that personal choice in the "free West" also have a rather limited scope, confined by other, differing sets of ideology.

Jameson has talked about the coercion experienced in our era of Late Capitalism in the Introduction to *Postmodernism: The Cultural Logic of Late Capitalism*. Multi-national Capitalism exercises its domination in a much softer form than the hard-hitting political purge of other ideologies. Two images that come to mind and help to articulate this comparison are contained in the 1933 classic film *King Kong* and the 2001 animation film *Final Fantasy*. The fear of the towering King Kong in the 1930s has been replaced by the threat imposed by amoeba-like "spirits" that float and flow in the air in the animation film *Final Fantasy*. These spirits engulf individuals by occupying the space around them. Human beings no longer die by being crushed under the heavy feet of King Kong. Instead, the spirits seep inside and corrupt human bodies, and the human souls are forced out. This kind of representation is best described by Jameson's term "a play of figuration" in relation to his concept of "Cognitive Mapping", to refer to the literary strategy of figurative distortion in the representation of something that is felt but cannot be named. The soft form of coercion in Late Capitalist society, including the domination of life by bureaucracy and multi-national businesses, with its cosmetic advantages of efficiency and cost-effectiveness, does not confront us as a threatening King Kong, but invades into our consciousness and takes control of our lives in a *Final Fantasy*-style.

Translating the self, bringing one's life in the past and the meaning generated from this past into the present life lived out in another cultural framework, does not guarantee successful anchorage of one's life in this other new framework. One also has to both experience and engage this new framework, in order to make meaning out of this new life. In order to experience and to engage, one needs to both appreciate and critique the reality of this new framework. But for someone such as "you" who has escaped ferocious political repression, it would probably feel unjustified, or even ungrateful, not to embrace the new life style. It is much more difficult to be critical of it. After all, by definition, political immigrants, or dissidents, who have come from countries outside the "Western democratic" system, are antagonistic toward their home countries, not their host countries in the West. Therefore it is even more difficult for them to articulate the specific form of coercion experienced in the Late Capitalist world. Problems that cannot be named, that one cannot pin down, can drive people in the direction of nihilism, since if people cannot put their finger on what is actually going wrong, there is very little to be done about it. This explains the two impulses existing in *One Man's Bible*, one of national allegory and the other nihilistic, corresponding to the treatment of life in China and the one outside it. Its lack of clarity and force in the representation of the present life outside and after China can therefore be interpreted as either incapability or unwillingness to provide a more insightful interpretation of life in the Late Capitalist West. The ability to provide a critical representation requires the writer to grasp the conditions of this new life in totality. Such kind of insights can only come with the willingness and the courage to face up to harsh reality. Not everybody can do it. But great writers such as Sartre, Camus and Beckett have done; and so too have responsible critics such as Marx, Benjamin, Fanon, Jameson and Baudrillard.

Nihilism is indisputably a major symptom of the modern era. Great literary works have been written on it. The immediate example that comes to mind is Ibsen's play *Hedda Gabler*. But unlike *One Man's Bible*, *Hedda Gabler* displays a distance between the text and the character. It is descriptive, even sympathetic, of the nihilistic tendency of the character without subscribing to it. Dostoevsky is even more critical of nihilistic attitudes in *The Possessed*. Both texts depict nihilism without being themselves nihilistic. But *One Man's Bible* embraces rather than analyses this nihilism. In fact almost all of Gao's dramatic writings produced outside China demonstrate an indulgence in the same nihilistic tendency. If one looks at his entire repertoire from the 1980s to date, it is easy to spot a gradual shift from national allegory to nihilistic writing. The most interesting thing about *One Man's Bible* is this continuum being compressed within one single text.

Exilic Nihilism

The nihilistic impulse mentioned in the previous section is notably characteristic of Gao Xingjian's writings after, but not before, the writer's exile. This simultaneity is more than a coincidence. Bakhtin's idea of the dialogic definition of the Self and the Other, i.e. of the necessity of an Other to define oneself, again inspires an understanding of this phenomenon. For Bakhtin, the identity of the Self is being formed and informed during the exchange of his "own speech" and the "alien" speech of the Other. (Bakhtin 1929 / Emerson 1985: 287) The body of Gao's texts produced in China is overtly political in nature. His advocacy of Modernist writing spoke directly against Socialist Realism sanctioned by the authority. The motif in his plays before 1986 of the conforming collective, the ruthless state authority and the manipulated masses have all variously represented the Other. This opposition against autocracy has already firmly defined the identity of these texts. If the writer's departure from China means freedom from state control and an autonomy for writing, the Other, which was essential to foreground the Self, is lost. There is an obvious change in the way the Self is constructed in Gao's works finished outside China.

Shengshengman bianzou [Variations on the Song Dynasty verse *Shengshengman*] (1987) was written for Jiang Qing, the same choreographer who commissioned *Nether City*, for another dance production which premiered in New York in 1989. The text is written as an extended verse in four sections. It elaborates on the rhythm created in the opening line of the Song Dynasty verse by Li Qingzhao with the use of reiterative locution[5]. Each of the sections of Gao's adaptation of the verse attempts to make use of reiterative locution and repetitive phrases to imitate one rhythmic pattern of *xiqu* music. Many of the original wordings in the Song Dynasty verse denoting the actions of searching and the sentiment of forlornness are retained in the first two sections. The third section, apart from traces of the source text, also consists of additional images of an individual being persecuted by others, without any indications of the content and nature of the persecution, let alone reflection on this persecution or the individual's emotions. The fourth section depicts an individual crawling along as time passes and finding nothing. The text ends with a sweeping denial of any meaning. The last eight lines are very short, containing only verbs that connote termination:

> everything has been used
> consumed
> settled
> wound up
> disposed of
> dealt with
> purged
> gone. (Gao 1987b/1996:94)

Again, there is no cause, no context, no descriptive or analytical dimensions in the idea of termination, except that they really are the lines at the end of the text. Surely one might excuse such one-dimensionality as the nature of a script intended to inspire a dance. There is no way to prove or disprove whether it is deliberately leaving space for the choreography.

Shengsijie (1991; French title by Gao as *Au bord de la vie*; translated into English as *Between Life and Death* by Gilbert Fong, 1999) is a woman's monologue. There is a male actor playing her lover but speaking no lines, and another actress playing all other female figures in her monologue, be it her mother in her memory or other figures in her imagination. Instead of "I", the main character is referred to by the actress herself as "she". According to the playwright's notes for performance, this means to create a distance for the actress from the character by allowing her to "enter and exit the character" (Gao 1991a/1995: 43). At the beginning of the play, the woman is arguing with her lover, complaining about his lack of understanding and care. A male figure is on stage but silent. She keeps talking without allowing him to respond and finally kills him. After the killing, she stays in the same room and starts reminiscing about her past. An atmosphere of claustrophobic enclosure is created. She recollects her relationships with her mother, her family and her lovers. The memory of her sexual experiences including a rape incident leaves her in disgust with her own body and a general feeling of abjection. The image of a Buddhist nun cutting up her own belly and rinsing her intestines, which first appears in *Soul Mountain* and is repeated here, is elaborated to allow potential for striking stage images, with the presence of an actress dressed up as a nun acting out the action (Gao 1990b: 309-310; Gao 1991a/1995: 32–34).[6] The inconsistent and neurotic speeches of the woman imbue the play from beginning to end with a nightmarish mood. Towards the end "she" speaks about the mental chaos "she" is feeling, expressing a lack of belief in any meaning in her life. Following this the final remarks about theatrical illusion are spoken from the actress's, rather than the character's, perspective, thus breaking the illusion before the curtain falls. But no further comment is made on the woman's psychological chaos and her disorientation in life. Nor is there any change of her psychological state from the beginning to the end of the play. What is created in this play is no more than a one dimensional image of a neurotic woman in grave trouble.

Immediately after *Between Life and Death*, another of Gao's plays *Duihua yu fanjie* (entitled in French by Gao as *Dialoguer, Interloquer*; translated as *Dialogue and Rebuttal* by Gilbert Fong, 1999) was finished in 1992. It was first put on by an Austrian theatre company. The Chinese version of the play was not published until 1994. It is a two-act three-hander. A woman and a man start a dialogue after their one-night casual sex. The content of their conversation is mostly to do with the sexual tension between them. Although they keep talking to each other, communication is minimal, partly because they are not consistent in things they say, and also because a lot of what they say does not follow the usual pattern of rational communication. Sometimes they talk about images and events in their imagination and memories, other times they rebut each other with irony and rhetorical questions. This impossibility of communication is symbolised throughout the play by a monk on stage trying to fulfill impossible tasks such as making a stick stand upright and resting an egg on its end. The monk makes comments on the situation between the couple by acting out these actions, but not interacting with them, breaking any dramatic illusion built up by the couple's acting. At the end of Act 1, the couple kill each other. But in Act 2, they are still talking to each other, despite being two corpses left lying in the room. The only difference is that now that they are not even able to leave each other anymore since they cannot physically remove themselves. The claustrophobic atmosphere is even more intense than that in *Between Life and Death*. Their speech pattern becomes increasingly irrational. Instead of using "you" and "I" as in Act 1, now "he" and "she" are used for both actors to refer to themselves and each other. Towards the end a number of speeches are written as unpunctuated repetitions of phrases that deny rational comprehension. Abundant Buddhist allusions are put in their speeches in Act 2. The general idea is that in life the heart and the mind are constantly troubled. Even in death the individuals cannot feel at peace as long as their spirits are conscious of themselves.

Yeyoushen (1993; French title by Gao as *Le Somnambule*; translated into English as *Nocturnal Wanderer* by Gilbert Fong, 1999) is another of Gao's plays written upon commission, this time by a French foundation. A scene showing passengers in a train compartment not having anything to do with each other is constructed as the outer frame for another scenario, vaguely indicated to be the content of a book read by one of the passengers, of a man walking in the street in the middle of the night. He encounters a number of people including a tramp, a scoundrel, a gangster and a female sex worker.[7] The characters are doubled up by the same actors who also play the passengers. These personas in the street get talking to each other, then at the end kill each other off for no specific reasons. One reading that this dual level structure generates is that these characters in the book are the repressed egos of the passengers. Again, there is nothing within the text to justify or explain why the relationship among these people develops in this particularly negative way. The text articulates a general lack of purpose and meaning of the characters' actions, which reads as almost contrived. Again, as in the other Gao plays of the same period, the nocturnal wanderer adopts "you", the second person address, to describe his own actions.

Neither does *Zhoumo sichongzou* (1995; French version *Quatre quatuors pour un week-end* by Gao; translated as *Weekend Quartet* by Gilbert Fong, 1999) deviate from this alternate use of the first, second and third person addresses to create distance between the actors and the characters they play. Like *Between Life and Death* and *Dialogue and Rebuttal*, the story has a European setting. Two heterosexual couples spent a weekend in a country villa. Their ages range from sixties to early twenties. Sex and relationships remain the main channel through which the characters relate to each other. Instead of having a structure as in a conventional play script with lines clearly designated to each character, this text indicates speakers as groups.[8] There are no indications of the individual speaker of each line under these groups. Formally it is possible to compare the script to an orchestrated score indicating the instrumental sections. But since the lines are written from very clear perspectives, it is very easy for readers to attribute them to individual characters. In terms of style, the lines are written in two modes: some are more like naturalistic conversations while others are more akin to confessions of innermost thoughts and desires; the former is realistic while the latter is psychological. They require the actors to alternate between realistic and stylised acting with considerable fluency. Again, reality is represented in two layers, a social one and a psychological one. At the end of the play, a more destructive ending signifying breakup of the couples and the possible suicide of one of the men is immediately followed by an alternative ending. The two couples bid each other goodbye in the most impeccably civilised manners when the weekend holiday draws to a close and the young couple go back to the city. All four of them have repressed the anguish they feel in life, which is connected with a lack of meaning and purpose in what they do, and the impossibility of happiness in purposeless lives like theirs. The dark "ending" that precedes this one can therefore be read as the desires the four people really want to fulfil but have repressed.

All these four plays express an intense existential crisis. The characters are either left in solitude or engaged in struggles for dominance and sexual tension with each other. In either case, they are each enveloped in cocoons of their own psychological enclosure. This is not the case in classic Existentialist works such as Sartre's *Huis clos* or Camus' *L'Étranger*, in which the protagonists' existential angst is contextualised in more realistic social scenarios. For example, in Sartre's *Huis clos*, Hell is presented as a rather "normal" situation similar to that of a bourgeois living room. In many Existentialist works, the Existentialist compulsion only unfolds gradually as the protagonists reflect on and arrive at the Existentialist conclusion. The development of events and the protagonists' gradual realisation are constructed with plots and descriptions rather than with repetitions of philosophical statements. By contrast, Camus' *Le Mythe de Sisyphe* is a fully elaborated philosophical essay. They *argue for* an Existentialist view on life rather than taking it for granted. Very often, even when such a view is established in these works, human endeavours to endow life with compassion and dignity are still valued highly. Famous examples are Camus' *La peste* and Beckett's *Waiting for Godot*. On the contrary, in the four of Gao's plays discussed here, existential crisis is the beginning and the end, presented as the only condition of life. All interactions among the characters are destructive. The only mode of relationship between the two sexes is sexual exploitation. Exploitation and competition are presented as fundamentals of human nature. There being no possibility of redemption, damnation is absolute since mutual or self-destruction is presented as the only possible pattern of human behaviour.

If these plays are read without regard to their conditions of production, they come across as not having made any statements about anything, as they themselves acknowledge. The characters of these plays have repeatedly announced that life is utterly meaningless, that each person must face his extinction in psychological isolation, and that such is the only condition of life. But if we contextualise these plays in the light of the change in the production contexts of Gao's writing, i.e., the authorial experience of exile, there is another possible reading of them. The impact of such estrangement from China on textual production prompts one to reflect on the relationship between literary production and its context.

Modern Chinese literature has a tradition of intensive interaction with national politics. In fact it was the social awareness of the May Fourth generation that induced the emergence of a self-conscious modern Chinese literature. Such a nationalist stance has been well-preserved throughout the century by left-wing writers, and is further legitimised by Mao's 1942 *Yan'an Talks*. After 1949, nationalist political discourse in one way or another has dominated literary production in China. Such is the case both for those works written according to the official line to serve the authorities, and those struggling against it and striving for autonomy in literary creation. In both cases, the literature is intensely reactive to the contemporary politics.

In many works of Chinese literature after 1949 that seemingly display opposite inclinations to the Party-assigned modes, it is the discursive tension between these two positions that gives them their significance. To raise repressed alternative voices already ascribes meaning to them, no matter what the concerns of these voices are. Gao Xingjian's works published in China definitely fall within this category. Although they never challenge the political hegemony of 1980s China in any fundamental way, the tendency in these plays and fictions to adopt innovative modes of expression has already constituted a subversive phenomenon against the domination of a highly controlled political authority on literature, and by extension on culture, and even life in general. The efforts displayed in Gao's early writings at promoting Modernism in China also acquire significance from the act of contradicting official positions, and of foregrounding the aesthetics of literary techniques, which is of secondary significance according to Mao's guidelines. To negate Socialist Realism is to negate the Maoist hierarchy of pragmatics over aesthetics, collective responsibility over individual autonomy. The slightly conservative ideology and the sometimes elitist and personal inclination in some of these works, as displayed in *Alarm Signal* and *The Other Shore*, has been allowed to pass without critique by literary critics, because they have adopted a position that is critical of the oppressive hegemony of state censorship. These works are well received perhaps not so much for their intrinsic formal and ideological values, but for the subversive power they imply and the impact they arouse by their very production under such conditions. However, the lack of sophisticated ideological reflection in Gao's early works means that the struggle for freedom they symbolise can only serve as a reactionary phenomenon. It also means that they have to be read in China in the shadow of an oppressive Other to acquire meaning. Once the creative subject has eschewed this oppressive Other, as Middle-aged Man does in *Fugitives*, the texts produced abroad display a lack of direction and relevance, since it is precisely the Other that defines a position for the earlier works in the repertoire; and therefore, it is the absence of the oppressive Other that brings about the disorientation in the later works. The restrictions imposed by this oppressive Other were left behind in China upon the author's departure, but his path to "freedom" has not led to new possibilities in literary creation in his particular case. On the contrary, the constant struggle for freedom in the choice of literary form against official censorship has lost all significance outside China. Further production of "formalist texts", as I shall refer to Gao's early repertoire, would now be stripped of any meaning. Such is the direct consequence of the lack of ideological reflection in these texts.

Nationalist interventionist writing in exile does not easily serve a subversive purpose. The South African writer Breyten Breytenbach once wrote in his exile in Europe about his sense of alienation that:

> You live and you write in terms of absence, of absent time. Not an imagined or remembered existence: more an absent presence ... You risk the rupture of silence: either because the break with your milieu is finally too traumatic, and the awareness of your declining faculties wears the few existing links down to nothing; or you lose the sense of inevitability... (Breytenbach 1985/1995: 229)

As far as Breytenbach is concerned, the writer in exile is trapped in a two-fold alienation, alienated from his new immediate environment, and alienated from the urgency that once prompted him to write in his native context. For some Chinese writers including Gao Xingjian, especially those who left China after the 1989 Tian'anmen Massacre, there is an even deeper sense of alienation since living in exile is also accompanied by their works being banned in the Mainland. Until at least the middle of the 1990s when the internet became more readily available in Chinese cities, the problems of inaccessibility between these writers and China were two-way. Any subversive voice raised against the state authority on the part of such writers is completely muted because of the absence of both writer and text in the national context. The resistance their literary production could generate is eliminated. Any impact they might make would be indirect and might even be appropriated by other institutions, especially when it is an overseas, or even a foreign readership that these works are specifically written for. The impact they make on the foreign public is through the mass media, regulated by the establishment that promotes and publicises them. On the one hand, such writing in exile could hardly exercise any immediate influence on affairs in the writers' native country. On the other, there is always the risk of being recuperated by the Western conservative Capitalist establishment into the anti-Communist discourse, which immediately undermines any subversive position.

Gao's writing was by no means the only victim of this double alienation. In a conference held in Chicago in 1990 on Chinese writing in exile, some participants reflected on the writing condition for Chinese writers living in exile at that moment in time. Writer, translator and literary critic Chen Maiping was concerned about the fact that many of them are writing to be translated, which might affect what they write (Lee 1993: iv). Gregory B. Lee's comments on Duoduo's situation in exile is along the same lines, when he observes that the poet was:

> ... now commodified, his "dissidence" now packaged; a dissidence always so simplistically projected by the Western media establishment as anti-Communist and pro-Capitalist sentiment, as the desire for the Western liberal notion of freedom . (Lee 1993: 70)

Himself a Chinese writer in exile, Chen Maiping expresses his view on the matter in a less direct way. He sees writing for translation as a means "which gives writers a voice of sorts and sometimes provides some financial relief". But both he and Lee were basically pointing to the same conclusion, namely Chinese writing by writers in exile being recuperated beyond the writers' control into the Western discourse of "anti-Communist and pro-Capitalist" binarism in order that they can nuzzle the hand that feeds them. It is perhaps with the aim of avoiding this recuperation that the four of Gao's plays discussed here shy away from the Chinese context that brings on the paranoia of the individual, namely the writer's personal experience of political prosecution. If this is the case, such resistance has to be deserving of respect, even though it results in the texts being unable to present a full picture of this existential crisis under the specific condition of exile. Thus a project of good critical potential has unfortunately degenerated into no more than a contrived nihilism.

Avoiding contemporary Chinese politics, however, does not mean that China is absent in these writings altogether. It has simply made its presence felt in the forms of myths, legends and cultural allusions. The majority of Gao's plays written in exile are rich in images of Chinese folklore and religions, not to mention those which are new interpretations of Chinese legends and mythologies. For many diasporic writers, writing about their native culture is a way to define their position in their host countries. It is no coincidence that a plethora of works by writers in exile make use of national myths, legends, history and customs as either themes or features. For some, they are material of their past to be translated into their present, so that their individual existence in the new host country is endowed with and enriched by the collective cultural past they once belonged to. As for others, they elaborate the differences between the native and the host cultures, and emphasise incongruities instead of seeking compromises. They stamp the presence of their native culture on their works to express the sense of alienation they feel in the foreign land. But in Gao's works, as in many others by Chinese writers in exile, the idea of China and their Chinese past very often become abstract because, to borrow Breytenbach's phrase, the writers are writing in an "absent presence" (Breytenbach 1995: 229). In many cases China is no more than an idea of a past and distant entity constructed in a text, or as Breytenbach describes such a form of writing, it is like "the tongue [that] keeps clacking against areas of dead palate" (Breytenbach 1995: 229). Many Chinese dissident writers in exile find themselves in a bind, obsessed by China, but unable to make effective utterances about China. They are confronted with the same question: Is there anything else to write except about China and their own dissidence?

The four plays discussed in this section demonstrate a change of direction away from interventionist literature. Gao himself has also announced closure during this period of his "homesickness" upon the completion of *Soul Mountain* and *Stories in the Books of Mountains and Seas* (2000: 15). But instead of engaging in other issues, these four plays show no more than a withdrawal from society to a personal enclosure, an interior solipsistic world cut off from communication with the outside. These texts represent such solitude as claustrophobic and their characters as anxious. The author's own claim to Buddhism and the proliferation of Buddhist images and symbols in the texts might encourage these texts to be read as being founded on a certain philosophical basis. Criticisms have been written on the Buddhist aspect in Gao's plays in this period.[9] However, I find it more appropriate to read them as texts about the experience of exile, in which disorientation and alienation combine to drive the characters into solitude they cannot break out of. The Buddhist state of spiritual peace is no more than an ideal, a goal the characters aspire to but cannot reach.

Ego as the Other

The first allusion to Buddhism in Gao's repertoire is made in *The Other Shore*. In that play, the crowd cross a river which is described as "stagnant" and "all it is about is to forget" (Gao 1986b: 240). This implies resemblance to the River of Oblivion. According to Buddhist belief, a soul has to cross the river after the body is dead in order to forget about the previous life and to join the *Samsara*, or the Wheel of Life. Then the soul can enter into another life. In the middle of the play there is a monk character appearing twice chanting a Buddhist prayer. The purpose of the prayer is to urge men and women to leave earthly desires behind and cross over to "the opposite shore". *Bi'an*, as the Chinese title of the play, or *Faramita* as the Buddhists call it, is a metaphor used in one of the most important concepts in Buddhism. When a believer acquires "real wisdom" and "wakes up from the earthly life", he is said to have reached *Faramita* and become Buddha, which means having achieved the state of emptiness and nothingness, or *Nirvana*, by not insisting on the existence of a Self. But in the play, as soon as the people have learnt the words "I" and "you", or have entered the mirror stage in Lacanian terms, they murder Woman and started struggling for domination among each other (Gao 1986b: 242). Instead of achieving Nirvana, the individual and the crowd return to life and engage once more in earthly pursuits. Indeed the main actions of the play start after this episode. It is also after this episode that the Other for Man is established as all other people who threaten his autonomy. But this other-people-as-Other is removed in Gao's texts written in exile, since the Other has taken an inward turn. In the absence of the oppressive Other and in the solitude of exile, the Self experiences an internal schizophrenic split and the "ego" is established as the ultimate Other.

The alternative use of the first, second and third person addresses as the narrative positions in *Soul Mountain* represents the first instance of this inward turn of the Other. As discussed earlier, the narrator's voice in that novel takes three forms, "I", "you" and "he", although they all indicate the same person. The second and third person points of view serve to indicate a self-reflexive process in which he finds an Other in himself — his ego [*ziwo*] that is examined and described in his attempt to achieve self understanding. In Chapter 26 of the novel, "I" concludes that the Self is the source of all problems and anxieties (Gao 1990b: 162). This is consistent with the plot of *The Other Shore* in which the moment of self-realisation is also the moment when trouble begins. Similarly in *Fugitives*, Middle-aged Man makes the pronouncement that he wants to "avoid myself" (Gao 1990a/Lee 1993: 135). But it is in *Soul Mountain* that the theme of the human ego is developed:

> The problems arise from this awakened ego in my heart, the monster that tortures me and takes away my peace. A man loves himself, hurts himself, becomes reserved, arrogant, happy and sad. He feels jealous and resentful. All are due to this "he". Ego is indeed the source of misery for human beings. (Gao 1990b: 162)

The idea of absence of self [*wu wo*] is the key to Buddhist Enlightenment. In Gao's texts, the Chinese idea of *wo* [the sense of the existence of oneself] and the psychoanalytic idea of the ego are collapsed into one another. Allusions to this idea are also revealed as abundant in Gao's entire repertoire written in exile. In *Soul Mountain*, "your" quest for Soul Mountain is identified as the goal because the geographical journey "you" takes is a metaphor for "I"'s narrative act of writing about his own state of mind in order to achieve an understanding of himself, or his ego. The aim of this self-analysis is to look for spiritual enlightenment. Soul Mountain [*lingshan*] suggests a connection with the famous story about Buddha stroking a flower [*lianhua weixiao*] at the famous "Meeting on Soul Mountain" [*lingshanhui*]. It is said that instead of giving an elaborate talk on enlightenment as his disciples had expected, he stroked a flower and smiled to demonstrate the state of enlightenment. What is shown is a state of mind in which there is no desire, not even the desire for self knowledge or the desire to achieve enlightenment. It is a state of emptiness and nothingness when the Self has forgotten about its own existence. It is the only way to free one from the earthly entities, the "colours of the world" [*se*] and the only path towards enlightenment according to Buddhist philosophy. This state of enlightenment is later elaborated in Zen philosophy. Reasoning is rejected as a means of reaching enlightenment. According to Zen philosophy, one can be enlightened [*dun wu*] through communication with nature and one's true self, but one can never understand enlightenment through analysis and study. Consequently, Zen Buddhism also rejects verbal means as a tool of reasoning. Ironically, according to this, the attempt of the narrator in *Soul Mountain* to seek enlightenment through narration is doomed to fail.

There are two reasons for such failure. Firstly, any attempt to seek enlightenment is an act of indulgence in the desire for it, instead of freeing oneself from all desire. This is a direction diametrically opposed to the goal. Moreover, in the process of narrating his state of mind, the narrated ego is made to be an Other. Meanwhile, it assures the existence of a Self to take up the act of narrating the Ego-Other. As Bakhtin puts it, the two are in formative relation. Instead of purging the Self as Zen philosophy exhorts its adherents to do, the plot has once again reinscribed it. The idea of flight becomes problematic since the whole process confirms what his character is supposed to be fleeing from. What is supposed to be a quest for Zen enlightenment in fact valorises and reaffirms the Self's existence. In this connection, it is worth recalling the extremely lyrical poem by the Zen master Huineng (638–713 A.D.) on the real state of enlightenment in response to the view that one has to often wipe the mirror of the heart so that it would not be masked by dust. Huineng's wisdom brings the desire for enlightenment in *Soul Mountain* into sharp relief. Such wisdom is best represented in the poem attributed to him in *Liuzu tanjing* (8th century A.D. ; translated into English as *The Platform Sutra of the Sixth Patriarch* by Philip Yampolsky, 2000):

Bodhi originally has no tree,
The mirror also has no stand.
Buddha nature is always clean and pure
Where is there room for dust?

(Liuzu tanjing, 8th Century / Yamplosky 2000: 132)

The same contradiction is found in both *Between Life and Death* and *Dialogue and Rebuttal*.[10] Another of Gao's plays, *Bayuexue* (2000; translated as *Snow in August* by Gilbert Fong, 2003), depicts the life of Huineng but is much more relaxed in comparison. This is to a large extent because the play itself extols the philosophy of Zen Buddhism. Once this goal is set, there can be no alternative but to depict the image of the greatest Zen master as the enlightened one. In this way, there can only be a rather limited parameter for the characterisation of this figure as a dramatic protagonist. The existential angst common in all of Gao's other main characters is absent in Huineng. The play shows in chronological order a number of events in his life. He is thoroughly enlightened even at his first appearance in the play when he is only a firewood vendor. His interaction with characters who are not enlightened makes his wisdom stand out. These characters include a nun who still clings on to earthly passion, and other followers of Master Hongren, who seek achievement and glory in the Buddhist hierarchy. A number of speeches are taken from stories about Huineng, and what he said and what he did. Some other speeches are written to imitate the style of Zen stories, in which ideas are expressed in seemingly irrelevant utterances and actions. They can only be understood if readers are willing to adopt logic and perspectives alternative from the rational ones of our daily life.

The subtitle of the play is "A Modern *Xiqu* in 3 Acts (8 Scenes)". In the production that Gao directed in Taiwan in 2002, although *jingju* [Beijing opera] players comprised the cast, they did not completely conform to the acting convention of *xiqu*. The incidental music was orchestral music composed by Xu Shuya. In a special issue of *Biaoyan yishu* [*Performing Arts*], the flagship performing arts magazine in Taiwan, featuring articles on this production, five out of the five articles are critical rather than complimentary. Most of them focus on the theatrical and technical side of the production. But a particularly poignant critique views the production from a Zen Buddhist perspective. It examines in detail the allusion to and elaboration on a number of Zen ideas in the play. The critic Lin Jufang is dissatisfied with the idealist treatment of Zen, and especially with the way Zen principles are taken as clichés without exploration of their profundity. It concludes with the view that the play is *"li chan yuan yi"*, literary meaning being very far from Zen enlightenment (Lin 2003: 39–40). I agree with critics that this text, along with his other plays written in exile in this period, does not demonstrate Buddhist enlightenment. At most one can only describe them as articulating an aspiration to seek without success, since the obsession on the search is self-defeating to the intention.

From *The Other Shore* to *Soul Mountain* and Gao's plays written in the 1990s there is a change in the relationship between the Self of the individual hero and his Other. The Other has turned from an external antagonistic opponent to the persona's ego, an internal component of his Self. These texts reveal themselves to be a claustrophobic repertoire. In exile, they are produced in solitude, neither making connection with their immediate environment, nor finding relevance to the context they are produced in. Yet the militant model of struggle between the Self and the Other lingers. Zen Buddhism is therefore used as the weapon to purge this ego. However, this internal Self/Other model is arbitrary and full of self contradictions. The way it is constructed does not valorise its claim. These texts have entered a crisis of utter irrelevance. They have not engaged in any real issues. Ironically, the only piece that has escaped this crisis is *Shunjian* (translated into English as *In an Instant* by Mabel Lee, 2004), a short prose piece the author wrote in 1991. It contains numerous paragraphs, each a snapshot of street scenes or of the subjective imagination of a person's mind. The piece does not have a theme. It is not about anything, but at least it engages with the subject's surroundings. It is free of the claustrophobia that characterises his other exile writing in existential crisis.

Yet I do not intend to dismiss these writings. On the contrary, I find them a very accurate reflection of the crisis of exilic existence, in which the advantage of autonomy is offset by the trauma of displacement, and the freedom of breaking away by the vertigo of loss of gravity. But there is a serious problem in these texts, namely, their absence of a critical attitude brought about by a lack of self-awareness of the exilic crisis. Even the consistent use of the third person functions to fetishise the ego rather than investigating it, since if there is no critical perspective in the content, clever manipulation of the narrative position cannot make the work critical.

What happens is that these texts fall victim both to China's ban and to the cultural consumerism of the Oriental Other in the West. Being mutually inaccessible (China with Gao and Gao with China), his writing is muted in the very location where profound meaning had been generated by its mere existence. To avoid being recuperated by Western discourses on China, Gao's writing in the 1990s has avoided China in order to avoid becoming what is typically regarded as dissident activist writing. It is a pity that instead of being critical of this situation and make meaningful utterances about it, these texts only find escape in sweeping nihilism, or the guise of Zen Buddhism. Worse still, these texts have not been able to engage with any other phenomena, probably because of the difficulty to imagine their readership at the time of their production. The intended readers are certainly not the Chinese in the Chinese mainland. There are some Taiwanese, some Hong Kong people, some overseas Chinese on different continents, some French and some Europeans who read them in translation, if they do eventually get translated. But none of these groups forms a sufficiently substantive readership to constitute a critical mass. The texts have become works produced from a non-position for no particular readers. Gao's body of work has been discontinued in China, but it is not going anywhere else. It has taken off in international space but has not found new ground to land on.

Crossing over Time

Many Chinese readers would remember first discovering Gao Xingjian's plays in the early to mid 1980s. Soon afterwards the Tian'anmen Square Massacre happened. Many overseas Chinese would remember joining marches and protests in support of those who demanded democracy in that vast country. They might even remember staying up all night on the 3rd of June 1989, listening to the radio and waiting for any development in events. Some literary students might also remember reading Gao's play *Fugitives* in the first issue of the revived literary journal *Jintian* [*Today*] in Stockholm,[11] feeling disoriented and not knowing what to make of it. There have subsequently been many re-evaluations of the student movement representing different opinions. The aftermath and consequences of the movement are still felt keenly. To this day, many people still made an effort to attend the annual commemoration of the massacre held in Hong Kong, the only one that has continued annually within the territory of China.

But the massacre only shows one aspect of China. There are many others. For example, many film audiences would remember watching Mi Jiashan's film adaptation of Wang Shuo's story *3-T Company* (1988). The witty and humorous touch was quite a change from the weighty sentiments of those root-searchers people were accustomed to. They might also remember watching Chen Kaige's *The Promise* (2005), feeling a sense of nostalgia for the critical edge in Chen's early films; and Li Shaohong's *Baobei in Love* (2004), pondering the blurring of boundaries between a critique and a celebration of the violence of urbanisation. Spanning the period in which these films were produced, Hong Kong was handed over to China; an advocate of independence was elected President of Taiwan; the New York twin towers fell; China had its embassy in Belgrade bombed by an American missile, joined the WTO, participated in the negotiations on the future of North Korea's nuclear programme, and built a huge network of expressways in Beijing to cope with the traffic during the Olympics. While the property prices are surging in Shanghai, poorly constructed and administered mines in areas including Heilongjiang and Liaoning Province continue to collapse, killing 12,204 people in 2003 and 2004 alone (Yan 2005); and warlord-like policemen in Guangdong opened fire at villagers who were protesting against corrupt officials and land seizures. Amidst all these developments there is the increasingly sinister American aggression enshrined in that nation's foreign policies.

Revisiting Gao's works in the new millennium I am struck by the change of context in which we read his later work. This is partly to be expected because, after all, these writings have been produced in very different circumstances. But the way China has been changing also imposes drastically different conditions on the production and reception of Chinese literature. For one thing, the conditions of lives in many Chinese regions are unrecognisable from the way things were in the 1970s and even the 1980s. For another, China's engagement with "the world" is different from what it was back then. In old Mao's words, China has made many "leaps forward", although not exactly in the way he envisaged. China has "opened up", whatever that means. The fact is that the relatively monolithic mode of politics and social life that Chinese state leaders once tried to maintain at all costs has become utterly impossible. The market is the new authoritarian power and consumerism the new ideology; yes, even in "Communist" China. Information technology and communications have assumed paramount importance in the new economy because they are instrumental in forming new consumption patterns. Certain books and magazines might still be hard to get in major bookstores, but urbanites are retrieving from the internet the most up-to-date information on consumer goods on a daily basis. Alongside consumers are activists and researchers forming discussion groups and exchanging data via email and on websites, as well as the more interested members of the public surfing and browsing on the net. There are bans on certain websites. But the speed of producing new sites and establishing new links outpaces the official censors, whose detection and banning of websites can only come after these web-sites have already been visited and their content circulated. Nowadays, wars for autonomy are not only fought with brute force, but also with speed and quick thinking. In a world where the centre finds it increasingly difficult to hold, hard-headed confrontation is not always the most efficient form of subversion. On the other hand, the state has long ceased to be the only force of totalitarianism. Facing the various conspiracies of state, bureaucracy, market and patriarchy, a critical subject would certainly find the subversive tools s/he employs bound up with other authoritarian institutions. Continuous and considerable re-positioning is necessary. Unfortunately, the lack of dialectical thinking in the depiction of the Self and the Other in Gao's works does not facilitate any re-positioning. Given a situation in which the Other has moved on but the Self has not, his more recent utterances seem to resemble fists punching thin air.

Part 5

Conclusion

8

Reading across Culture

Crossing over Language

One phenomenon that has accompanied the "opening up" of China is improved mobility of people, in addition to that of information and goods. Travelling both into and out of China is much easier now compared to the 1980s. One incident that comes to mind is of course Gao Xingjian's departure to Germany in 1987. It was extremely difficult to get a visa to travel abroad. He would not have got official approval to leave the country had it not been for the intervention of a sympathetic Party member occupying a considerably influential position. It is almost ironic to juxtapose this incident with the landmark development in 2003 of the policy to minimize visa control for people to travel to Hong Kong from the Mainland. What was once considered potentially subversive is now promoted as government policy. With this new policy, residents registered in selected provinces can easily obtain short-term tourist visas to visit Hong Kong without applying through their work units or joining organised tours. Nowadays it is easy for Mainlanders to come to Hong Kong, the capitalist city that was once considered dangerous because it was the place many dissidents found temporary abode and shelter before they moved abroad. Since the city's sovereignty was ceded back to China in 1997, China has taken a hands-off approach to it. This new policy of minimum control is driven, not by political, but by economic concerns. It is an attempt to boost business of the retail market of the former colony by encouraging Mainland tourists to spend money there. Moreover, to meet the need for China's participation in international business, many more people are getting trained abroad and more expatriates are also employed to work in the Mainland. As distance and time are both compressed in the shrinking postmodern world, communication seems to be so smooth between nations and cultures. It is easy to create the illusion of a world in which people are becoming more similar. This illusion is possible as long as the media continues to suppress the presence of the population of "less developed" regions who are living in poverty, suffering as the result of the greed and cynicism of multi-national enterprises backed by their nations' ambitions for economic expansion. It is in such a world that language has tremendous political potential. Publication in diverse languages can function to remind people of the heterogeneity of the real lives lived out by real people who are left behind by the market-driven and hi-tech new world.

Yet this potential of language as resistance can only remain a theoretical possibility, since in the actual international book markets, most literature written in "minor" languages is not in mainstream circulation. Even if it were, the chances that it could be widely read in the original languages are slim. With the dominance of the English language, people are increasingly dependent on English translations to get to know "other" literatures. Rarely nowadays do we meet comparativists like Leo Spitzer who could read in twenty-one languages. The result is that works by writers of "minor" languages are received through translation into "strong" languages among the international readership. In fact Gao Xingjian's success is very revealing of the power of translation. A number of critics and writers have remarked on the role that translation has played in his international status.[1] It was a wonderful moment of sly humour when Liu Ching-chih, an academic from the field of translation studies, proposed renaming the Nobel Prize in Literature the "Nobel Prize in Literary Translation". He recounts an incident in a public seminar in 1991 when he asked Göran Malmqvist about the absence of a Chinese writer in the Nobel Prize list and the latter's answer was:

> "lacking good translations". I remarked: "then the Novel Prize in literature should be changed to the Nobel Prize in Literary Translation". To this, he said that "it is not possible to revise Nobel's will". On reflection, it is rather ironical: Gao Xingjian won the Nobel Prize in Literature and Göran Malmqvist was the translator of Gao's works — does that mean the latter's translation was the decisive factor for the former to become a winner of this Prize? It must be. This example has further proved that the Prize should be renamed the "Nobel Prize in Literary Translation" and I think Göran Malmqvist should share the Prize with Gao. And then, it will be even more embarrassing, since Göran Malmqvist was one of the Selection Committee members for the Prize. (Liu 2002: 62–63).

To prove the importance of translation being a decisive factor in Western reception of "other" literatures, Liu relates another story in which literature professor Huang Zuyu wrote to the Swedish Royal Academy concerning the "neglect" of Chinese literature demonstrated by that body. Huang received a reply from the Standing Secretary of the Academy explaining "that the problem lay in the language barrier and that assessing the literary works concerned had entirely depended on translation" (Liu 2002: 62–63). Like other works in "minor" languages, Gao's works are essentially received abroad through translation. Translation is surely a powerful instrument. The value of translation is beyond doubt since its very aim is to facilitate understanding between people of divergent cultures, who would not otherwise be able to communicate. But anybody who has any experience of translation realises that a translation does *not* equal the source text. Translation is not a magical invisible lens through which beholders decipher the foreign symbols, would suddenly see the text "as it is". Translators need to tear apart the source text and fit the information piece by piece into the semantic fields and syntactical structures of the target language. In literary translation, the convention of literary writing, including generic forms, rhetorical devices and expectations of the literary readership in the target culture, often determine the form a translation needs to take. The source text is necessarily re(/de)formed in translation.

Gao Xingjian's remark on the French translation of *Soul Mountain* is very revealing of the difficulties one often encounters in translation. One thing he has discussed with his French translator is how the absence of tenses and moods in Chinese verbs creates an ambiguity in the time frame of events and in the sense of their reality. He suggested putting all the verbs in the present tense in the French translation only to meet the translator's categorical objection on the ground that it would be "terrible French" (Gao 1998: 155). The result is the inevitable explicitation, or making explicit, of ambiguities, which so often occurs in translation, as observed by translation critics such as Vinay and Darbelnet, Eugene Nida and Blum-Kulka (Klaudy 2000: 80–84). Exactly the same is evident in the English translation by Mabel Lee, the only English translation in circulation and approved by the writer himself. The translation endeavours to create the same ambiguity, but the English language simply does not support it. Let's recall the opening sentences of Chapter 41 of the novel already discussed in Chapter Five of this book. The chapter opens with three points of time in comparison: when "I" arrives at a village; two years before that when the old shaman dies; and on the occasion of the last ritual the shaman performs before he dies. Since Chinese verbs have no tense markers, the narrative presence is able to be shifted backward twice within the three opening sentences rather smoothly and subtly. The more realistic narrative present of the journey taken by "I" is blended into the legendary past of the shaman's life and the mythic world of the old shaman's folk religion. This paragraph is rendered as follows in Lee's English translation:

> His death takes place two years before I come here. At the time he is the last surviving Master of Sacrifice among the hundred Miao stockades, but for several

decades there has not been an ancestor sacrifice on such a grand scale. He knows it will not be long before he will return to Heaven... (Gao 1990b: 251 / Lee 2000: 237)

The paragraph does not follow the usual pattern of tense sequence required by English grammar. All the actions, including those taken by "I", the death of the shaman two years before that, and the ritual he performs before his death are all presented in the present tense. The reason for not following the usual tense sequence in English is undoubtedly the translator's awareness of the original's manipulation of the time-frame. But putting all events and actions in the present conflates all three periods into one. The result is a flattening of the temporal landscape, which has been skilfully created in the original. The flexibility in the shifting of what constitutes "narrative presence" is missing. Moreover, this very unusual breaking of grammatical convention in English tense usage reads as an anomaly rather than a subtlety as it does in the source text. The historic present, used for the events in the shaman's life-time, only works after readers have got over the awkward tenses of the first sentence. The ambiguity in the Chinese text is an attempt to realise the flexibility in making meaning within the convention of the source language, but in the translation the same ambiguity has become the cause for breaking the linguistic convention of that target language. Such moments inappropriately confer on the translation an appearance of being linguistically more daring than the source utterance.

Another difficult element to deal with in translation is cultural specificity. It often causes such serious problems of intranslatability that textbooks and training manuals frequently single it out for separate discussion (Newmark 1988; Hatim 2001). It is therefore easy to understand the enormous difficulty the translator faces in translating a novel as loaded with cultural elements as *Soul Mountain* is. For example, the ethnic elements in the novel are extremely culturally specific. Gao has also remarked on his deliberate use of a mixture of Chinese dialects in the novel (Gao 1998: 156). But quite understandably such style is not created in the translation, simply because it is not possible to write Chinese dialects in English. There are arguments for and actual examples of adopting regional dialects of English. But there are also arguments against this kind of parallelism. In the end it comes down to the translator's personal choice, and sometimes the individual requirements of the text being translated.

One can easily find abundant examples to show that a translation simply is *not* the source text. But they must not be used to convict translation as an out-and-out imposter. In fact the very categorisation of texts as translation means they never claim to replace the source text. A translation stands in for the source text without replacing it. Translation is the best possible sign to highlight the absence of the source text. It is a marker of absence and difference. Russell West's Derridean description of translation offers considerable clarification of the issue:

For translation is predicated upon an ineradicable specificity and difference that cannot be overcome — indeed, which launches the translative task in such a way as to preclude the completion of that task. Translation is predicated upon its own impossibility, and it is this impossibility that drives it and, paradoxically, establishes its very condition of possibility. (West 2004: 235–236)

The problem tends to arise with the concept of "equivalence" in translation studies, which gives the illusion of sameness between the source and the target texts. It has sent translation off on a mission that has no chance of being accomplished, for the simple reason that "鞋", or "*xie*", just is not "shoe"; and "one" is neither "*uno*" nor "*una*". Each word carries unique phonetic and semantic qualities and inspires different semantic associations and phenomenological experiences. Each and every sign is unique. The differences between the reading experience of source text and that of the corresponding translation are not only of a hermeneutic, but also a phenomenological nature. This is why the concept of "equivalence" has been constantly qualified and revised in recent translation studies (Kenny 2000: 77–80).

Translation is extremely useful as long as we do not insist on the fantasy of a translation being "the same" as the source text, as long as we do not pretend that it is doing what it cannot. The very nature of translation is a means of communication between two otherwise uncommunicated subjectivities. Like any acts of interpretation, a translation illuminates certain aspects of a text, while other aspects may be played down, or even missed out, or lost, so to speak. To insist that a translation is equivalent to the source text is a deliberate suppression of elements, which are not or cannot be expressed in the target language and the target culture.

How to Read a Culturally Different Book?

To return translation to its rightful place, its readers need to be aware that there are areas and aspects of the source text that remain in the dark, hence unavailable to them. They probably need to accept that there are aspects of the source text which are not conveyed by the translation, and acknowledge their existence in another culture and other circumstances. On the other hand, for readers of translation to acknowledge that what they see is no more than the partial truth means admitting imperfect knowledge, and it takes not only honesty, but also courage, because in our "developed" world dominated by an information economy, knowledge constitutes power.

Indeed translation studies since the 1990s has emphasised translation as an institution plagued with the interplay of different powers rather than as a purely linguistic activity. Specifically, colonial and post-colonial translation activities are understood by Tejaswini Niranjana as a field where displacement, power negotiation and transfer take place. (Niranjana 1992:2) Apart from the necessary linguistic and cultural non-equivalence between a source text and its translation, she highlights a text being "displaced" in translation. Translation necessarily implies reception within another framework, alternative from the one from which the source text is generated. She is particularly critical of the result of such displacement of colonial translation of Indian literature. She describes the phenomenon of colonial elites reading Indian literatures in English such as in the case of young Gandhi as "translation as interpellation" (Niranjana 1992: 11). Indian history and Indian cultural experience is being recontextualised in the colonial language before it is being told to the colonised themselves. The knowledge about their own culture and history is mediated by the language and culture of their colonisers.

The politics of intepellation identified by Niranjana is historically particular and is only one example of many politics contexualising translation. Many other translation projects are equally affected by different circumstances. Fundamentally, however, the more widespread problem of power struggle that translation has become entangled with is the representation of a nation, a culture, or a people, to foreigners. In the globalised academia and book market of our contemporary era, literature's participation in the international arena directly affects its prospects for development. Yet international participation hardly comes without a price. Texts are now being represented by agents, a phenomenon beyond the writers' own control. As David Damrosch observes, it is the norms of the target system that "profoundly shape" the translation and circulation of foreign texts (Damrosch 2003: 26). The selection and methods of translation of foreign texts depend heavily on how well the finished products will fit into a new cultural space. Damrosch locates the targeted cultural space as an international readership for the category of writing he calls "world literature", a concept often traced back to Goethe's coinage of *Weltliteratur* in 1827 in a conversation with his young friend Johann Peter Eckermann. Damrosch has noted and adopted a modern twist given by Guillén to Goethe's vague and utopian concept, that is, in order to be qualified as World Literature, a text does not only have to be read beyond home, but also has to enter into mainstream circulation and be "actively present within a literary system beyond that of its original culture" (Damrosch 2003: 4). Here, Even-Zohar's theories of Transfer and Polysystem are evoked. This makes norms in the target system the overriding factor in translation and transfer, and also manipulation in the process of translation even more powerful in his model of World Literature. Consistent with this train of thought, Damrosch repeatedly stresses that a text manifests different things at home and abroad.

However, a curious contradiction arises in Damrosch's theory. On the one hand he takes a piece of Chinese Tang poetry as an example to invalidate the imposition of unsuitable models of reading. In his opinion, "even carefully scholarly attempts to read a foreign work in the light of Western critical theory are deeply problematic". But on the other hand, he contends that "looking at such new contexts [of reception], the generalists will find much of the specialist's information about the work's origins is no longer relevant and not only can but should be set aside" (Damrosch 2003: 287). I have no intention of advocating the tyranny of authenticity or indigenous ownership of a text. But to eradicate in one stroke any relevance of the meaning(s) generated by a text in its original context appears to be a somewhat simplistic mode of reading, to put it mildly. Surely there is room for a more responsible mode of reading, and at the very least one can nurture an awareness of possible different readings, especially at the homebase of the text. Damrosch does not seem to see the need to challenge institutionalisation of what Lawrence Venuti calls the "invisibility" of translation (Venuti 1995). Damrosch suggests that "to use translations means to accept the reality that texts come to us mediated by existing frameworks of reception and interpretation. We necessarily work in collaboration with others who have shaped what we read and how we read it" (Damrosch 2003: 295). It is a pity if the awareness of the truth of translation as non-equivalence only results in indiscriminate "acceptance" and in deeming specialist knowledge on the text irrelevant. If translation is used in this way to prompt amnesia, it is made to function as the accomplice of violent appropriation. In such case, translation does not forge communication, but promotes arrogant disrespect for other subjectivities. It then makes the world of a translation reader smaller rather than bigger. But this is not the only way of translating or reading a translation. There is much translators can do to prompt their readers' awareness of the possibility of understanding their texts in other frameworks. Kwame A. Appiah and Theo Hermans both support "thick translation", meaning context-based translation, of concepts practiced mostly in academic translation (Appiah 2000; Hermans 2003). Their theories are further elaborated and put into practice by Martha Cheung in her translation of discourses on translation in China (Cheung 2004, 2006). After all, the modes of translation come down to the (man-made) parameters allowed for each text-type and personal choice made by individual translators.

Also dealing with World Literature, Christopher Prendergast calls for a mode of reading that is both dialectical and historicising. He places World Literature within our context of globalisation rather than taking it as a transcendental utopian endeavour, and examines how the idea is contested from different perspectives. He points out that what he calls a literary "international *rendezvous*" does not "necessarily constitute a polite get-together" (Prendergast 2004: 4). He is much more sensitive to the sentiments of the "being read" and concludes that "in today's conditions, we are more likely to break up and diversify this story [of World

Literature] and its subjects according to the plurality of human cultures" (Prendergast 2004: 3). In a cultural space where diversity is given its place, translation will play a role much more progressive that than conceded by Damrosch. In fact the improved means of communication is making our world increasingly complicated and we are finding grids of reception framework superimposed upon one another in different media channels. Translation can be taken as points of reference for different interpretations substantiated by different structures of reception. It can serve as a reminder rather than an erasure of difference. Perhaps it is only now, so many years after the appearance of his article, that Walter Benjamin's wish to see translations juxtaposed with one another on the same reading horizon to make up a vision of universal language can be finally seen as critical rather than utopian. A dialectical and historicising mode of reading is needed not only for textual translation but also for cultural translation including transfer of writing and thinking, and even behavioural paradigms between cultures. It is only when we acknowledge differences and incongruities that we begin to really see each other, rather than seeing the image of ourselves everywhere.

Let us now return to the adventure of Gao Xingjian's literary repertoire. How do we understand his works within the frameworks of World Literature, and of literary and translation politics? It is important to note that the most significant reception of his later works is through their translation. While the translations are being canonised in the Western literary system by the Nobel Prize, the effect has not made a significant rebound back to the Chinese literary polysystem, the cultural homebase of the language in which Gao's works are written. The Chinese ban on his works remains in place; his Chinese readership remains limited. In fact, it is the translation of his works into English that has become most active since the author was awarded the prize. His works still operate mostly in translation, existing as shadows of their own figures. There are unavoidable discrepancies between the cultural framework of the production of these Chinese language texts and the reception framework of the translation. One (mis)reading that is symptomatic of this discrepancy is the diverse interpretations of the sense of alienation the exiled subject experiences in many of Gao's later works, which has already been discussed in Chapter Seven of this book. Most of these works talks about China as a distant entity, either in the near past when the narrative is about the Cultural Revolution, or in the ancient past, when China is embodied in myths and legends. When the reading of these works takes place in the West within the Western cultural systems, where China is a distant entity, the narrative subject would seem to be very much *in situ*, rather than displaced. The cause of the exilic alienation is therefore being suppressed. This decontextualised alienation is then conveniently recuperated into the Existentialist discourse of the French and European polysystems. The circumstantial alienation expressed in these texts is interpreted as something fundamental to human existence. What is more, this can be interpreted as an Existentialism "with Chinese characteristics". It therefore valorises the universality of this branch of philosophy the West has embraced. It nurtures a comfortable illusion of seeing the Other in the image of Oneself.

In an interview with the BBC shortly after being awarded the Nobel Prize, Gao said:

> To some extent, I'm disappearing as a person and becoming a symbol. Of course this symbol is what a lot of Chinese people having been wishing for. People see it as an affirmation of Chinese writers or Chinese literature, or of the Chinese people. (BBC Interview 2001)

It is true that Gao has disappeared as a person and become a symbol, but not in quite the way he suggests in his speech. What is being celebrated is not Chinese literature, but a repertoire of Chinese writing Gallicised, made to fit into a Western image of "good" Chinese literature. Sadly Gao has once again been used as a chess piece in political games, a situation which he has tried so hard to evade. This time, the politics is one of representation. In his Nobel lecture, he emphasises his writings as personal, individual and autonomous. But the fact is that once they are published, they are placed in the public sphere, subject to use and manipulation by all kinds of forces and powers. One might find it illuminating to read against this background the intense emotion invested in the condemnation of commercialism and consumerism dominating art and the avant-garde in his latest play *Kouwen siwang* [Seeker of death] (2004; French title by Gao as *Le Quêteur de la mort*; translated into English as *The Man Who Questions Death* by Gilbert Fong, 2007). In this play, a man is locked in a modern art museum and meets the personification of death. The two characters debate the purpose and meaning of first modern art, and then life. A decontextualised reading of the play would simply assert that it reiterates the point made by various art theorists on how the avant-garde has been tamed by a contemporary commercialism and a consumerist popular culture that is devoid of critical awareness. But if it is mapped onto the crisis of Gao's writings being recuperated into the politics of representation in the arena of so-called World Literature, the play has the potential to generate a more specific and profound reading. Yet, similar to other plays Gao has written since the mid 1990s, ideas are spoken as abstract concepts and the dramatic situation is presented as transcendental and fundamental to the human condition. Once again, a potentially acute critique is tamed because the particular conditions that trigger the critique are not explored in the text.

A descriptive study of Gao's works should probably stop here. Yet one cannot but be intrigued by the peculiar pattern that has been developed in these works in which the object of critique is always absent. Is it a case of deliberate avoidance to mimic the situation in which the individual does not possess a comprehensive understanding of his own situation? Or are his works the very expression of a passionate soul who is suffering the emotional consequence of a situation he himself does not comprehend? Or could it be a cynically clever writing strategy to shun the commitment of passing judgment on the situation? There is no point speculating on intention, but I would say that a reading of these texts taking into account all contextual information, in other words, a non-reductive reading, makes the reading a more rewarding experience.

As a final remark, what lesson can be gained from the experience of reading Gao's *oeuvre*? Our condition of reading today is one informed by globalisation. An important question we need to ask ourselves as readers is identical to the title of Gayatri Spivak's article, "How to read a culturally different book?" (Spivak 1994). It may be wise to follow Prendergast's advice to be sensitive to the subjectivities of the "being read" and to do the decent thing, which is to acknowledge and respect the diversity of human conditions. Does it therefore mean there is no viability in the concept of a World Literature? This would depend entirely on how one imagines such a designation. Any attempt to select and collect all the "great" works in the world on the part of a single agent and to bring them together in a space it creates, be it the Roman Empire or the United States, would be highly suspect. One always needs to historicise projects, be they creative or critical. One might argue that it is exactly in the era of globalisation that certain conditions of life are shared among people of previously diametrically different cultures. This, however, is only a partial truth. No doubt Western Capitalism has spread its influence across the globe, but not everybody occupies an equal position in the world's economic and political interplay. Different nations, and different groups of people within a nation, relate differently and perform differently under the situation of globalisation. Thus, in the reading of a culturally different book, if one pays attention to difference, it will be a more rewarding experience, for both the reading subject and the one being read.

The central issue, therefore, does not depend on whether we have, or want, a World Literature. The issue is whether people read as "world readers". The corollary is therefore in the mode of reading. Good readers have the ability to follow the numerous linguistic and structural innuendos of a narrative and go out towards the unfamiliar world presented in a text. They are able to, or at least make an effort to, establish empathy with unfamiliar "Others". Translators and publishers have much to offer in preparing for this kind of "world reading". They can provide footnotes, para-textual material, thick translation, or simply make the translators visible. These practices have to be encouraged. Sometimes they might retard smooth reading, but if smooth reading implies regressive consumerist superficial reading, one should not want to facilitate it in the first place. Indeed this is equally true of the need for historicised, sophisticated reading of unfamiliar, older works within one's own cultural parameters.

Ultimately there is a lesson to learn from the variegated reception of Gao's writing. In its commendation the Swedish Academy appreciates these works within its own framework of literary criticism which aspires to be, but falls short of being, universal, as the negative reception of this award to Gao from various Chinese literary circles attests. On the other hand, many radically negative comments on Gao's works see no value of Chinese literature except as a manifestation of nationalism. These readings too have failed to acknowledge other frameworks of reception. Indeed neither of these two perspectives facilitates sufficient understanding of Gao's works. As cultural translations his early works are produced between frameworks, between the Realist and the Modernist. Those works engage with both and therefore need to be read in relation to both simultaneously. As exile writing his later works are also produced between two frameworks, namely China (the past, memory) and France (the present, reality). But these latter works do not engage with either, therefore end up being neither here nor there. They also need to be read in relation to both frameworks simultaneously. Readers today are empowered by Deconstruction Theory to conceptualise space between locations. "World readers" who are able to read beyond a single framework would not be sufficiently gullible to take Gao's latter writings as celebrations of political and spiritual trancedence, nor would they see them only as literary consumables, tailor-made for the globalised market. Instead, they will find it possible to read those works as expressions of a diasporic subject who is unable to relate to either past or present, as utterances that fall between discourses, as ink dances in limbo.

Notes

CHAPTER 1

1. Gao started to get published in 1979. His only publication in that year was the first part of the novella *Hanye de xingchen* [Stars on a cold night]. The second part was published in the second issue of the same journal in 1980. His essay *"Guanyu Ba Jin de chuanshua"* [Hearsay about Ba Jin] was published in *Huacheng* (Guangzhou), No. 6, 1980, although it is listed in some biographies of Gao under 1979.

2. One example is Richard Freeman's description of the "translation" of the British National Health Service into other societies. Each country has made adjustments to the service so that it fits into the social structure of that country. (Freeman 2002) Another example is noted by John Sallis. The term *Übertragung* in psychoanalysis is rendered into "translation", making the point that dream-content is a translation [*Übertragung*] of the dream-thought into another expression. (Sallis 2002: 7–8).

3. As mentioned earlier, some earlier Chinese writings have already shown influences of European Modernism. Marvelous critical works on the early instances of Modernism in Chinese literature in May Fourth writings have been produced by scholars including Leo Ou-fan Lee, David Der-Wei Wang and Gregory B. Lee on the works they have identified as Modernist by writers such as Lu Xun, Dai Wangshu, and urban writers in Shanghai such as Liu Na'ou, Shi Zhecun and Mu Shiying. Across the Taiwan Strait, Chen Yingzhen, among other critics, has also written on early Modernist writings in Taiwan. Gao's writings are definitely not the first instance of Modernism in Chinese literature, but they are the first of such attempts after the Cultural Revolution. In this way they represent something "new".

CHAPTER 2

1. It is important to differentiate between Gorkian Socialist Realism and Mao's later revision of it. Mao's 1942 "Talks at the Yan'an Conference on Literature and Art" document laid down the main rule of Maoist revolutionary writing. It stipulates that

revolutionary literature should be easy to read, and should mirror reality. It should not contain difficult literary devices, so that the majority of people could understand and enjoy it. This idea was then escalated to function as criteria for censorship from the 1950s onwards, which dominated the arts and literature until the early 1980s.

2. The term refers to people returning to positions from which they had been removed during the Cultural Revolution.

3. They are: "*Bali guanju suibi*" (Notes on Parisian theatre), "*Nisi — weilanse de yinxiang*" (*Nice — a blue impression*), "*Bali yingxiangji*" (*My impressions of Paris*), "*Bajin zai bali*" (*Ba Jin in Paris*), "*Yidali suixiangqu*" (*An Italian rhapsody*) and "*Menghai — shi de sanwen*" (*Dreaming of the sea — a poetic prose piece*). See Bibliography for publication details.

4. It is possible to argue that the selection of material to be described already constitutes an interpretation of the external reality, but this is not the position adopted in Gao's article.

5. They are Chapters 4, 5, 6, 7, 8, 9 and 16. They are also arranged in the right chronological order in terms of their dates of publication.

6. There is no numbering for the chapters in the book. The numbers are added here for convenience in discussion.

7. There are no intertextual studies which compare their translation and creative work to date, although such studies would bring important insights for translation studies. The main difficulty for such a study would be to identify the titles they have translated and to isolate their translation from the editing imposed on the texts. The only way may be to obtain manuscripts from the translators/writers themselves. But the possibility of acquiring such material is low because in most cases there are no copies of their translation as they were handwritten at a time when the computer was not available to every translator.

8. Leo Ou-fan Lee has given a comprehensive analysis of the relationship between literary experiments and ideological dissidence in this period in an article entitled "The Politics of Techniques: Perspectives of Literary Dissidence in Contemporary Chinese Fiction" (1985).

CHAPTER 3

1. Bradbury and McFarlane, among other critics, have given a very comprehensive account of Modernism of this strand in their seminal work *Modernism — A Guide to European Literature 1890–1930*.

2. According to Terry Siu-han Yip's chronology (2001), this piece was completed in July 1982, although it was not published until 1984.

3. This was a spontaneous movement that took place in the mid 1980s of cultural reflection by academics, artists, writers and the media. Many of their works adopt highly critical attitudes towards traditional Han-Confucian culture and attribute the unsatisfactory development of the nation to this cultural mode. For details see Han Shaogong, "*Wenxue de 'gen'*" [The 'roots' of literature] (1985); Ah Cheng, "*Wenhua zhiyue zhe renlei*" [Man conditioned by culture] (1985); Chen Sihe, "*Dangdai wenxue zhong de wenhua xungen yishi*" [The conscious search for cultural roots in contemporary literature] (1986) and Li Shulei, "*Cong xunmeng dao xungeng*" [From the search for dreams to the search for roots] (1986).

CHAPTER 4

1. Studies on formal features of these plays have been done by Ma Sen (1989), William Tay (1990), Li Jianyi (1991), Xiaomei Chen (1995), Kwok-kan Tam (2001), and Quah Sy Ren (2004).
2. Run Sheng (1983) and Qu Liuyi (1984) have written comprehensive summaries on the debates on these two plays.
3. A useful reference on the accusations against Gao is his article *"Geri huanghua"* (1992; translated into English as "Wilted Chrysanthemums" by Mabel Lee, 2007).
4. All translations of names in *Bus Stop* are taken from Geremie Barmé's translation of the play.
5. All translations of names and extracts of *Alarm Signal* are taken from Shiao-Ling S. Yu's translation of the play.
6. In Roubicek's translation, *Liang duizhang*, literary Team Leader Liang, is changed to "Leader Zhang".
7. For detailed analysis of the formal features of Gao's play, see Quah, Sy Ren (2004).
8. Gao has in many occasions explained his intention for this kind of alienation. For a detailed study of theatrical devices in Gao's play, see Quah (2004).

CHAPTER 5

1. Torbjörn Lodén summarises the six creative tenets of *Soul Mountain* into: 1. The recreation of a literary language; 2. Alienation; 3. Primitivism; 4. Anti-Confucianism; 5. Scepticism; and 6. Chinese and western myths (Lodén, 2001: 268–272).
2. Pascale Casanova in her book *The World Republic of Letters* also uses the expression "Translated Men". There she refers to authors who are read in dominant languages through translation, self-translation or adopting a foreign language in their writings. (Casanova 2004: 206) My use of the expression here is related but different.

CHAPTER 6

1. The article was published later in the same year in *Mingbao Monthly* in Hong Kong with the new title *"Guojia shenhua yu geren diankuang"*, literally "The myth of the nation and insanity of the individual".
2. For a detailed description of the formal features of Gao's plays, also see Quah, 2004.
3. According to Yip's chronology, this play was written in Beijing in 1987 (Yip 2001:321).
4. The story of Zhuangzi testing his wife's fidelity has not made any appearance in any biography of the philosopher or in his own writing. Apparently he is used as the protagonist of this story because his writing about confusions of identity in his famous writing about "Butterfly Dream" in *"Qiwu"* [Unity with the Cosmos] is associated with the omnipotence of the husband in controlling life and death and in assuming a double identity to test his wife.

CHAPTER 7

1. One of the criticisms most representative of this position is by Aijaz Ahmad (Ahmad 1994: 95–122).
2. This episode coincides with the events narrated in Gao's early short story "You Must Stay Alive".

3. The comparable circumstances of these two characters are also observed in K. K. Tam's analysis of the novel (Tam 2001: 299).

4. On the other hand, cultural and economic domination has taken another form in the "West". It is so enmeshed in consumerism and the overpowering ideologies of "progress" and "development" that it becomes very difficult to recognise. Perhaps this is why different literatures speak about coercion in different ways.

5. This is a Chinese poetic device of repetition of the same word to produce special sound effects. In Li Qingzhao's verse, seven consecutive pairs of reiterative locution are applied to open the verse. Lin Yutang's brilliant translation entitled *Forlorn* recreates in the opening lines not the same but equally interesting sound effects:

   "So dim, so dark,
   so dense, do dull,
   so damp, so dank,
   so dead!"

6. In the 2003 Hong Kong production of the play by No Man's Land Theatre Company directed by Tang Shu-wing, the nun played by Lindzay Chan was placed right in the middle of the second level of the two-tiered stage at least 10 feet above the stage floor. Strong lights were cast on her acting out the mime gestures of splitting her belly, taking out the intestines and washing them. Awesome facial expressions of pains and joy merging together to render a most striking stage image.

7. This character is identified as *jinü*, "prostitute", in the play.

8. However, in the French script, speeches are designated as belonging to individual actors/characters.

9. A comprehensive review on the monk figures in Gao's plays in this period is found in Huang Meixu's article "*Shitan Gao Xingjian xiju zhong de chandao renwu*" [A preliminary investigation on the Buddhist and Taoist monk figures in Gao Xingjian's plays].

10. Literary critic Henry Zhao has elaborated on the Buddhist and Zen themes in Gao's plays written in the 1990s and propounded the theory of them being a kind of Zen/*Xieyi* Theatre (Zhao, 2000).

11. The journal was first published in 1978 but suspended in 1980 in Beijing. It was later revived in Stockholm by diasporic writers living there including Chen Maiping and others. Before internet journals became widespread and easily accessible, *Jintian* remained the most important periodical airing works by writers in exile who were not read in China anymore.

CHAPTER 8

1. One example of such a view is Nie Hualing's response to Gao's being awarded the Nobel Prize when interviewed by a magazine. Nie, as a writer herself and co-founder of the International Writing Programme of University of Iowa, is extremely experienced and knowledgeable in the promotion of international writings. She suggests the award to Gao "shows the importance of translation" (Chen Haoquan 2000: 14).

Gao's Works Cited

Gao, Xingjian (1979). *Hanye de xingchen* [Stars on a cold night]. *Huacheng*. No. 3, pp. 146–218.

—— (1980b). "*Falanxi xiandai wenxue de tongku*" [The agony of Modern French literature]. *Waiguo wenxue yanjiu* [Foreign literature studies]. No. 1, pp. 51–7.

—— (1980c). "*Faguo dangdai wenxue de yige zhuti – zhuiqiu: ping liangpian faguo duanpian xiaoshuo*" [A theme in contemporary French literature – quest: on two French short stories]. *Shiyue* [October]. No. 3, pp. 249–51.

—— (1980d). "*Faguo xiandaipai renmin shiren Puliewei'er he ta de Geciji*" [The French Modernist poet Prévert and his *Paroles*]. *Huacheng*. No. 5, pp. 221–5.

—— (1980e). "*Ni yiding yao huozhe*" [You must stay alive]. In *Gei wo laoye mei yugan* [Buying a fishing rod for my grandfather] (1989), pp. 12–36.

—— (1981a). *Xiandai xiaoshuo jiqiao chutan* [A preliminary exploration of the techniques of modern fiction]. Guangdong: *Huacheng chubanshe* [Huacheng press].

—— (1981b). "*Youzhi gezi jiao hongchunr*" [A pigeon called Red Beak]. *Shouhuo* [Harvest]. No. 1, pp. 205–54.

—— (1981c). "*Pengyou*" [Friends]. In *Gei wo laoye mai yugan* [Buying a fishing rod for my grandfather] (1989), pp. 1–11.

—— (1981d). "*Yu, xue ji qita*" [Rain, snow and other things]. In *Gei wo laoye mai yugan* [Buying a fishing rod for my grandfather] (1989), pp. 37–54.

—— (1982a). *Juedui xinhao* [Alarm signal]. In *Gao Xingjian xiju ji* [Collection of plays by Gao Xingjian] (1985), pp. 11–83.

—— (1982b). "*Lushang*" [On the road]. In *Gei wo laoye mai yugan*. [Buying a fishing rod for my grandfather] (1989), pp. 55–66.

—— (1982c). "*Ershiwu nian hou*" [Twenty-five years later]. In *Gei wo laoye mai yugan* [Buying a fishing rod for my grandfather] (1989), pp. 67–75.

—— (1983a). "*Xiejiang he tade nü'er*" [Shoemaker and his daughter]. In *Gei wo laoye mai yugan* [Buying a fishing rod for my grandfather] (1989), pp. 95–100.

—— (1983b) *Chezhan* [Bus stop]. In *Gao Xingjian xiju ji* [Collection of plays by Gao Xingjian] (1985), pp. 84–135.

—— (1983c). *"Yuen'en si"* [Yuan'en Temple]. In *Gei wo laoye mai yugan* [Buying a fishing rod for my grandfather] (1989), pp. 144–54.

—— (1984a). *Xiandai Zhezixi* [Sketches of modern *xiqu*]. In *Gao Xingjian xiju ji* [Collection of plays by Gao Xingjian] (1985), pp. 136–86.

—— (1984b). *"Huadou"* [Huadou]. *Renmin wenxue* [People's literature]. No. 9, pp. 19–32.

—— (1985a). *Dubai* [Monologue]. *Xinjuben* [New playscripts]. No. 1, pp. 85–90.

—— (1985b). *Yeren* [Wild man]. *Shiyue* [October]. No. 2, pp. 142–69.

—— (1985c). *Gao Xingjian xiju ji* [Collection of plays by Gao Xingjian]. Beijing: *Qunzhong chubanshe* [The masses press].

—— (1985d). *"Chehuo"* [An accident]. In *Gei wolaoye mai yugan* [Buying a fishing rod for my grandfather] (1989), pp. 224–35.

—— (1986a). *Gei wo laoye mai yugan* [Buying a fishing rod for my grandfather]. In *Gei wo laoye mai yugan* [Buying a fishing rod for my grandfather] (1989), pp. 241–59.

—— (1986b). *Bi'an* [The other shore]. *Shiyue* [October]. No. 5, pp. 238–51.

—— (1987a). *Mingcheng* [Nether city]. *Nüxingren* [Female people]. Oct, pp. 204–29.

—— (1987b). *Shengshengman bianzou* [Variations on the Song Dynasty verse Shengshengman]. In *Zhoumo sichongzou* [Weekend quartet] (1996), pp. 89–94.

—— (1989). *Gei wo laoye mai yugan* [Buying a fishing rod for my grandfather]. Taipei: Unitas Press.

—— (1990a). *Taowang* [Fugitives]. *Jintian* [Today]. No. 1, pp. 41–64.

—— (1990b). *Lingshan* [Soul mountain]. Taipei: *Lianjing wenxue chubanshe youxian gongsi* [Lianjing literature press Co. Ltd.].

—— (1991a). *Shengsijie* [Between life and death]. In *Gao Xingjian xiju liuzhong: di wu ji* [Six plays by Gao Xingjian: Vol. 5] (1995), pp. 1–42.

—— (1991b). *"Wenxue yu xuanxue – guanyu Lingshan"* [Literature and Metaphysics – about *Soul mountain*]. A paper delivered at Institute for Oriental Languages, University of Stockholm, January, 1991.

—— (1991c). *Shunjian* [In an instant]. *Zhongshi wanbao* [China evening times], 1/9/1991.

—— (1992a). *"Geri huanghua"* [Yesterday's blossoms]. In *Meiyou zhuyi* [No-isms] (2000), pp. 158–66.

—— (1992b). *"Xu"* [Preface]. In Lao Hong. *Luowu dai* [The generation of naked dance]. Tainan: *Wenhua shenghuo xinzhi chubanshe* [New knowledge for a cultural life press], pp. 1.

—— (1992c). *"Wenxue yu xuanxue – guanyu 'Lingshan'* [Literature and Metaphysics – about *Soul Mountain*]. *Jintian* [Today]. No.3, pp. 203–15.

—— (1993a). *"Guojia shenhua yu geren diankuang"* [The myth of the nation and insanity of the individual]. *Ming Pao Monthly*. Aug, pp. 114–7.

—— (1993b). *Shanhaijing zhuan* [Stories in the books of mountains and seas]. Hong Kong: Cosmos Books.

—— (1993c). *Yeyoushen* [Nocturnal Wanderer]. In *Gao Xingjian xiju liuzhong: di wu ji* [Six plays by Gao Xingjian: Vol. 5] (1995), pp. 47–122.

—— (1993d). *"Meiyou zhuyi"* [No-isms]. In *Meiyou zhuyi* [No-isms] (2000), pp. 1–6.

—— (1993e). *Duihua yu fanjie: Gao Xingjian xiju liuzhong: di liu ji* [Dialogue and Rebuttal: Six plays by Gao Xingjian: Vol. 6] (1995). Taipei: *Dijiao chubanshe* [Dijiao press].

—— (1995) *Gao Xingjian xiju liuzhong* [Six plays by Gao Xingjian]. Taipei: *Dijiao chubanshe* [Dijiao press].

—— (1996). *Zhoumo sichongzou* [Weekend quartet]. Hong Kong: New Century Publishing.

—— (1998). "*Xiandai hanyu yu wenxue xiezuo*" [Modern Chinese language and literary writing]. *Hong Kong Drama Review*. No. 1, pp. 147–59.

—— (1999). *Yigeren di shengjing* [One man's bible]. Taipei: *Lianjing wenxue chubanshe youxian gongsi* [Lianjing literature press Co. Ltd.].

—— (2000). *Meiyou zhuyi* [No-isms]. Hong Kong: Cosmos Books Ltd.

—— (2000a). *Bayuexue* [Snow in August]. Taipei: *Lianjing wenxue chubanshe youxian gongsi* [Lianjing literature press Co. Ltd.].

—— (2001). *Yeren* [Wild Man]. Taipei: Unitas Publishing Co. Ltd.

—— (2004). *Kouwen siwang* [Seeker of death]. Taipei: *Lianjing wenxue chubanshe youxian gongsi* [Lianjing literature press Co. Ltd.].

English Translations of Gao's works cited (arranged by chronological order of publication, under names of translators):

Ng, Mau-sang trans. (1983). "Contemporary Technique and National Character in Fiction". *Renditions*. No. 19 and 20, pp. 55–8.

Barmé, Geremie trans. (1983). *The Bus-stop. Renditions*. No. 19 and 20, pp. 379–86.

Roubicek, Bruno trans. (1990). *Wild Man: A Contemporary Chinese Spoken Drama. Asian Theatre Journal*. Vol. 7, No. 2 (Fall), pp. 184–249.

Lee, G. B. trans. (1993). *Fugitives*. In *Chinese Writing and Exile*. G. B. Lee ed. (1993). Illinois: The Centre for East Asian Studies, The University of Chicago, pp. 89–138.

Aspfors, Lena and Lodén, Torbjörn trans. (1995). "The Voice of the Individual". *Stockholm Journal of East Asian Studies*. No. 6, pp. 71–81.

Yu, Shaio-ling, S. trans. (1996). *Alarm Signal*. In *Chinese Drama after the Cultural Revolution, 1979-1989: An Anthology*. Shaio-ling S. Yu ed. (1996). New York: The Edwin Mellen Press, pp. 159–289.

Yu, Shaio-ling, S. trans. (1996). *The Bus Stop*. In Shaio-ling S. Yu ed. (1996), pp. 233–91.

Riley, Jo trans. (1997). *The Other Side*. In *An Oxford Anthology of Contemporary Chinese Drama*. Martha Cheung and Jane Lai eds. (1997). Oxford: Oxford University Press, pp. 149-184.

Besio, Kimberly trans. (1998). *Bus Stop: A lyrical comedy on life in one act*. In *Theatre and Society: An Anthology of Contemporary Chinese Drama*. Haiping Yan ed. (1998). London: M.E. Sharpe, pp. 3–59.

Fong, Gilbert trans. (1999). *The Other Shore*. In *The Other Shore* (1999). Hong Kong: The Chinese University Press, pp. 1–44.

—— trans. (1999). *Between Life and Death*. In *The Other Shore* (1999), pp. 45–80.

—— trans. (1999). *Dialogue and Rebuttal*. In *The Other Shore* (1999), pp. 81–136.

—— trans. (1999). *Nocturnal Wanderer*. In *The Other Shore* (1999), pp. 137–90.

—— trans. (1999). *Weekend Quartet*. In *The Other Shore* (1999), pp. 191–254.

Lee, Mabel trans. (2000). *Soul Mountain*. New York: HarperCollins Publishers.

Lee, Mabel trans. (2002). *One Man's Bible*. New York: Perennial.

Fong, Gilbert trans. (2003). *Snow in August*. Hong Kong: The Chinese University Press.

Lee, Mabel trans. (2004). "The Temple". In *Buying a Fishing Rod for My Grandfather* (2004). New York: HarperCollins Publishers, pp. 1–16.

—— trans. (2004). "In the Park". In *Buying a Fishing Rod for My Grandfather* (2004), pp. 17–32.

—— trans. (2004). "Cramp". In *Buying a Fishing Rod for My Grandfather.* (2004), pp. 33–42.

—— trans. (2004). "The Accident". In *Buying a Fishing Rod for My Grandfather* (2004), pp. 43–60.

—— trans. (2004). "Buying a Fishing Rod for My Grandfather". In *Buying a Fishing Rod for My Grandfather* (2004), pp. 61–88.

—— trans. (2004). "In an Instant". In *Buying a Fishing Rod for My Grandfather* (2004), pp. 89–122.

—— trans. (2007). "Literature and Metaphysics: About *Soul Mountain*". In *The Case for Literature* (2004). New York: HarperCollins Publishers, pp. 82–103.

—— trans. (2007). "The Voice of the Individual". In *The Case for Literature* (2004), pp. 126–39.

—— trans. (2007). "Wilted Chrysanthemums". In *The Case for Literature* (2004), pp. 126–39.

Bibliography

Adorno, Theodor and Horkheimer, Max (1986). *Dialectic of Enlightenment*. J. Cumming trans. London: Verso.

Ah Cheng (1985). "*Wenhua zhiyue zhe renlei*" [Man conditioned by culture]. In *Wenyibao* [Literature and arts post], 6 July 1985, p. 2.

Ahmad, Aijaz (1994). *In Theory: Classes, Nations, Literatures*. London, New York: Verso.

Álvarez, Román and Vidal, M. Carmen-África eds. (1996). *Translation, Power, Subversion*. Clevedon, Philadelphia, Adelaide: Multilingual Matters Ltd.

Apollonio, Umbro ed. (1973). *Futurist Manifestos*. Robert Brain et al trans. London: Thames and Hudson.

Appiah, Kwame Anthony (2000). "Thick Translation". In Lawrence Venuti ed. (2002), pp. 417–429.

Apter, Emily (2004). "Global Translatio: The 'Invention' of Comparative Literature, Istanbul, 1933". In Christopher Prendergast ed. (2004), pp. 76–109.

Artaud, Antonin (1977). *The Theatre and Its Double*. V. Corti trans. London: John Calder.

Barker, Francis, Hume, Peter and Iversen, Margaret eds. (1994). *Colonial Discourse / Postcolonial Theory*. Manchester: Manchester University Press.

Baker, Mona ed. (2000). *Routledge Encyclopedia of Translation Studies*. London and New York: Routledge.

Bakhtin, Mikhail (1984). *Rabelais and His World*. Helene Iswolsky trans. Bloomington: Indianna University Press.

—— (1985). *Problems of Dostoyevsky's Poetics*. C. Emerson ed. and trans. Minneapolis: University of Minnesota Press.

—— (1986). *Speech Genres and Other Late Essays*. C. Emerson and M. Holquist, M. eds. V. W. McGee trans. Austin: University of Texas Press.

Baoweng Laoren ed. (1992). *Jingu qiguan* [Marvelous stories of ancient and modern times]. Beijing: *Renmin wenxue chubanshe* [People's literature press].

Barmé, Geremie and Lee, Bennett eds. and trans.(1979). *The Wounded: New Stories of the Cultural Revolution*. Hong Kong: Joint Publishing Co.

BBC Interview with Gao Xingjian. On-line article: http://www.bbc.co.uk/worldservice/arts/highlights/010316-xingian.shtml

Beckett, Samuel (1972). *Our Examination round his Factification for Incamination of Work in Progress*. London: Faber and Faber.

—— (1972). *Waiting for Godot*. London: French.

Besemeres, Mary (2003). "Cultural Translation and the Translingual Self in the Memoirs of Edward Said and André Acimen". In Magda Stroinska and Vittorina Cecchetto eds. (2003), pp. 19–32.

Bergson, Henri (1971). *Time and Freewill: an Essay on the Immediate Data of Consciousness*. F. L. Pogson trans. London: George Allen and Unwin.

—— (2004). *Matter and Memory*. Nancy Margaret Paul and W. Scott Palmer trans. New York: Dover Publication.

Bradbury, Malcolm and McFarlane, James eds. (1976). *Modernism: A Guide to European Literature 1890–1930*. Harmondsworth: Penguin Books.

Breytenbach, Breyten (1985). "Letter from Exile". In John Simpson ed. (1995), pp. 229–230.

Brook, Peter (1972). *The Empty Space*. Harmondsworth: Pelican Book.

Budick, Sanford and Iser, Wolfgang eds. (1996). *The Translatability of Cultures*. Stanford: Stanford University Press.

Butler, Judith (1990). *Gender Trouble*. London and New York: Routledge.

Camus, Albert (1954). *The Stranger*. Stuart Gilbert trans. New York: Vintage Books.

—— (1960). *The Plague*. Stuart Gilbert trans. Harmondsworth: Penguin Books.

—— (1975). *The Myth of Sisyphus*. Hamish Hamilton trans. Harmondsworth: Penguin Books.

Carbonell, Ovidio (1996). "The Exotic Space of Cultural Translation". In Román Álvarez and M. Carmen-África Vidal eds. (1996), pp. 79–98.

Casanova, Pascale (2004). *The World Republic of Letters*. M. B. DeBevoise trans. Cambridge, Massachusetts and London: Harvard University Press.

Cassirer, Ernest (1961). *The Philosophy of Symbolic Forms*. R. Manheim trans. New Haven and London: Yale University Press.

Chen, Haoquan (2000). "*Zhuming zuojia kan Gao Xingjian huo Nuojiang*" [Famous writers on Gao Xingjian being awarded the Nobel Prize]. In *Dangdai wenyi* [Contemporary literature and arts]. Dec, p. 14.

Chen, Huiying (1993). "*Fang juzuojia Gao Xingjian*" [An interview with Gao Xingjian the playwright). *Xingdao ribao* (Singtao Daily), 3 November 1993.

Chen, Sihe (1986). "*Dangdai wenxue zhong de wenhua xungen yishi*" [The search for cultural roots in contemporary literature]. In *Wenxue pinglun* [Literary criticism]. No.6, pp. 24–33.

Chen, Xiaomei (1995). *Occidentalism: A Theory of Counter-discourse in Post-Mao China*. New York: Oxford University Press.

Cheung, Martha (2004). "On Thick Translation as a Mode of Cultural Representation". The IATIS Conference, Seoul, Korea, 12 August 2004.

—— (2006). *An Anthology of Chinese Discourse on Translation — from the Earliest Times to the Buddhist Project*. Manchester: St. Jerome.

Chuang Tzu (1964). *Chuang Tzu : Basic Writings.* Burton Watson trans. New York : Columbia University Press.

Cooper, Merian C. and Schoedsack, Ernest B. dirs. (1933). *King Kong.* Hollywood: MGM.

Damrosch, David (2003). *What Is World Literature?* Princeton: Princeton University Press.

Davis, Geoffery V., Marsden, Peter H., Ledent, Bénédicte and Delrez, Marc eds. (2004). *Towards a Transcultural Future: Literature and Society in a 'Post-colonial' World.* Amsterdam and New York: Rodopi.

De Beauvoir, Simone (1987). *The Second Sex.* H.M. Parshley ed. and trans. Harmondsworth: Penguin Books.

Denton, Kirk A. (1996). *Modern Chinese Literary Thought: Writings on Literature, 1893–1945.* Stanford: Stanford University Press.

Dolby, William ed. and trans. (1978). *Eight Chinese Plays from the 13th Century to the Present.* New York: Columbia University Press.

Duoduo (1992). "Meiyou" [There is no]. *Jintian [Today].* No. 2 (1999), pp. 34–36.

Esslin, Martin (1961). *The Theatre of the Absurd.* Harmondsworth: Penguin Books.

Even-Zohar, Itamar (1978). "Translated Literature in the Polysystem". In Lawrence Venuti ed. (2001), pp. 192–197.

—— (1990). "Translation and Transfer". *Poetics Today.* 11:1.

—— (1997). "The Making of Culture Repertoire and the Role of Transfer". *Target.* Vol. 9. No. 2, pp. 355–363.

Fong, Gilbert ed. (2000). *Xin jiyuan de huawen xiju — de'erjie huawen xijujie (xianggang 1998) yantaohui lunwenji* [Chinese language theatre in the new millennium — the second Chinese language theatre festive (Hong Kong 1998) conference proceedings]. Hong Kong: Hong Kong Theatre Association and Hong Kong Theatre Project.

—— (2005). *'Bayuexue — quannengxiju — chan'* [*Snow in August* — total theatre — Zen]. *Hong Kong Drama Review.* No. 5, pp. 375–390.

Fang, Keqiang (1989). "*Xungenzhe: yuanshiqingxiang yu banyuanshizhuyi*" [The searchers of roots: an inclination for nature and semi-primitivism]. *Shanghai wenxue* [Shanghai literature]. No.3, pp. 64–69.

Freeman, Richard (2002). "Transfer as Translation", On-line article: http://www.pol.ed.ac.uk/freeman/workingpapers/transfer_as_translation.pdf

Gan Yang ed. (1989). *Zhongguo dangdai wenhua yishi* [Cultural ideologies in contemporary China]. Hong Kong: Joint Publishing Co.

Gao, Wensheng (1990). *Zhongguo dangdai xiju wenxue shi* [History of contemporary Chinese theatrical writings]. *Guangxi: Guangxi remin chubanshe* [Guangxi people's press].

Gibson, Walter (1977). *Bruegel.* New York and Toronto: Oxford University Press.

Goldblatt, Howard (1990). *Worlds Apart: Contemporary Chinese Writing and Its Audience.* New York: M.E. Sharpe.

Han, Shaogong (1985). "*Wenxue de 'gen'*" [The 'roots' of literature]. *Zuojia* [Writers]. No.4, pp. 2–5.

—— (1992). *Homecoming? And Other Stories.* Martha Cheung trans. Hong Kong: Renditions Press.

Hatim, Basil (2001). *Teaching and Researching Translation.* Harlow: Pearson Education Ltd.

Hegel, Robert E. and Hessney, Richard C. eds. (1985). *The Expression of Self in Chinese Literature.* New York: Columbia University Press.

Hermans, Theo (2003). "Cross-cultural Translation Studies as Thick Translation". *Bulletin of SOAS*, Vol. 66. No. 3, pp. 380–389.

Hironobu, Sakaguchi dir. (2001). *Final Fantasy*. Hollywood: Columbia Pictures.

Hsu, Tao-ching (1985). *The Chinese Conception of the Theatre*. Seattle: University of Washington Press.

Huang, Meixu (2000). "*Shitan Gao Xingjian xiju zhong de chandao renwu*" [A preliminary investigation on the Zen and Buddhist monk figures in Gao Xingjian's plays]. In Gilbert Fong ed. (2000), pp. 296–309.

—— (2005). "*Cong Fang Zixun di 'Bayuexue — quannengxiju — chan' tanqi*" A discussion after Gilbert Fong's "*Snow in August* — total theatre — Zen"]. *Hong Kong Drama Review*. No. 5, pp. 391–398.

James, William (1952). *The Principles of Psychology*. Chicago, London, Toronto, Geneva, Sydney, Tokyo: Encyclopaedia Britannica, Inc.

Jameson, Fredric (1986). "Third-world Literature in the Era of Multinational Capitalism". *Social Text*. Fall, pp. 65–88.

—— (2000). *The Jameson Reader*. Michael Hardt and Kathi Weeks eds. Oxford: Blackwell Publishers Ltd.

Jia, Pingwa (1999). *Selected Stories by Jia Pingwa*. Beijing: *Zhongguo wenxue chubanshe* [Chinese literature press].

Jia, Xinmin ed. (1992). *Ershi shiji zhongguo dashi nianbiao* [A chronology of major events in China in the 20th Century]. Beijing: *Remin daxue chubanshe* [People's university press].

Jiang, Qing (1990). "*Chong pi 'Da pi guan'*" [To hack "*To Hack the Coffin*" again]. *Nüxingren* [Female People]. Sept, pp. 147–150.

Jiao, Juyin (1985). *Jiao Juyin xiju sanlun* [Essays on the Theatre by Jiao Juyin]. Beijing: *Zhongguo xiju chubanshe* [China theatre press].

Joyce, James (1939). *Finnegan's Wake*. London : Faber and Faber.

—— (1960). *A Portrait of the Artist as a Young Man*. Harmondsworth: Penguin Books.

Kahler, Erich (1987). *The Inward Turn of Narrative*. Richard and Clara Winton trans. Illionois: Northwest University Press.

Kenny, Dorothy (2000). "Equivalence". In Mona Baker ed. (2000), pp. 77–79.

Kinkley, Jeffrey C. ed. (1985). *After Mao: Chinese Literature and Society 1978–1981*. Cambridge, Mass: Council on East Asian Studies, Harvard University.

Kinney, Anne Behnke (2002). *Traditions of Exemplary Women: A project with translation*. University of Virginia.On-line material: http://etext.virginia.edu/chinese/lienu

Klaudy, Kinga (2000). "Explicitation". In Mona Baker ed. (2000), pp. 80–84.

Lao Hong (1992). *Luowu dai* [The generation of naked dance]. Tainan: *Wenhua shenghuo xinzhi chubanshe* [New knowledge for a cultural life press].

Lao She (1991). *Lao She Quanji* [The Complete Works of Lao She]. Beijing: *Renmin wenxue chubanshe* [People's literature press].

Lee, Alison (1990). *Realism and Power: Postmodern British Fiction*. London and New York: Routledge.

Lee, Gregory B. ed. (1993). *Chinese Writing and Exile*. Illionois: the Centre for East Asian Studies, The University of Chicago.

—— (1996). *Troubadours, Trumpeters, Troubled Makers: Lyricism, Nationalism, and Hybridity in China and Its Others*. Durham, N.C.: Duke University Press.

Lee, Leo Ou-fan (1985). "The Politics of Techniques: Perspectives of Literary Dissidence in Contemporary Chinese Fiction". In Kinkley ed. (1985), pp. 159–190.

—— ed. (1988). *Xin ganjue pai xiaoshuo xuan* [Collection of stories by the "New Sensual"]. Taipei: *Yunchen wenhua shiye gongsi* [Yunchen culture Co.].

Li, Jianyi (1991). "Gao Xingjian's *The Bus-Stop*: Chinese Traditional Theatre and Western Avant-garde". Diss. University of Alberta.

Li, Jiefei ed. (1992). *Xunzhao de shidai* [The era of search]. Beijing: Beijing *shifandaxue chubanshe* [Beijing Normal University press].

Li Shulei (1986). "*Cong 'xunmeng' dao 'xungen'*" [From 'the search for dreams' to 'the search for roots']. *Dangdai wenxue sichao* [Contemporary literary thoughts]. No. 3, pp. 42–49.

Li, Tuo ed. (1993). *Zhongguo xungen xiaoshuo xuan* [A collection of Chinese fiction in search of cultural roots]. Hong Kong: Joint Publishing Co.

Liang, Yiqi (2002). "*Cong Yigeren di shengjing kan Gao Xingjian bieshuyige di xushi tese*" [A look at Gao Xingjian's unique narrative style through a study of *One Man's Bible*]. *Daxue shidai* [University Times]. No. 3, pp. 73–77.

Lin Gufang ((2003). "*Li chan yuan yi! — chanzhe kan 'Bayuexue'*" [Indeed far from Zen! — A Zen follower's perspective on *Snow in August*]. *Biaoyan yishu* [Performing arts]. No. 6, pp. 39–40.

Lin, Kehuan (1987). "*Gao Xingjian de duoshengbu yu fudiao xiju*" [Gao Xingjian's polyphonic and polytonal drama]. In Xu Guorong ed. (1987), pp. 145–170.

Liu, Ching-chih (2002). "*Fanyi yu nobe'er wenxue jiang*" [Translation and the Nobel Prize in Literature]. *Zhongguo Fanyi* [Chinese translators journal]. Vol. 23. No.6, pp. 43–44.

Liu, Xinwu (1977). "Class Counsellor". In Geremie Barmé and Bennett Lee eds. and trans. (1979), pp. 147–178.

—— and Wang, Meng, et. al. (1981). *Prize Winning Stories from China 1978–1979.* Beijing: Foreign Languages Press.

Lodén, Torbjörn (2001). "World Literature with Chinese Characteristics: On a Novel by Gao Xingjian". In Tam ed. (2001), pp. 257–276.

Lu, Tonglin ed. (1993). *Gender and Sexuality in Twentieth-Century Chinese Literature and Society.* Albany: State University of New York Press.

Lu, Xinhua (1979). "The Wounded". In Geremie Barmé and Bennett Lee eds. and trans. (1979), pp. 9–24.

Lu Xun (1956). *Lu Xun: Selected Works.* Xianyi and Gladys Yang trans. Beijing: Foreign Languages Press.

Luk, Y. T. (1987). "Chinese Theatricalism and Modern Drama". *Comparative Literature Studies.* No. 3, pp. 291–301.

Ma, Jian (1995). "*Xianshi shehui yu shenghuozhong de geren — tan Gao Xingjian de xiju Bi'an*" [Society in reality and individual in life — on Gao Xingjian's drama *The Other Shore*]. *Hong Kong Economic Journal,* 15 April 1995, p. 16.

Ma, Sen (1989). "The Theatre of the Absurd in China: Gao Xingjian's *The Bus-Stop*". In Tam ed. (2001), pp. 77–88.

Mao, Zedong (1983). "Talks at the Yan'an Conference on Literature and Art". Bonnie S. McDougall trans. *Philosophy East and West.* Vol. 33, No. 1, pp. 87–93.

—— (1991). *Mao Zedong xuanji* [Selected writings of Mao Zedong]. Beijing: Renmin chubanshe [People's press].

Madsen, Peter (2004). "World Literature and World Thoughts: Brandes/Auerbach". In Christopher Prendergast ed. (2004), pp. 54–75.

Malmqvist, Göran (2000). "Presentation Speech for the 2000 Nobel Prize in Literature". At Stockholm Concert Hall. 10 December 2000.

Malraux, André (1984). *Man's Fate*. Haakon M. Chevalier trans. New York: Random House.

—— (1990). *Anti-memoirs*. Terence Kilmartin trans. New York: Holt.

Marinetti, F. T. (1913). "Destruction of Syntax — Imagination without Strings — Words-in-Freedom". Robert Brain et al trans. In Umbro Apollonio ed. (1973), pp. 95–106.

McDougall, Bonnie S. (2005). "Gained in Translating and Being Translated in Beijing in the 1980s". A paper delivered in conference *International Discussion on Cross-Culture, Translation, and World Literature*. Centre for Cross-Cultural Studies. 22 April 2005, Hong Kong.

Miller, J. Hillis (1996). "Border Crossings, Translating Theory: Ruth". In S. Budick and W. Iser eds.(1996), pp. 208–223.

Min, Ze (1984). "*Duidai xifang xiandaipai wenti de yuanze fenqi*" [Fundamental differences among various stances on the issue of Western Modernism]. *Wenyi yanjiu* [Studies on literature and arts]. No. 1, pp. 40–46.

Mo Yan (1993). *Red Sorghum*. Howard Goldblatt trans. London: Heinemann.

Murdoch, Iris (1969). *Sartre*. London and Glasgow: Collins.

Newmark, Peter (1988). *A Textbook of Translation*. Harlow: Pearson Education Ltd.

Niranjana, Tejaswini (1992). *Siting Translation: History, Post-structuralism, and the Colonial Context*. Berkeley, L.A., Oxford: California University Press.

Prendergast, Christopher ed. (2004). *Debating World Literature*. London and New York: Verso.

Prévert, Jacques (1965). *Selections from Paroles*. Lawrence Ferlinghetti trans. Harmondsworth: Penguin Books.

Qian, Zhongwen (1987). *Xianshizhuyi he Xiandaizhuyi* [Realism and Modernism]. Beijing: *Renmin chubanshe* [People's press].

Qu, Liuyi (1984). "*Ping huaju 'Chezhan' ji qi piping*" [An analysis of the drama *Alarm Signal* and the criticism it has received]. *Wenyi bao* [Literature and arts post]. No. 7, pp. 29–33.

Quah, Sy Ren (2004). *Gao Xingjian and Transcultural Chinese Theater*. Hawaii: Hawaii University Press.

Robbe-Grillet, Alain (1965). *For a New Novel*. R. Howard trans. Illinois: Northwest University Press.

—— (1965). *Snapshots; and, Towards a New Novel*. Barbara Wright trans. London: Calder and Boyars.

Ru, Zhijuan (1979). "A Story out of Sequence". Fan Tian and John Minford trans. In Liu Xinwu, Wang Meng, et. al. (1981), pp. 302–333.

Run Sheng (1983). "*Guanyu huaju 'Juedui xinhao' de taolun zongshu*" [A summary of the debates on the drama *Alarm Signal*]. *Zuopin yu zhengming* [Works and debates]. No.3, pp. 41–42.

Said, Edward (1993). *Culture and Imperialism*. London: Chatto and Windus.

Sallis, John (2002). *On Translation*. Bloomington: Indiana University Press.

Sartre, Jean-Paul (1995). *No Exit, and three other plays*. Stuart Gilbert trans. New York : Vintage Books.

—— (1965). *Nausea*. Robert Baldick trans. Harmondsworth: Penguin Books.

Sha, Yexin (1983). *The Imposter*. Daniel Kane trans. *Renditions*. Nos.19 and 20, pp. 333–369.

Shi, Junbao et. al. (1978). *Eight Chinese Plays from the 13th Century to the Present*. William Dolby trans. New York: Columbia University Press.

Simpson, John ed. (1995). *The Oxford Book of Exile*. Oxford: Oxford University Press.

Spence, Jonathan ((1981). *The Gate of Heavenly Peace*. London: Faber and Faber.

Spivak, Gayatri (1994). "How to read a culturally different book?" In Francis Barker, Peter Hume and Margaret Iversen eds. (1994), pp. 126–150.

Stroinska, Magoda and Cecchetto, Vittorina eds. (2003). *Exile, Language and Identity*. Frankfurt am Main: Peter Lang.

Su, Wen (1932). "*Guanyu Wenxin yu Hu Qiuyuan de wenyi lunbian*" [About the debate between Literary News and Hu Qiuyuan on literature and arts]. *Xiandai* (*Les contemporains*). Vol. 1, No. 3, pp. 375–385.

Sun, Qingsheng (1994). *Zhongguo xiandai xiju sichao shi* [A history of the trends of thoughts in modern Chinese drama]. Beijing: Beijing University Press.

Tam, Kwok-kan (1986). "Drama of Paradox: Waiting as Form and Motif in *The Bus-Stop* and *Waiting for Godot*". In Tam ed. (2001), pp. 40–66.

—— ed. (2001). *Soul of Chaos*. Hong Kong: Chinese University Press.

Tan, Chulian (1996). *Zhongguo xiandaipai wenxue shilun* [A historical account on Chinese Modernist literature]. Shanghai: *Xuelin chubanshe* [Scholar press].

Tay, William (1990). "Avant-garde Theatre in Post-Mao China: *The Bus-Stop* by Gao Xingjian". In Howard Goldblatt ed. (1990), pp. 111–118.

—— (1984). "Wang Meng, Stream-of-consciousness, and the Controversy over Modernism". *Modern Chinese Literature*. Vol. 1, No.1, pp. 7–21.

The Confucian Analects (1991). In *The Four Books*. James Legge trans. Hunan: Hunan Press.

The Platform Sutra of the Six Patriarch: the Text of the Tun-huang Manuscript. (1967) Philip B. Yampolsky trans. New York: Columbia University Press.

The Classic of Mountains and Seas (2000). Anne Birrell trans. Harmondsworth: Penguin Books.

The Traditions of Exemplary Women (2002). Anne B. Kinney trans. On-line material: http://etext.virginia.edu/chinese/lienu/browse/LienuIntro.html

Tian, Xuxiu ed. (1988). *Duoshengbu de juchang* [Polyphonic theatre]. Shijiazhuang: *Huashan wenyi chubanshe* [Huashan literature and art press].

Tung, Constantine (1987). *Drama in the PRC*. Albany: State University of New York Press.

Venuti, Lawrence (1995). *The Translator's Invisibility*. London and New York: Rouledge.

—— ed. (2000). *The Translation Studies Reader*. London and New York: Routledge.

Wang, Anyi (1989). *Baotown*. Martha Avery trans. New York: W.W. Norton and Co. Ltd. Inc.

Wang, Shifu (1935). *The Romance of the Western Chamber*. S. I. Hsiung trans. London: Methuen.

Wang, Zuolin (1990). *Wo yu xieyi xijuguan* [Myself and my idea on a theatre like freehand brushwork]. Liu Jiang ed. Beijing: *Zhongguo xiju chubanshe* [China theatre press].

Wei, Minglun (1985). *Pan Jinlian*. Shiao-Ling S. Yu trans. In Shiao-Ling S. Yu ed. (1996), pp. 97–158.

West, Russell (2004). "Translator in Transit: Postcolonial Identities in Transformation on the Pacific Rim: Annamarie Jogose's *In Translation*". In Geoffery V. Davis, Peter H. Marsden, Bénédicte Ledent and Marc Delrez eds. (2004), pp. 231–248.

Williams, Raymond (1952). *Drama from Ibsen to Brecht*. London : Chatto & Windus.

——— (1994). *The Politics of Modernism*. London and New York: Verso.

Xiao, Yun (1984). *"Guanyu huaju 'Chezhan' de zhengming"* [Debates on the drama *The Bus-stop"*. *Xiju luncong* [Discussion on drama]. Vol. 3, pp. 126–128.

Xu, Guorong ed. (1987). *Gao Xingjian xiju yanjiu* [Studies on Gao Xingjian's drama]. Beijing: *Zhongguo xiju chubanshe* [China theatre press].

Yan, Hua (2005). *"Liangnian wan'er kanggong cansi"* [12,000 miners have met tragic death in two years]. Asian Times on Line. 24 February 2005, http://www.atchinese.com/2005/03/0324rep.htm

Yang, Xianyi and Yang, Gladys eds. (1999). *Selected Stories by Zhang Chengzhi*. Beijing: *Zhongguo wenxue chubanshe* [Chinese literature press].

Yip, Terry (2001). "A Chronology of Gao Xingjian". In Tam ed. (2001), pp. 311–340.

Yu, Shiao-Ling S. ed. (1996). *Chinese Drama after the Cultural Revolution, 1979–1989*. New York: The Edwin Mellen Press.

Yuan, Ke (1982). *Shenhua lunwenji* [Collection of essays on myths]. Shanghai: *Shanghai Guji chubanshi* [Shanghai classics press].

——— (1988). *Zhongguo shenhuashi* [A history of Chinese mythology]. Shanghai: *Shanghai Guji chubanshi* [Shanghai classics press].

——— (1996). *Yuan Ke shenhua lunji* [Collection of essays on myths by Yuan Ke]. Sichuan: *Sichuan daxue chubanshe* [Sichuan University press].

Yue, Ming-bao (1993). "Gendering the Origins of Modern Chinese Fiction". In Lu, Tonglin ed. (1993), pp. 47–66.

Zhang, Bojin ed. (1969). *Guoju dacheng* [Collection of national theatre]. Taipei: National Drama Promotion Committee, Ministry of Defence.

Zhang, Chengzhi (1984). "Rivers of the North". In Xianyi and Gladys Yang eds. (1999), pp. 44–365.

Zhang, Heng (1982). "Western Metropolis Rhapsody". David R. Knechtges trans. In *Wen xuan, or Selections of Refined Literature*. Princeton: Princeton University Press.

Zhang, Xudong (2000). *"Chengren de zhengzhi yu bei chengren de qidai"* [The politics of recognition and the expectation to be recognised]. *Twenty-first Century*. No. 62 (Dec), pp. 18–23.

Zhao, Henry Y. H.(2000). *Towards a Modern Zen Theatre*. London: School of Oriental and African Studies, University of London.

Zheng, Min (1991). *Zaochen, wo zai yuli caihua* [Morning, I gather flowers in the rain]. Hong Kong: Breakthrough Ltd.

Zhou li zheng yi [The legitimate interpretation of Zhou Rites] (1987). Sun Yi annotated. Beijing: *Zhonghua shuju* [China books company].

Zhu, Qiong'ai (1993). *"Wei dongfang xiju kaipi xinlu — juzuojia Gao Xingjian tan chuangzuo lilun"* [Opening up a new way for eastern theatre — Gao Xingjian the playwright on creativity]. *Hong Kong: Hong Kong Economic Journal*. 29 October 1993, p. 15.

Zhu, Xi ed. (19—). *Lunyu* [Kongzi's Analects]. In *Sishu jizhu* [The Four Classics: with annotations]. Shanghai: *Zhonghua shuju* [China books company].

Index

OTHERS